Early American
Herb Recipes

Early American Herb Recipes

Alice Cooke Brown

DOVER PUBLICATIONS, INC.
Mineola, New York

Bibliographical Note

This Dover edition, published in 2001, is an unabridged republication of the original edition published by the Charles E. Tuttle Company, Inc., Rutland, Vermont and Tokyo, Japan, in 1966.

Library of Congress Cataloging-in-Publication Data

Brown, Alice Cooke.
    Early American herb recipes / Alice Cooke Brown.
        p. cm.
    Originally published: 1st ed. Rutland, Vt. : C.E. Tuttle Co., [1966].
    Includes bibliographical references and index.
    ISBN-13: 978-0-486-41875-9
    ISBN-10: 0-486-41875-8
        1. Herbs. 2. Cookery. I. Title.

TX718.H4 B76 2001
641.6'57—dc21

                                                                    2001028859

Manufactured in the United States by Courier Corporation
41875807   2014
www.doverpublications.com

Contents

Illustrations 7

Acknowledgments 9

Preface 11

CHAPTER ONE: Herb Gardens and Borders 15
HISTORICAL BACKGROUND, 15
PICKING AND PRESERVING HERBS, 19

CHAPTER TWO: Medicinal Uses of Herbs 23
HISTORICAL BACKGROUND, 23
GLOSSARY OF OLD MEDICINAL TERMS, 45
MATERIA MEDICA CLASSIFICATION, 46
COLLECTING OF MATERIA MEDICA, 46
RECIPES FOR REMEDIES, 47
LIST OF DISEASES AND REMEDIAL HERBS, 62

CHAPTER THREE: Toiletries, Perfumes, Pomatum.......................... 67
HISTORICAL BACKGROUND, 67
COLOGNE RECIPES, 70
DEODERIZER RECIPES, 70
HAIR TONIC RECIPES, 71
PERFUME RECIPES, 71
POMADE RECIPES, 72
SOAP RECIPES, 74
TOILET WATER RECIPES, 75
TOOTH BRUSHES AND POWDERS, 75

CHAPTER FOUR: Culinary Uses of Herbs 77

    MEAT RECIPES, 80

    GRAVY AND SAUCE RECIPES, 89

    SOUP RECIPES, 94

    FISH RECIPES, 104

    FOWL RECIPES, 107

    VEGETABLE RECIPES, 111

    VINEGAR RECIPES, 113

    SALAD RECIPES, 115

    PICKLE RECIPES, 120

    BEVERAGE RECIPES, 125

CHAPTER FIVE: Other Household Uses of Herbs 135

    CONFECTIONS, 137

    CONSERVES AND PRESERVES, 139

    PASTRIES, CAKES AND PIES, 140

    PUDDING RECIPES, 142

Bibliography 145

Index 149

Illustrations

PLATES

Page

1. Herb-bordered walk at the Shelburne Museum, Shelburne, Vermont 14
2. Lemon balm in the herb garden of the Shelburne Museum 14
3. Print, "Gathering Watercresses" from Peterson's Magazine, March, 1864 19
4. Interior of the apothecary shop at the Shelburne Museum 24
5. Entrance to the apothecary shop at the Shelburne Museum 24
6. Prescription counter of the Shelburne Museum apothecary shop............. 25
7. Compounding room furnace, Shelburne Museum apothecary shop 27
8. Herb drawers from the Hollis Drug Store on Union Street in Boston 29
9. An old Indian mortar and pestle 32
10. European mortar and pestle of the 17th century 33
11. Old English brass mortar and pestle probably used in the navy 33
12. A collection of various mortars and pestles 39
13. Drugstore advertisement of the 19th century 43
14. Title page of an 1826 medical book for seamen 49
15. Various samples of packaged herb teas 53
16. An 1864 cover from Peterson's Magazine 66
17. "The Damask Rose," an engraving from an 1864 issue of Peterson's Magazine ... 66
18. Various packaged herb products used in the 19th century 73
19. Preparing herbs at the Little Stone Cottage of the Shelburne Museum 76
20. Frontispiece from The London Complete Art of Cookery, published in 1797 81
21. Title page from The Family Hand-Book 91
22. Replica of an old apothecary shop at the Shelburne Museum 95
23. Specimens of roots and chips used in the dying of cloth 137

7

SKETCHES OF EARLY AMERICAN HERBS

These sketches are facsimile reproductions of the engravings that appeared in the 1849 edition of Dr. W. Beach's *The American Practice Condensed, or the Family Physician; Being the Scientific System of Medicine; on Vegetable Principles, Designed for all Classes.*

Almonds, *p.16*
Aloe, *p.17*
Asarabacca, *p.30*
Balsam of Tolu, *p.31*
Barberry, *p.34*
Bayberry, *p.35*
Beth-root, *p.36*
Bittersweet, *p.37*
Black Alder, *p.41*
Black Hellebore, *p.41*
Blood-root, *p.42*
Blue Flag, *p.44*
Boneset, *p.45*
Burdock, *p.45*
Camphor Tree, *p.47*
Capsicum, *p.48*
Castor Bean, *p.50*
Catnip, *p.50*
Celadine, *p.51*
Chamomile, *p.52*
Cicuta, *p.54*
Cloves, *p.55*
Cohosh, *p.56*
Comfrey, *p.57*
Common Elder, *p.57*
Copaiba, *p.58*
Dandelion, *p.59*
Devils' Bit, *p.59*
Dwarf Elder, *p.61*
Elecampane, *p.61*
Euphorbia, *p.62*

Fern, Male, *p.65*
Flowering Ash, *p.65*
Foxglove, *p.68*
Garden Nightshade, *p.69*
Gentian, *p.72*
Golden Seal, *p.74*
Guaiacum, *p.78*
Henbane, *p.79*
Hops, *p.82*
Horehound, *p.83*
Indian Turnip, *p.84*
Ipecacuanha, *p.85*
Jalap, *p.87*
Juniper, *p.87*
Ladies Slipper, *p.88*
Liquorice, *p.89*
Liverwort, *p.90*
Lobelia, *p.92*
Mandrake, *p.93*
Marsh Mallows, *p.96*
Mullein, *p.98*
Mustard, *p.98*
Oak, *p.101*
Olive Tree, *p.101*
Pennyroyal, *p.102*
Peppermint, *p.103*
Pine, *p.104*
Pink-root, *p.105*
Plantain, *p.106*
Pleurisy-root, *p.106*
Poke, *p.109*

Polypody, *p.109*
Poppy, *p.112*
Prickly Ash, *p.113*
Red Raspberry, *p.114*
Rhubarb, *p.114*
Rose, *p.115*
Saffron, *p.115*
Sarsaparilla, *p.116*
Sassafras, *p.117*
Seneca Snake-root, *p.119*
Senna, *p.119*
Skullcap, *p.120*
Skunk Cabbage, *p.121*
Slippery Elm, *p.122*
Solomon's Seal, *p.123*
Spearmint, *p.124*
Spikenard, *p.125*
Stramonium, *p.127*
Striped Alder, *p.127*
Sumac, *p.129*
Swamp Dogwood, *p.129*
Tanzy, *p.130*
Virginia Snake-root, *p.130*
Water Horehound, *p.133*
White Wood, *p.139*
Wild Carrot, *p.138*
Wild Indigo, *p.138*
Witch Hazel, *p.139*
Wormwood, *p.141*
Yellow Dock, *p.141*

Acknowledgments

A DEBT OF GRATITUDE is owed a number of individuals who helped to make this book a reality. Mr. Charles V. S. Borst of the Charles E. Tuttle Company in Rutland, Vermont has provided invaluable assistance in discovering additional sources of information, and as a consultant in innumerable capacities.

Mr. Sterling Emerson, Director of the Shelburne Museum, is especially thanked for making possible a photographic insight into the important herb resources at the museum. Among others at the museum to whom great appreciation is owed are Mr. Frank H. Wildung, consultant regarding the apothecary's preparation and use of herbs and the selection of artifacts for photographic purposes; Mrs. Daisy Williams, an herb enthusiast of long standing, who so generously offered additional sources of information and graciously appeared in costume as she sifted the herbs before the hearth in the Old Stone House; and Einars J. Mengis, staff photographer.

Many thanks go to Dr. Alan S. Wilson, Vice Chancellor for Administration at the University of Hartford, for his remarks many years ago concerning the importance of bringing to light the many uses made of herbs in early American life. Dr. Wilson is himself an herb specialist of long standing and has one of the finest herb gardens in New England, at his home in Glastonbury, Connecticut.

Mr. Arthur F. Winslow, also of the University of Hartford, is especially thanked for the personal interest he took in locating so many rare and unusual books, pamphlets, and documents relating to the study of herbs. It is through his efforts and those of Mr. Borst at the Charles E. Tuttle Company in Rutland, Vermont that the author has been able to bring together what is considered perhaps the finest collection of rare sources now in existence.

Botanical information concerning the early use of herbs provided by Mrs. Peter Cascio of West Hartford, Connecticut is greatly appreciated by the writer. Insight into the location of available sources relative to the many ways in which herbs were utilized and prepared by the Indians has been most helpful.

A debt of gratitude is owed President Raymond Withey and Dean Andrew Vargish of Green Mountain College in Poultney, Vermont for their stimulating interest in the preservation and perpetuation of early American life.

Preface

PRIOR TO THE PUBLISHING of cook-books in the eighteenth century, the house-wife depended on her memory and her manuscript recipes. At times, like the hymns which were sung also from memory before any were printed with music, a strange con-glomeration would result. An occasional family was fortunate enough to possess a copy of Dr. William Salmon's *The Family Dictionary: or Household Companion.* This was one of the most sought-after books of its kind among the English-speaking colo-nists. It was originally printed in London during the 1690's; it had additional edi-tions in the early eighteenth century. Since Dr. Salmon was convinced that good food was essential to good health, his book con-tained recipes for the preparation of meals, as well as for remedies. The latter were "fitted for curing most diseases incident to men, women, and children," many of which included herbs.

Home remedies were the chief reliance of the household. The mother of the family tended to treating the aches and pains with her own prescriptions, good or bad by present-day standards. Nearly every house had a small herb garden where the ingredi-ents for home-grown and home-made remedies could be obtained. She could con-coct remedies for jaundice, hysterics, coughs, sore throat, colic, consumption, toothache, corns, and many other health problems. When one considers how often it is difficult to keep alive someone ill with the flu or tuberculosis with the most advanced modern drugs, one can't help but wonder about the chances of a patient of yesteryear who relied on Hoarhound for "lung complaints" or Life Everlasting for fevers and influenza. Some of the remedies seem fantastic and beyond the remotest stretch of the imagina-tion; some are ludicrous, and others are founded on sound principles and undoubt-edly produced excellent results. All the re-cipes here collected are authentic and offer accurate insight into contemporary medical thinking from the seventeenth century through the period of the Civil War. Each is transcribed just as it appeared in the original source; this explains the unusual spelling and grammatical construction.

If the housewife had time, energy, and pride in matters of good grooming, she made her own cologne, perfume, pomade, soap, tooth powder, and tooth brushes. For the men in the family, she concocted shaving materials and lotions to promote the growth of hair.

But her prime responsibility was to prepare, cook, and serve the family meals. It will be observed from examining the recipes which follow, herbs were used extensively. Not only did they add zest, but these were days prior to scientific refrigeration. Highly spiced and flavored dishes were a necessity when foods were growing rancid or spoiled. Also, especially the British, who had relied heavily on herbs both for food and medicinal remedies, included herbs for purposes of health protection.

One interesting and exciting way to approach the American past is through reconstructing the vivid moments of everyday living around the fireside where the mother could be seen bustling about preparing a meal. These are lives like ours in their moments of laughter, whimsy, or anxiety— busy, perhaps gathering herbs in the garden or adding them to a special dish. Nothing can be more fascinating than experiencing our heritage through original recipes, for these are among the most authentic and provocative materials of our culture.

Over five hundred recipes have been compiled here from original sources collected by the writer over a period of many years. These reflect the tremendous importance of herbs to the rigorous survival of our forefathers and afford factual insight into vital aspects of early American life.

"The discovery of a new dish does more for the happiness of man than the discovery of a star."
BRILLAT-SAVARIN, *Physiologie du Gout*

There is to me
A daintiness about these early flowers,
That touches me like poetry. They blow out
With such a simple loveliness among
The common herbs of pasture, and they breathe
Their lives so unobtrusively, like hearts
Whose beatings are too gentle for the world.

Would you be strong? Go follow up the plough;
Would you be thoughtful? Study fields and flowers;
Would you be wise? Take on yourself a vow
To go to school in Nature's sunny bowers.
Fly from the city; nothing there can charm—
Seek wisdom, strength, and virtue on a farm.

J. L. BLAKE, *The Farmer's Every-day Book*

Plate 1. *Herbs border the walk leading to the Apothecary Shop at the Shelburne Museum, Shelburne, Vermont. The shop, a replica, was built as an addition to the original country store, which served originally, c. 1840, as the Shelburne Post Office. (Courtesy Shelburne Museum, Inc.) Plate 2. Lemon balm predominates in this portion of the Shelburne Museum's herb garden. (Courtesy Shelburne Museum, Inc.)*

14

CHAPTER ONE

Herb Gardens and Borders

Speak not—whisper not:
Here bloweth thyme and bergamot; . . .
Dark-spiked rosemary and myrrh,
Lean-stalked, purple lavender. . . .
                    WALTER DE LA MARE,
                    The Sunken Garden

HISTORICAL BACKGROUND

THE EARLY HOUSEWIVES of America, like their counterparts abroad, all lived in close affiliation with Nature, for tending their herb gardens must have promoted just such a relationship. As will be evident in the variety of recipes which follow, our grandmothers—and theirs—found countless ways in which to utilize herbs. The herb garden was an essential adjunct to the farmstead. One can imagine the delight with which these early homemakers set out their herb gardens, for they knew well three important uses to which these plants could be put—medicinal, culinary, and for their aromatic fragrance.

Those gardens which were carefully planned were most attractive. With relatively little effort an herb garden could be planted that would vie with any flower garden.

A number of writers on gardens and gardening had helpful suggestions as to planning. Hyll in 1577, Surflet in 1616, Lawson the following year, Blake in 1664, and Langley in 1728 all provided such information. Thomas Hyll in *The Gardeners Labyrinth* (1577) lists a great many herbs which should be grown, and says, "What rarer object can there be on earth, (the motions of the Celestial bodies except) than a beautiful and Odoriferous Garden plot Artificially composed. . . . But now to my Garden of Flowers and Sweet Hearbs and first the Rose. . . . Of all the flowers in the Garden, this is the chief for beauty and sweetness." Richard Surflet in his *Maison Rustique* (1600) suggests that "The Garden shall be divided into two equall parts. The one shall containe the hearbes and flowers used to make nosegaies and garlands. . . . . .

Almonds

The other part shall have all the sweet-smelling hearbes, whether they be such as beare no flowers, or if they beare any, yet they are not put in Nosegaies alone, but the whole hearbe with them. . . . and this may be called the Garden for hearbes of a good smell."

Lawson in his *Country House-wifes Garden* (1617) points out that "the number of formes, mazes and knots is so great and men are so diversely delighted, that I leave every House-wife to herselfe, especially seeing to set down many, had been but to fill much paper; yet lest I deprive her of all delight and direction, let her view these few choyse, new formes and note this generall, that all plots are square, and all are bordered about with Privet, Raisins, Feaberries, Roses, Thorns, Rosemary, Bee-flowers, Isop, Sage or such-like."

Lawson explains why it is necessary to have two sorts of gardens. "Herbs are of two sorts, and therefore it is meet (they requiring divers manners of Husbandry) that we have two Gardens; a Garden for flowers, and a Kitchin garden; or a Summer garden: not that we mean so perfect a distinction, that we mean the Garden for flowers should or can be without herbs good for the Kitchin, or the Kitchin garden should want flowers, nor on the contrary; but for the most part they would be severed: first, because your Garden-flowers shall suffer some disgrace, if among them you intermingle Onions, Parsnips, etc." William Lawson adds, "Though your Garden for flowers doth in a sort peculiarly challenge to itself a perfect, and exquisite form to the eyes, yet you may not altogether neglect this, where your herbs for the pot do grow: And therefore some here make comely borders with the herbs aforesaid; the rather, because abundance of Roses and Lavender, yield much profit and comfort to the senses: Rosewater, Lavender, the one cordial (as also the Violets; burrage (borage) and Bugloss) the other reviving the spirits by the sense of smelling, both most durable for smell, both in flowers and water."

Stephen Blake in *The Compleat Gardener's Practise,* (1664), mentions a few patterns or designs for gardens but urges the gardener to create his own, "which probably may please your fancy better than mine." One of the designs which appeared in Blake's book was a favorite called "the Lover's Knot." Underneath it, he wrote:

Here I have made the true Lovers Knott
To try it in Mariage was never my Lott.

It is obvious from the writings of Batty Langley in his *New Principles of Gardening,* (1728), that he did not find attractive the formal designs of parterres and knots. "Since the pleasure of a Garden depends on the variety of its parts, 'tis therefore that we should well consider of their disposition to present new and delightful scenes at every step which regular Gardeners are incapable of doing. Nor is there anything more shocking than a stiff regular Garden; where, after we have seen one quarter thereof the same is repeated."

There are interesting listings of available and desirable herbs in England in the late sixteenth and early seventeenth centuries. In 1577, Hyll lists angelica, anise, chamomile, clary, costmary, Dutchbox, elecampane, fennel, feverfew, hyssop, lovage, marjoram, mints, rosemary, rue, sage, savory, tansy, and thyme.

Richard Surflet in his *Maison Rustique,* (1600), includes among his herb listing: anise, balm, basil, chamomile, costmary, Good King Henry, horehound, hyssop, jasmin, lavender, marjoram, mints, mugwort, nepeta, pellitory, pennyroyal, rosemary, rue, sage, savory, southernwood, sweet balm, tansy, thyme, wild marjoram, and wormwood.

William Lawson in *The Country House-wife's Garden,* (1617), notes bee-flowers (borage), clove-gilliflowers, cowslips, daisies, hyssop, lavender, lilies, pinks, rosemary, roses, sage, southernwood, and thyme, thus including also a number of herbs as well as "roses".

Four years prior to Lawson's publication, Markham in his *English Husbandman* sug-gests, "Germander, Issope, Pinke-gilly flowers, Time, but of all hearbes Germander is the most principallest best for this purpose."

Dr. Catherine Fennelly, editor of the Old Sturbridge Village Booklet Series, and Rudy Favretti in one of these booklets entitled, *Early New England Gardens* concur as to those herbs known to have been available in New England prior to 1800. Included in their listing are the following: anise, angelica, balm, sweet basil, borage, catmint, camomile, chervil, chicory, chives, clary (Salvia sclarea), coriander, costmary, dill, fennel, horehound,

Aloe

hyssop, marjoram, mustard, parsley, pennyroyal, pepper-grass, purslane, rosemary, rue, sage, winter savory, sorrel, tansy, thyme, teasel, watercress, woad, wormwood.

One would do well today to duplicate such an early New England garden or at least have an herb border or a delightfully scented "Lavender Walk." Guests will never cease to be charmed by the beauty of the soft mauve blossoms backed by the silver leaves and their beautiful spikes, as they exude their exquisite scent in an early fall evening—recalling other evenings long ago!

John Winthrop did just that, when he recalled memories of old England as he remarked in his *Journal*, "And there came a smell off the Shore like the Smell of a Garden."

If one examines the early Plymouth records, assignment of mesesteads *and* garden plots will be noted. Surflet refers to just such a delight, when he writes of the "Garden for hearbes of a good smell," in his *Maison Rustique*, (1600).

No one housewife was likely to grow all herbs known to exist in the early days. Her basic ones were probably mint, sage, parsley, thyme, and marjoram, for they were easy to grow and had so many culinary uses.

Curious folklore has come down through the ages regarding some herbs. For example, sage is supposed to grow well only where "the woman rules"—perhaps the supposed hen-pecked husband was consoled when he detected its flavour in the turkey stuffing. To transplant parsley meant bad luck, so this had to be grown from seed, planted very deep, "for it must visit the 'nether' regions three times to obtain permission to grow in the earth." *Hyssop,* said to "avert the Evil Eye," was also an attractive and aromatic herb to be included in the garden.

The mandrake, or May apple, was supposed to bring good fortune, if it were left untouched for three days, then soaked in warm water which was later sprinkled over the household and farm belongings. This practice was performed four times a year. In between dunking ceremonies, the dry herb was kept wrapped in a silk cloth among one's best possessions. The demand for mandrake became so great, that the basic herb began to be transformed commercially into various forms and figures. Someone thought of planting grass seed in the root's top to make hair for a mandrake's head. Despite the fake, man-made, mandrake figures, people continued to consider them good luck and went on purchasing them. Herbalists like William Turner were disgusted. In 1568, he wrote, "The rootes which are conterfited and made like little puppettes and mammettes, which come to be sold in England in boxes with heir, and such forme as a man hath, are nothying elles but folishe feined trifles, and not naturall. For they are so trymmed of crafty theves to mocke the poor people with all, and to rob them both of theyr wit and theyr money."

Gerard in 1597 shows his disgust, also, when he criticizes those "idle drones that have little or nothing to do but eate and drinke" and have dedicated "some of their time in carving the roots of Brionie forming them to the shape of men and women."

In 1710, Dr. Salmon adds, "Sometimes (tho not often) three of those Roots have been observed, which some by Transplant-

Plate 3. *"Gathering Watercresses," reproduced from the March 1864 issue of Peterson's Magazine.*

ing have Occasionally cut off for humor or admiration sake, and to amuse Fools . . . "

Gerarde wrote in his herbal (1597), "But this is to be reckoned among the old wives fables . . . touching the gathering of Spleenewoort in the night, and other most vaine things, which are founde heere and there scattered in the old writers books from which most of the later writers do not abstaine, who many times fill up their pages with lies and frivolous toies, and by so doing do not a little deceive yoong students."

Despite all the folk lore and unavailability of all the herbs she may have wanted, never-

theless in those days when womenfolk lived very busy but often lonely lives, their herb gardens were a source of pleasant recreation as well as a supply of vital medicinal and culinary ingredients.

PICKING AND PRESERVING HERBS

The work done by the Shakers when they turned to the commercial production of herbs is similar to the labor of the housewife as she prepared herbs from her own garden. Dr. Edward D. Andrews in *The Community Industries of the Shakers* (1933) describes the processes performed by the Shaker sisters as, "cleaning roots, picking and 'picking over' flowers and plants, cutting sage, cleaning bottles, cutting and printing labels, papering powders and herbs, and 'dressing' or putting up extracts and ointments."

Sister Marcia Bullard, a Shaker, offers interesting insights concerning herbs as they were tended in the Civil War era.

We always had extensive poppy beds and early in the morning, before the sun had risen, the white-capped sisters could be seen stooping among the scarlet blossoms to slit those pods from which the petals had just fallen. Again after sundown they came out with little knives to scrape off the dried juice. . . .

There were the herbs of many kinds. Lobelia, pennyroyal, spearmint, peppermint, catnip, winter-green, thoroughwort, sarsaparilla and dandelion grew wild in the surrounding fields. When it was time to gather them an elderly brother would take a great wagonload of children, armed with tow sheets, to the pastures. Here they would pick the appointed herb—each one had its own day, that there might be no danger of mixing—and, when their sheets were full, drive solemnly home again. . . . We had big beds of sage, thorn apple, belladonna, marigolds and camomile, as well as of yellow dock, of which we raised great quantities to sell to the manufacturers of a well-known 'sarsaparilla.' . . . In the herb shop the herbs were dried and then pressed into packages by machinery, labeled and sold outside. Lovage root we exported both plain and sugared and the wild flagroot we gathered and sugared too. On the whole there was no pleasanter work than that in the 'medical garden' and 'herb shop.'

Today, one can gain much helpful information relative to the growing of herbs from The Herb Society of America. One of their excellent publications is entitled, *A Primer for Herb Growing*. Herein, it is pointed out that most herbs used today originated from the shores of the Mediterranean "and east-ward to India. In these lands it is hot and sunny. Therefore in order to be given a situation similar to their native habitat, herbs, with the exception of a few species, should be planted in a well drained, sunny place, where the soil is friable, and alkaline, in colloquial language, 'sweet.' "

In this same publication the Herb Society offers its suggestions as to "Harvesting and Drying." These will be cited so that one can compare modern instructions with those of the Shakers as described for the Civil War era, and those which follow gleaned from early times.

Where the leaves of the herb are the part to be used, they have the best flavor when harvested just before the flowers open. Most herbs should be harvested on a clear morning, when the leaves are no longer wet with dew. The flowers or leaves should be cut with sharp knife or scissors, leaving enough foliage for new growth. The leaves should be carefully washed and the excess water shaken off. They can be dried on wire or cheese cloth frames, or tied in bunches and hung up from a clothes line in an airy dark place like an attic. If too much sun comes into the room or attic, the bunches can be covered over with paper bags cut open at the bottom for sun fades the green of the leaves. The herbs on the screens should be dry within the week, the bunched herbs take longer. They should be labelled before drying. When thoroughly dry, the leaves should be stripped from the stems and placed in air tight containers and kept away from strong light.

One finds general agreement among the various instructions, except the early house-wife did not have available some of the more modern equipment. Whereas drying them "hung from a clothes line in an airy dark place like an attic" is suggested above, herbs were often suspended from the barn rafters, blossom end down, in the early days.

If one examines one of Miss Leslie's recipes which follows, it will be noted that she attempts to speed up the drying process by placing them in an oven, not so hot that they will scorch or burn.

Let us see what other directions were offered in the early "receipt books" and "directories" as to the picking and preserving of herbs.

DIRECTIONS ON HERBS: All herbs should be carefully kept from the air. Herb tea, to do any good, should be made very strong.

Herbs should be gathered while in blossom. If left till they have gone to seed, the strength goes into the seed. Those who have a little patch of ground, will do well to raise the most important herbs; and those who have not, will do well to get them in quantities from some friend in the country; for apothecaries make very great profit upon them. . . .

Few people know how to keep the flavor of sweet-marjoram; . . . It should be gathered in bud or blossom, and dried in a tin-kitchen at a moderate distance from the fire; when dry, it should be immediately rubbed, sifted, and corked up in a bottle carefully.

American Frugal Housewife, 1833

TO DRY HERBS: By drying herbs with artificial heat as quickly as possible, you preserve their scent and flavour much better than when they are dried slowly by exposing them to the sun and air; a process by which a large portion of their strength evaporates. All sorts of herbs are in the greatest perfection just before they begin to flower. Gather them on a dry day, and place them in an oven, which must not be hot enough to discolour, scorch, or burn them. When they are quite dry, take them out, and replace them with others. Pick the leaves from the stems, (which may be thrown away,) and put them into bottles or jars; cork them tightly, and keep them in a dry place. Those that are used in cookery should be kept in a kitchen closet.

Miss Leslie's Complete Cookery, 1839

TO EXTRACT THE ESSENTIAL OIL OF FLOW-ERS: Take a quantity of fresh, fragrant leaves, both the stalk and flower leaves; cord very thin layers of cotton, and dip them in fine Florence oil; put alternate layers of the cotton and leaves in a glass jar, or large tumbler; sprinkle a very little fine salt on each layer of the flowers; cover the jar close, and place it in a window exposed to the sun. In two weeks a fragrant oil may be squeezed out of the cotton. Rose leaves, mignonette, and sweet scented clover, make nice perfumes.

The Improved Housewife or Book of Receipts, 1858

TO EXTRACT ESSENCES FROM FLOWERS: Procure a quantity of the petals of any flowers which have an agreeable fragrance; card thin layers of cotton, which dip into the finest Florence or Lucca oil; sprinkle a small quantity of fine salt on the flowers, and lay them, a layer of cotton, and a layer of flowers, until an earthen vessel or a wide-mouthed glass bottle is full. Tie the top close with a bladder, then lay the vessel in a south aspect to the heat of the sun, and in fifteen days, when uncovered, a fragrant oil may be squeezed away from the whole mass, little inferior (if that flower is made use of) to the *dear* and *highly valued* Otto or Odour of roses.

Family Receipt Book, 1819

TO KEEP PARSLEY FOR WINTER USE: Gather large, good sprigs, and if at all dusty, wash them; shake off the water dry as you can, and lay into a jar a handful of parsley and a handful of salt. When to be used, throw them into cold water to freshen and to remove the salt.

Young Housekeeper's Friend, 1846

TO PRESERVE AROMATIC AND OTHER HERBS: The boxes and drawers in which vegetable matters are kept, should not impart to them any smell or taste; and more certainly to avoid this, they should be lined with paper. Such as are volatile, of a delicate texture, or subject to suffer from insects, must be kept in well-covered glasses. Fruits and oily seeds, which are apt to become rancid, must be kept in a cool and dry, but by no means in a warm and mosit place.

Family Receipt Book, 1819

TO PRESERVE HERBS: All kinds of herbs should be gathered on a dry day, just before, or while in blossom. Tie them in bundles, and suspend them in a dry, airy place, with the blossoms downwards. When perfectly dry, wrap the medicinal ones in paper, and keep them from the air. Pick off the leaves of those which are to be used in cooking, pound and sift them fine, and keep the powder in bottles, corked up tight.

Kitchen Directory, 1846

TO PROPAGATE HERBS BY SLIPS AND CUTTINGS: Many kinds of pot-herbs may, in July, be propagated by cuttings or slips, which may be planted out to nurse on a shady border for a few weeks, or till they have struck root, and may then be planted out where they are to remain. If made about the middle, or end of the month, they will be ready for transplanting before the end of August, and in that case will be well established before the winter. The kinds are marjoram, mint, sage, sorrel, tansy, tarragons, and thyme.

Mackenzie's 5,000 Receipts, 1829

QUINTESSENCE OF LAVENDER, OR OTHER AROMATIC HERB: Take off the blossoms from the stalks, which must be cut fresh at sun-rising in warm weather; spread the blossoms on a white linen cloth, and lay them in the shade for twenty-four hours; after which, stamp or bruise them; then put them, immersed in warm water, into the still, near a fire, and let them infuse for the space of five or six hours, so closely covered that nothing may exhale from it; after which time, take off the covering, and quickly put on the helm, and lute it carefully. You must, in the beginning, draw over half the quantity of the water you put in. If you take away the receiver, you will see the quintessence on the surface of the water, which you may easily separate from it. Then put the distilled water back again, and distil it over again, till there appear no more of the quintessence on the water. You may distil this water four or five times over, according as you perceive the quintessence upon it.

The best distilling utensils for this work are those for the *balneum marioe*, or sand bath; meanwhile you may, after the common method, distil the ingredients on an open fire. But if you intend to make quintessence for waters, you may make use of common salt, in order to extract the more quintessence of any blossom.

Take four pounds of blossoms of any aromatic plant and infuse in it six quarts of water. If you use salt to bring your infusion to a ferment, add half a pound of common salt to it.

Family Receipt Book, 1819

TO REMOVE HERBS AND FLOWERS IN THE SUMMER: If you have occasion to transplant in the summer season, let it be in the evening after the heat is past, plant and water the same immediately, and there will be no danger from the heat next day; but be careful, in digging up the earth, you do not break any of the young shoots, as the sap will exude out of the same to the great danger of the plants.

Family Receipt Book, 1819

SWEET HERBS: should be dried, and the stalks thrown away, and the rest be kept in corked large mouth bottles, or small tin boxes.

Beecher's Domestic Receipt Book, 1857

AS TO THE HERBS: Angelica, Mint, Balm, Wormwood, and the like, they ought to be gather'd in their prime, and gently dried; the proportion is more or less in quantity, according as you will have the Water in strength of the Herb; for one is stronger than another, and a handful of Wormwood will go further than two or three of another Herb.

The Family Dictionary: or Household Companion, 1710

CHAPTER TWO

Medicinal Uses of Herbs

It is medicine, not scenery, for which
A sick man must go a-searching.
SENECA, Epistulae ad Lucilium

HISTORICAL BACKGROUND

THERE WERE EARLY MARRIAGES and large families in the early days. The usual-sized family was one having ten or twelve children. Some families consisted of twenty or twenty-five. Patrick Henry, for example, was one of nineteen children and John Marshall was the first of fifteen.

Even though life expectancy was not high in the 1700's, there were people like Sarah Thayer, who when she died in 1751 had 66 male and 66 female descendants. Sarah Tuthel of Ipswich, Massachusetts lived to see from seven out of sixteen children, 127 grandchildren and great-grand-children. Another New England woman, before she died in her hundredth year, could count 500 descendants, 205 of whom were alive; and one grand-daughter had been a grandmother

for nearly fifteen years. What produced this magic longevity and productivity? Was it that these were the people who knew and made use of the medicinal virtues of the herbs?

To-day in many parts of the world there is a renewed interest in integrating elements of medical folklore with modern scientific knowledge. The words, "renewed interest" are used quite intentionally, for Dr. W. Beach writes in 1846: "Both the untutored savage and the beast are taught, by reason and instinct, to use those vegetables which are scattered so richly around them, to relieve their diseases."

Bosman, in his *Description of the Coast of Guinea* in reference to different herbs employed by the natives, says: "I have seen several of my countrymen cured by these medicines, when *our own physicians were at a loss what to do.*" Then, he adds: "I have several times observed the negroes cure such extensive and dangerous wounds with these herbs, that I have looked on with amazement."

Plate 4. *Interior view of the Apothecary Shop at the Shelburne Museum. In the showcases are displayed such packaged items as "Pink Pills for Pale People," "Wendell's Ambition Pills," "Pure White Face Powder," "Saturday Night Nerve, Brain, and Muscle Tonic," "Mother Gray's Powders," "Pear's Glycerine Soap," "Toothache Wax," fuller's earth (still used as a baby powder), an antidote for chewing tobacco, and leeches. (Courtesy Shelburne Museum, Inc.)*

Plate 5. *Lavender, tansey, and mints are among the plantings in the herb border at the entrance to the Shelburne Museum Apothecary Shop. The shop is well stocked with drugs, spices, herbs, and patent medicines. (Courtesy Shelburne Museum, Inc.)*

An early writer, Le Vaillant, in his *Travels into the Interior Parts of Africa*, wrote interestingly of the use of herb remedies of the natives. "Upon one occasion they cured him of a violent attack of quinsy, after he had given up his case as hopeless. His tongue and throat were so swelled that he could only speak by signs; and his breathing became so much impeded that he expected to be suffocated. In the meantime he was visited by a party of savages, who, feeling an interest in

24

his situation, pledged themselves to cure him. He had at this time despaired of his life for nearly a week. The remedy was a hot local application of a certain herb. It was also to be used as a gargle. The poultice was renewed several times in the night, and the gargle still more frequently repeated. When day appeared he was greatly eased: he could breathe more freely, and the swelling and inflammation of the throat were abated. By the third day he found himself cured. He then went out to examine the plant by which he had been restored to health."

Le Vaillant quotes the native as saying, "Nothing in the country was more common; it grew all around the camp, and was to be met with in every direction." Writes Le Vaillant, "He describes it as a species of sage, about two feet high, with a pleasant smell and balsamic taste."

Marsden in his history of Sumatra writes, "The art of healing among the Sumatrans

Plate 6. *The prescription counter of the Apothecary Shop at the Shelburne Museum, showing its balances, pill-making equipment and labeled stock bottles of the most commonly used ingredients in compounding prescriptions. (Courtesy Shelburne Museum, Inc.)*

consists almost entirely in the application of simples, in the virtues of which they are *surprisingly skilled*. All the old men and women in the country are physicians, and their *rewards depend upon their success."* Marsden adds, "The Sumatrans have a degree of botanical knowledge that surprises a European. They are in general, and at a very early age, acquainted not only with the names, but the qualities and properties of every shrub and herb among that exuberant variety with which their country abounds."

Dr. Beach in his *American Practice, or the Family Physician* (1846) writes, "How much more natural is it to look to the field and the forest for plants and roots to cure our complaints, than to dig in the bowels of the earth and procure certain metals, which prove poisonous and destructive even in obtaining them, and much more so after having been subjected to a chemical process."

Later, Dr. Beach adds, "The Indians of North America know how to treat their complaints, both in physic, surgery, and midwifery, related by Count La Sallee, Washington Irving, Catling, Lewis and Clark, and numerous others. It is the same in the East Indies, South Sea Islands, Patagonia, Africa, & c."

The early settlers arrived bringing with them an age-long knowledge of herbs and their uses. Many herbs found here, they had known in England or Europe. But curiously enough, as opportunities arose to become acquainted with the American Indian culinary and medicinal practices, it was found that they, too, used herbs, extensively.

Among the potherbs for which the Indians had high regard was the marsh marigold, especially the youngest shoots which they boiled. The history of the marigold has its origins long before the Christian era. The Romans named its European counterpart, Caltha; this was the name used by Linnaeus. The species found native to America is the palustris, meaning "of the marshes."

The Indians also used the water parsnip, or cow parsnip, sometimes referred to as Indian rhubarb, as another potherb. This plant grew in great abundance in certain areas, such as New England and along one of the Canadian rivers, called the Parsnip River. Because there are many relatives in this same botanical family, and because some of its members are as poisonous as the hemlock which Socrates drank, we do not make use of the cow parsnip, as the Indians did. The Indians learned to know the blossom first, and then familiarized themselves with it in the early spring.

The Indian also used poke, or pokeberry, by cutting the very young shoots far above the ground, and boiling them. The roots were considered to be too poisonous for use. In the markets of Philadelphia at the turn of the nineteenth century, pokeweed shoots were being sold as spring greens. It has been recorded that they were on sale, also, in Louisiana and Florida.

The milkweed used by the Indians was a very safe herb for Indian and settler alike to eat. Their shoots are delicious once they have been boiled in two waters so that the milky liquid which has an unpleasant flavor can be removed. In the early spring, the Indians ate the first shoots. In summer, they used the milkweed blossoms for sweetening. On cool nights, the nectar inside the blossoms becomes mixed with dew. By shaking the

Plate 7. *Furnace in the compounding room of the Apothecary Shop at the Shelburne Museum showing equipment for the percolation and distillation of medicinal compounds, including glass and metal percolators, copper funnels, dippers, etc., with native herbs strung overhead. Such furnaces were often placed behind fireplaces in old houses and were used for boiling clothes and making up stock feed as well as for extracting the essence of important herbs. Many of the items shown came from the Peck Drug Store in Burlington, Vermont (1806–1957). (Courtesy Shelburne Museum, Inc.)*

27 ✦ MEDICINAL USES OF HERBS

flowers over a pot before the dew and nectar have evaporated or dried, a delicious sweetening can result. Fried milkweed pods still considered quite a delicacy by some of our Western Indians were a use made of this potherb later, when the blossoms changed into pods. Pleurisy root is another name for the milkweed. It had tremendous medicinal qualities and, as such, was cultivated by the Delaware Indians. In fact, the medicinal values of this plant were so great that the whole species was named after Aesculapius, the great Greek physician.

Fireweed, a native plant, was dug in the early spring for its underground shoots, which would then be boiled. The tender leaves of the fireweed which came a little later in the spring also made an excellent potherb.

The Forest Potawatomi were very fond of the flavor of the oxalis. Because its juice was sour, sweentening was added to its leaves and eaten for a dessert. Another member of the oxalis family, the ladies sorrel or creeping oxalis, was a favorite of the Iroquois, especially the leaves. Farther west, in the Nebraska area, it was the flowers, leaves, and even the bulbs of the violet woodsorrel which were eaten with such delight.

Many of the pigweeds were used by the American Indians. Among these, was a western variety, called Mexican tea, and another which took on the name of Fremont, in remembrance of the explorer.

As soon as the imported lambsquarters, a member of the goosefoot family, began to grow in America, a number of Indian tribes adopted it as a potherb. It is allied with the spinach family, and as such is a good green

boiled. The Navajos and the Digger Indians of California are among those who made extensive use of the pigweeds.

Other native herbs were often used by the Indians in their raw state, rather than as potherbs. Even the seeds were used, first being dried, ground, and then mixed with cornmeal and salt to be formed into a sort of pancake or bread. Among some of the Indians, the pigweed flowers, too, were used as part of the green salad.

The Indians made use of the bulb of the Jack-in-the-pulpit. The early settlers referred to this plant as Indian turnip, for they found that it was used extensively and its flavor and shape resembled the turnip. The solid bulb of the Jack-in-the-pulpit was the "turnip" part. It contains a very bitter juice, and so can not be eaten raw. It must be either boiled or baked to free its starch from its bitter taste and to make it sweeter and more edible. The Indians even made use of its berries by boiling them with venison when they were ripe and red.

Very little has survived in recorded form of herb recipes used by the Indians. One of the few collectors of such information was a man named John Monroe who in the early 1700's compiled a number of recipes and directions for making many of the Indian discoveries in the medical arts.

Monroe says of the following salve recipe that it will heal any sore. "Take ten pounds of hog's lard, one quart of tobacco juice, one handful of dog mackimus, one handful of sweet elder, one handful of arsmart, one handful of bittersweet, one handful of white Solomon's seal, one handful of fir bark, one handful of tamarack bark, six ounces of

Plate 8. *These apothecary's herb drawers came from the Hollis Drug Store on Union Street in Boston, presumably established in 1826, as noted in a newspaper advertisement for horse liniment citing that date for the establishment of the store. These drawers were used for such herbs as burdock, saffron, senna, snake root, sassafras, poke root, chicory, arnica, scullcap, calamint, and alkanet. (Courtesy Shelburne Museum, Inc.)*

beeswax, six ounces of resin, one pound of honey, one quart of New England rum and two ounces of common shoemaker's wax. Collect these in the month of June and boil them together, or take one-half the quantity of each sort."

Nearly every colonial home had its medicine chest of household remedies in which medicinal herbs were often used extensively. But not all recipes included herbs. Take, for example, an ointment used in the

colonial period for sprains, strains, rheumatism, and lame back, in which there were assembled, "good sized live toads, four in number; put into boiling water and cook very soft; then take them out and boil the water down to one-half pint, and add fresh churned, unsalted butter one pound and simmer together; at the last add tincture of arnica two ounces."

Or, a remedy for ulcers devised by Governor Winthrop and recommended highly in

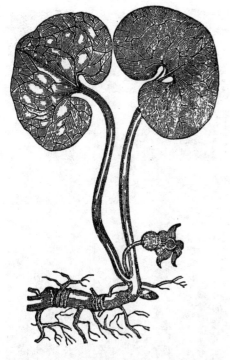

Asarabacca

asthma," he might find essence of peppermint of great help.

Also, a number of "cures" could be purchased in the apothecary shops found in the larger communities. For example, one was urged to buy Lignorum Anti Scorbutic Drops as "perfect cures" for "the most inveterate scurvy, leprosy, pimpled faces of ever so long standing, so as never to return again; also the king's evil, fistulas, old obstinate sores or ulcers, and may be taken by persons of the most delicate constitutions, without the least injury, in any season or climate, without hindrance of business." Stoughton's Cordial Elixir was "good for the stomach" and Asthmatic Drops served as "a never failing medicine for the most confirmed asthma and the longest standing, and all sorts of consumptions;" according to the advertisement, one bottle should be adequate. Hull's Colic Pills were to be taken "till they operate." Huxham's Tincture was "useful in low fevers."

The doctor's remedies were often no better than the ordinary household variety. Some of the so-called "cures" are a little shocking when compared with today's standards. Dr. Salmon offered the following directions for making a liniment to treat sciatica in his *Family Dictionary* in 1710. "Take three new whelped Puppies, Earthworms one pound, Leaves of Rosemary, Laurel, Lavender, Mother of Thyme and John's Wort, of each a handful; boil them in common Oil and Red Wine, then strain and press them strongly out, and to the Liquor add of yellow Wax and Goose Grease, of each ten ounces."

For the rheumatism, Dr. Salmon prescribes taking "Chymical Oil of Aniseeds,

1656 which consisted mainly of "one ounce of Crabbe's eyes and four ounces of strong wine vinegar." John Winthrop, Jr.'s recipe for curing the ague is as follows: "Pare the patient's nails when the fever is coming on; and put the parings into a little bag of fine linen—; and tie that about a live eel's neck, in a tub of water. The eel will die and the patient will recover."

Some of the remedies were more pleasant. One could prevent hysterics by eating specially seasoned caraway seeds on bread and butter each day.

Sunburn could be alleviated by an ointment made from elder flowers and hog's lard. If one was seized with "fits of spasmodic

Balsam of Tolu

Observations of Dr. Alexander Hamilton concerning the physicians of New York were that they "study chiefly the virtues of herbs, and the woods there furnish their shops with all the pharmacy they use."

Even though calomel, quinine, and a few other medicines were being used by some of the better doctors by the middle of the eighteenth century, "bleed, purge, and sweat" still remained the most frequently used treatment for nearly any ailment, from a sore throat to the most fatal fever. George Washington died more from unnecessary bleeding than from his serious case of quincy or laryngitis. One Charleston physician is said to have advised: "Bleed and purge, bleed and purge—and, if your patient stays with you, bleed and purge some more."

A Quaker doctor's description of prevailing practice may be characteristic of the times:

> When patients come to I
> I physicks, bleeds and sweats 'em,
> Then—if they choose to die,
> What's that to I—I lets 'em.

and of Rosemary, of each 6 drops, mix it with as much Tobacco, as will fill a pipe, and so smoak it. Repeat it again in a second Pipe, and smoak it as before; and if the Pains cease not, repeat it the third time, and if they be inveterate, the fourth time. It cures it, and gives present Ease as if it was by enchantment."

There were numerous problems with teeth in these days before dentists. Dr. Salmon gives this advice for keeping the teeth "from Rotting or Aching. Wash your Mouth every Morning with Juice of Limons, mix'd with a little Brandy; and afterwards rub your Teeth with a Sage-Leaf, and wash your Teeth after Meat with fair Water mix'd with Brandy."

Medicinal herbs were vended in the backwoods regions by the drug peddlers, who later handled all sorts of patent medicines. Since Philadelphia was an active center for the selling of drugs, many of the peddlers representing the local drug firms would go about crying out their sassafras, bergamot, sweet basil, and wormwood along Chestnut Street, near Independence Hall.

Hawthorne met one of these medicine vendors, "a Dr. Jacques, who carried about with him recommendatory letters in favour of himself and drugs, signed by a long list of

Plate 9. *Indian mortar and pestle. (Courtesy Shelburne Museum, Inc.)*

people. I believe he comes from Philadelphia."

Many such peddlers became renowned for selling "materia medica" in the backwoods areas and were frequently addressed as "Doctor," especially in the South where the pharmacists received similar distinction.

The Yankee drug peddler was the basis for the later introduction of the Medicine Man and the Medicine Show. Richardson Wright in his *Hawkers and Walkers in Early America* describes the medicine man as one who "Carrying the nostrums of some drug house, sets himself up wherever the people gather, in the public square or at country fairs. . . . His flow of language is comparable only to the Fourth of July oratory of present-day senators, although in horrors it sometimes attains the blood-curdling colour of the sermons once preached by Jonathan Edwards."

By the time the Shakers introduced the commercial production of herbs, it was no longer necessary for a housewife to have her own herb garden. Many more varieties became available. Therefore, medicinal herb recipes became more comprehensive in scope at a time when medical science was expanding in the direction of a greater utilization of herbs.

Professor Benjamin Silliman of Yale in one of a series of letters from Lebanon, in the spring of 1832, wrote "They (the New Lebanon Shakers) take great pains in drying and packing their medical herbs, and so highly are they valued that they have frequent orders for them from Europe to a very large amount."

A mid-nineteenth century catalog of the New Lebanon Society listing various "medicinal plants, barks, roots, seeds, flowers and select powders" emphasizes that the Shaker medicinal herb industry was first established in 1800 "being the oldest of the kind in the country."

Eldresses White and Taylor, in their *Shakerism, Its Meaning and Message,* point out that the Shakers were "the first in this country to introduce botanical medical practice, the first roots, herbs and vegetable extracts for medicinal purposes placed on the market having borne the Shaker stamp." The preparing of herbs and roots for general sale by the Shakers was not initiated before around 1820, when Dr. Eliab Harlow and Dr. Garrett K. Lawrence, a botanist of the New Lebanon Society, focused their attention on herbs and roots and introduced a more systematic and scientific method of collecting, preparing, and conducting the business.

In the 1820's, Thomas Corbett of Canterbury, New Hampshire, was one who bought large amounts of balm, sweet marjoram, sassafras bark, poppy capsules, pleurisy root, and red rose.

In 1827, orders were placed for boxes of herbs, extracts, peppermint oil, and such items as basil, horehound, sage, thyme, borage, and hyssop.

The following verse follows the title of a catalog prepared by the United Society of Shakers at New Lebanon, New York:

A blade of grass—a simple flower
Culled from the dewy lea;
These, these shall speak with touching power,
Of change and health to thee.

Plate 10. *European mortar and pestle of the 17th century, possibly used in the Pennsylvania Dutch area. It was located recently in Westchester County, New York. (Courtesy Shelburne Museum, Inc.)*

Plate 11. *English brass mortar and pestle probably used in His Majesty's naval service. (Courtesy Shelburne Museum, Inc.)*

At New Lebanon the Shaker society had fifty acres devoted to gardens of sage, savory, marjoram, horehound, rue, borage, hyssop, pennyroyal, and other plants. Dr. Andrews in *The New York Shakers and Their Industries* notes that "nearly 200 varieties of indigenous plants were collected, and 30 or 40 other varities were brought from the South and West and from Europe."

By the middle of the nineteenth century, the medicinal herb industry had expanded greatly. Methods of preparing plants to be marketed were put on a large-scale basis.

The extract business had become very

extensive by the Civil War era. And the annual output of pulverized herbs and roots or powders was in excess of 7,000 pounds. The supply and demand for various ointments, tinctures, and oils such as that of wormwood had also increased.

New Lebanon and Watervliet, New York, as well as Harvard, Massachusetts, Canterbury, New Hampshire, Enfield, Connecticut and New Hampshire, and New Gloucester, Maine all had flourishing herb industries where herbs were grown and prepared for pharmaceutical use. Union Village, Ohio was the location of that state's largest medicinal herb and extract industry.

Dr. Samuel Thomson, an authority frequently resorted to in the medical recipes which follow, was an itinerant herb doctor from New Hampshire, and author of *A New Guide to Health*. According to Johnston in his

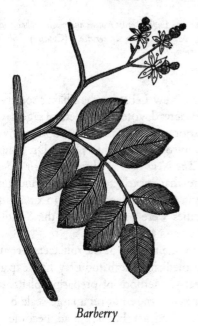

Barberry

Notes on North America (1851), the Thomsonian Medical System had a strong impact on the Shaker herb industry, for it "makes use of herbs only."

Man has used herbs throughout recorded history and possibly "ever since the world began" to cure his ill health. One finds in the *Apocrypha: Ecclesiasticus,* xxxviii, 4 this statement: "The Lord hath created medicines out of the earth; and he that is wise will not abhor them." On the other hand according to Ovid, 43 B.C.—18 A.D., "Medicine sometimes injures, sometimes restores health; showing which plant is healthful and which harmful." Virgil, the Roman poet, wrote in his Aeneid, "He preferred to know the power of herbs and their value for curing purposes, and, heedless of glory, to exercise that quiet art." Even in Shakespeare's *The Merchant of Venice,* one is told, "In such a night Medea gather'd the enchanted herbs that did renew old Aeson." Dr. Salmon in his Preface to his *Family Dictionary,* in 1710, writes, "We have in this book chiefly taken notice of some few Garden Herbs, or Plants, which have a respect to the Table, for Sallets, Pickles, & c. And some few others of Principal Account in Curing common Maladies, which Ladies and Gentlewomen may easily apply to the Benefit of their poor Neighbours, upon many Accounts: . . ."

Salmon adds this comment: "As to the choice of Medicines here treated of, they are Excellent, and the best Compositions of the Kind, extracted out of heaps of Voluminous Authors. And they have a few other Qualifications which go along with them, as being, 1. Few in Number. 2. Cheap. 3. Common, or easily to be had. 4. Easily prepared. 5.

Effectual. 6. Safe in Operation. 7. Small in Dose. 8. Durable, so as not to be hurt by Time. These are true Qualifications, which a set of Medicines, fitly prepared for Family Use, ought to consist of; and any of which being wanting, must make them so much the less valuable and desirable."

Among the herbs used by Dr. Salmon are parsley water, fennel, poppy, savory, nasturtium cresses, garlic, marjoram, marrigold, tarragon, thyme, basil, sage, and mints.

Parsley water "distilled from the Leaf, Root and Stalks, in Balneo Mariae, being gathered in the beginning of the Spring," is recommended by Salmon in that "it attenuates, opens, cleanses, and is Hepatick and Diuretick."

As for fennel, or dill to pickle, "Let your Water boil, then having your Fennel tied up in Bunches, half a dozen walms will be enough; drain it, and let your Pickle be Vinegar."

Dr. Salmon gives directions for two kinds of poppy syrup. One was made infusing the fresh flowers of red poppies in warm spring-water, strained, adding sugar, and "boiling it to a thickness over a gentle Fire." This syrup is "chifly used for Fevers, Pleurises, and Quinsies, and other Diseases, especially of the Brest, that need cooling Medicines." Syrup made from black poppies is suggested by the doctor for "Frensies, or to those that are restless, and cannot sleep well, as also for Catarrhs and coughs."

As for savory, satureia, "The winter kinds is preferred." They are used, "Either by a strong *Infusion* in Sherry, White Lisbon, Canary, or Madera Wine; or in their *Tincture,* being extracted by a good Digestion in

Bayberry

good Brandy, or a choice Sugar Spirit; or in a Pouder." As for the use of savory, "They strengthen and restore the Head, Brain, Nerves, Stomach, Womb, and other Viscera when diseased."

Dr. Salmon includes both external and internal uses for nasturtium cresses. "Used outwardly, beaten up with Lard to cure Scabs in the Head, and other Parts of the Body" and inwardly for such ailments as "Swellings and Diseases of the Spleen, to provoke the Courses, and expel the Dead Child." In 1577, John Grange, in *The Golden Aphroditis,* wrote, "Eat well the cresses." Cress was supposed to help the memory.

Garlic appears to have been considered a versatile herb by the doctor for it was described as helping "the Bitings of Mad Dogs, and other Venemous Creatures:" being a "good Preservative against the Plague;" easing "Pains in the Teeth" and ears. Among its adverse qualities, however, he points out that it "causes strange Fancies and Visions in the Head; therefore let those (troubled with Melancholy) take it inwardly with great Moderation."

Marjoram is mentioned as an herb from which "a rare Conserve" can be prepared using the tops and tenderest parts of sweet marjoram, two handfuls or more; "bruise it very well in a Wooden Bowl or Mortar; add twice the weight in Sugar, boil it up with Marjoram Water till the Sugar comes to the thickness of a Syrup; then put in the beaten Marjoram, and it will be a rare Conserve."

A conserve can be made also of marigold by taking six ounces of these fresh gathered flowers, "Syrup of Limons two ounces; beat them well together, to a Mash or Pulp: Being well beaten, add Syrup of Limons, enough to make it into a fit Body for keeping." Suggested uses include its being an excellent water for inflamed eyes, or for headache.

Dr. Salmon suggests many uses for tarragon, one of which is as a "pultice." He describes this herb as "one of the hot, Spicy Materials of our Sallets, propagated both by Seed and rooted Slips, and springs again several times after it is cut." As for its culinary use, "Gather for Sallets that which is fresh, bright and tender, and tops of the Stalks, not the Leaves which are almost blackish, tough, and old, or lye near the ground, or grow near the bottom of the Stalks. It is generally eaten with Lettice, Purslane, Endive and

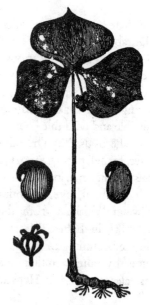

Beth-root

Succory, instead of Rochet, . . ." Among its virtues are noted that it strengthens a weak stomach, invigorates the blood, "and is good for old People."

Thyme is discussed in considerable detail. Among its uses are to purge "the Internals," to ease the pains of gout; it is good also "for Diseases in the Bladder," for "the Sciatica," and it is even suggested as an alleviant for "those that are troubled in mind, and much given to Frights and Fears upon slight occasions."

Garden basil is described as that herb which "comforts the Heart, and expels Melancholy, moves the Courses, and cleanses the Lungs." He includes, also, an ointment made of Basil which is "an excellent Balsam for all green wounds."

Salmon mentions four kinds of sage: the red, the green, the variegated, and the sage of

Bittersweet

virtue. He considers the red and the sage of virtue to be the best. Red is especially good for "a very wholesome and pleasant Sallet in Spring-time, being well washed and dipped in Vinegar and Salt, and so eaten with new Bread and Butter; and its Leaves are a proper Ingredient in all other cold Sallets, provided it is not supream." He cites sage as being good especially for "the Head, Brain, Memory and Dimness of Sight." It is also "good against all Paralytical Affections of the whole Body." He concludes by referring to Blanchard who said that these kinds of sage "make a good medicament against the French pox. They are propagated by Slips, which are planted in April or May." Thomas Cogan in 1596, in his *Heaven of Health*, wrote: "Of all the garden herbs none is of greater virtue than sage."

Among mint concoctions, the doctor includes mint syrup and mint water, recommending them as a remedy for nose bleed, fortifying the blood, restraining vomiting and hiccoughs, headache and earache, biting of mad dogs, etc. As an aid to digestion, "those that affect much Milk, to prevent the curdling of it in their Stomachs, would do well to chew Mint in their Mouth, and swallow the Juice after it."

A curious recipe contains a mixture of rosemary, bawm, cloves, nutmeg, claret, eggs, and sugar for one inclined to have a miscarriage.

This was typical of the information which the early American housewife had regarding the use of herbs; that is, if she was fortunate enough to have access to a copy. Otherwise, she relied on memory, her own jottings, word-of-mouth relays, or Indian recipes, until the time came when a greater availability of household books was made possible with the publishing of such in this country.

According to Joseph Taylor's *Nature the best Physician; or, a Complete Domestic Herbal* (1818), leaves of betony, dried and made into powder, were considered a good ingredient for snuff. It would occasion sneezing. If one removed blackberry roots from the earth in February or March and boiled them with honey, an excellent remedy for dropsy would result. An extract made from decocting burdock root was found successful in cases of the gout, asthma, and jaundice.

According to Geoffrony as quoted by Taylor in his Domestic Herbal, chervil is also excellent against the dropsy. The juice should be expressed from the fresh herb, or put into an earthern pan and exposed to a "violent heat, after which the juice must be pressed out. Dose is three or four ounces every fourth hour."

Taylor writes, "Many troubled with the asthma, cut the (Colt's-Foot) leaves small, and mix it with tobacco for smoaking, and affirm they found great benefit thereby. . . . Consumptive children have been cured by eating the leaves boiled and buttered, or made into a strong tea and sweetened with sugar."

As for special virtues of sweet fennel, Taylor suggests that the whole plant, as well as its seeds, "is greatly cried up against dimness of the eyesight, especially for those who have hurt their eyes by reading in the night time; for this purpose the powder of the seeds should be taken, every morning fasting, with sugar."

Lavender is recommended as being "good in catarrhs, apoplexy, palsy, spasms, vertigo, lethargy, and trembling of the limbs. The dose of the flowers or seeds, is from a scruple to a drachm: or the infusion may be drank in the same manner as tea. The dose of the conserve of the flowers is half an ounce, and of the essential oil from two drops to six on sugar."

An ointment of marsh-mallows is described by Taylor as being an excellent emollient.

Wild or sweet marjoram "helps digestion, . . . , and is employed in baths for the feet." A marjoram tea is good for asthma or a violent cough. When taken as snuff, it "will make the nose run considerably."

As for mustard, some apply it "outwardly to cure the hyp-gout, and also lay it on the feet, mixed with other things, in dangerous fevers."

Taylor cites many uses for the common white onion. "When boiled and mixed with honey, (the onions) are good in disorders of the lungs, arising from a thick clammy phlegm. Many use them when roasted to ripen boils: likewise when bruised with salt they are good for burns and scalds, and for culinary purposes, their uses are too well known to be here described."

"Both wine and sugar may be extracted" from parsnip roots; and "if land is sown with them to feed cattle, they will cause them to yield abundance of milk, and cows, sheep, and lambs, will eat of them as freely as they do of their fodder in general."

A diuretic can be concocted from a conserve of the tops of pennyroyal; it is also useful in cases of "the gravel and jaundice. It is generally taken as a tea, or the juice sweetened with sugar-candy."

Taylor's head-ache remedies include "a juice made of the leaves and flowers of primroses, and equally mixed with milk." This has been done to cure an "inveterate head-ache when everything else has failed. . . . It is also thought good for the night-mare."

Among saffron's great virtues, Taylor mentions that "it refreshes the spirits, is good against fainting fits, and palpitation of the heart. It strengthens the stomach, helps digestion, cleanses the lungs, and is good in coughs. . . . The dose must be taken in moderation, for if too large, it produces heaviness of the head and sleepiness."

Sage tea is considered very good "against the apoplexy, epilepsy, palsy, and trembling of the limbs. . . . It was held in such high estimation among the ancients, that they

Plate 12. *Various mortars and pestles. The center one, standing about fifteen inches high, is of English origin and was made from lignum vitae, a very hard wood. The one at the lower left was made from a burl. The stone mortar and pestle, at the lower right, is of Indian origin and was used only for crude materials. The brass set, to the left of the stone one, is dated 1706 and was probably used in His Majesty's naval service. The one at the top left, hand fluted and decorated throughout, dates back to the 17th century and probably was made by a German wood carver. (Courtesy Shelburne Museum, Inc.)*

have left us a Latin verse which signifies— 'why should a man die, whilst he has sage in his garden.'"

An oil made from St. John's wort is produced "by infusing the flowers in olive oil." Taylor recommends it highly "against pain, and as a balsam. The flowers give their latent red colour very beautifully to the oil in this preparation. An infusion of the fresh tops is good in the jaundice."

As for the medical values of sorrel, primarily they are to "cool and quench the thirst, and the decoction is a serviceable drink in fevers. It is excellent against the scurvy."

An extract made from strawberries, sweetened with honey, "is an excellent gargle for sore throats."

Thyme is "said to strengthen the brain, and to attenuate and rarify clammy humours. They help digestion, and may be of some service in shortness of breath: but they are chiefly used in the kitchen as pot-herbs."

"An infusion of it (Mother of Thyme) made and drank in the manner of tea is pleasant, and is an excellent remedy for headaches and giddiness. . . . It certainly cures that troublesome disease the nightmare. A gentleman afflicted terribly with that complaint took a strong infusion of it by way of remedy, and was free from it many years. Afterwards, the disorder returned, but always gave way to the same remedy."

One of Taylor's cough and cold remedies is supplied by turnips. "When (they are) cut in slices raw, and sugar placed between, the juice drawn therefrom, and administered in colds, and when a cough is troublesome, has been found very efficacious to many."

Liquorice "was directed by the old physicians to be sucked frequently by persons in dropsies, to abate their thirst, and prevent their drinking too often; and this is singular, that whereas the sweet of sugar, in whatever form, makes persons thirsty afterwards, the sweet of liquorice, which is at least equal to it, does not. . . . A kind of beer may be brewed with liquorice in the place of malt, and it will have a considerable strength and an agreeable flavour."

As for the dwarf piony, Taylor discloses that "there is an opinion, that being hung about the necks of children, it will prevent the convulsive disorders to which they are liable in cutting their teeth. . . . The opinion . . . is as old as Galen: he names a girl who was kept free from the epilepsy eight months by wearing a piony root about her neck, and immediately was seized with the disease on dropping it."

Taylor cites also some unique qualities of chickweed. "The young shoots and leaves of chickweed, when boiled, can hardly be distinguished from spring spinach. They are also deemed refrigerating, and nutritive, and an excellent food for persons of a consumptive habit of body."

Several medical books and collections of recipes for good health were published in the 1840's. One of these was Dr. Robely Dunglison's *New Remedies: the Method of Preparing and Administering Them.* . . . published in Philadelphia in 1841. In writing of a method to cauterise, Dr. Dunglison gives the following direction: "By the term *moxa,* the Chinese and Japanese designate a cottony substance, which they prepare by beating the dried leaves of the artemisia chinensis, a kind of mugwort. With this down they form a cone, which is placed upon the part intended to be cauterised, and is set fire to at the top. This mode of exciting counter-irritation has been long practiced by the Chinese and Japanese, . . . , but (according to Kaempfer's *History of Japan,* translated by Scheuchzer) it was not much employed in Great Britain and France until about the commencement of the seventeenth century, when it was introduced through the agency of a physician who had resided in India."

Dr. Beach's remedy for rheumatism as cited in his *American Practice Abridged, or The Family Physician,* (1846) includes the use of burdock which "is used as an alterative. The seeds or the root enter into the *alterative syrup.* It is administered, in the form of decoction, in salt rheum, herpes, ulcers, and rheumatism, and in all diseases of the skin. . . . The root or seeds may be given in the form of a decoction or infusion, which is made by boiling 2 ounces of the fresh root in three pints of water to two; which, when intended as a diuretic, should be drank in the course of two days. The root enters into a medical beer, which is good to purify the blood." The writer was told recently by an herb druggist of a woman whose entire fortune had been spent attempting to gain relief from arthritis. She had even tried the "gold treatment." At length, she contacted the apothecary for an herb remedy. Hesitant to suggest anything, knowing that she had already consulted world renowned specialists, but at her insistence, he mentioned trying Burdock Tea. Her recovery was said to be a miracle. All the townspeople called on her to witness what had happened. Although the writer can make no guarantee, this herb tea is certainly worth a "try".

Dr. Robert Christison who wrote *A Dispensatory, or Commentary on the Pharmacopoeias of Great Britain (and the United States)* (1848) mentions chamomile as an effective herb remedy for dyspepsia. "The most fre-

Black Hellebore

quent application of this drug (Chamomile) at present is as a bitter tonic in dyspepsia. . . . An excellent antacid stomachic in ordinary cases of dyspepsia attended with acidity, consists of two fluid ounces of a fresh infusion, and 10 or 20 grains of bicarbonate of soda, taken half an hour before each meal.

The simple infusion, under the familiar name of chamomile tea, is the most esteemed of domestic remedies for stomach complaints."

Mrs. Sarah J. Hale in *The Way to Live Well, and To Be Well While We Live* (1849) has this suggestion regarding an earache. This, she writes, "is usually caused by a sudden cold. Steam the head over hot herbs, bathe the feet, and put into the ear cotton wool wet with sweet oil and paregoric."

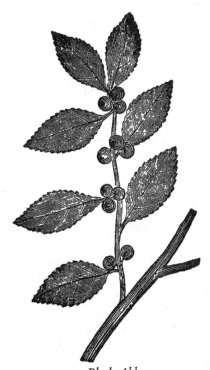

Black Alder

America's first herbal (1801) by Samuel Stearns recommends hasty pudding for those sick people who need a light diet and "cannot bear heavy materials for their suppers." Another name for this dish, which can be made "in Haste," is mush or "sapawn." Stearns' directions follow:

"It is made by boiling wheat, rye, Indian (corn), barley, or oat flour, in water, to a proper consistence, stiring the mixture as it boils, to prevent anempyreuma. It is eaten with milk, or with butter, or butter and molasses, or sugar, & c."

Blood-root

Another rare source in this regard is Dr. George K. Bagley's *The Family Instructor, or Guide to Health:* (1848) "containing the Names and Description of the Most Useful Herbs . . . with A Large List of Recipes, which have been carefully selected from Indian Prescriptions, and from those who were cured by the same after every other remedy had failed."

Dr. Bagley's recipes include Indian Hemp, or Water Nerve Root; Indian Meal Gruel and Indian Tea, for the sick; and Indian Milkweed, or Bitter Root. Among his herb recipes are included the descriptions and uses for wood sorrel, hoarhound, balm of Gilead, hyssop, dandelion, sweet Sicily, borage, mustard, tansy, horse radish, summer savory, senna, and life everlasting.

Bagley mentions wood sorrel as being "good for all inflammation, to quench thirst, and strengthen a weak stomach, restore a lost appetite, and stop vomiting."

Hoarhound is suggested as a fine thing for "lung complaints." Also, "a cold tea made of the leaves, is good to prevent children from coughing nights."

Bagley states that "The oil from the buds (of balm of Gilead) is one of the best remedies for healing a new cut that is known."

The doctor suggests hyssop as being "useful as a gargle in sore throat."

For bilious complaints, Dr. Bagley suggests dandelion. "This herb, root and branch, should be taken, steeped in pure water a sufficient length of time to get out the strength; then strain the liquor from the herb, and continue to simmer the whole till quite thick."

As for sweet Sicily, "This is one of the best

herbs known in a syrup for a cough, it being of a loosening nature."

Borage "Makes a cooling drink in cases of internal inflammation—produces gentle moisture without heating the body. It is sometimes used in rheumatism (or arthritis) and diseases of the skin."

As for mustard seed, Bagley writes, "I find mustard very serviceable in all cases where a blister is necessary. Take rye meal, mix it with vinegar, cover the surface of the poultice with pulverized mustard, and apply it. There is not the danger from mustard poultices that there is from common blisters."

Tansy is recommended for "bruises when pounded with a little spirits; also for hysterics and weak veins."

The doctor suggests horse-radish as being "used in dropsy and general debility of the system. . . . It is also useful in hoarseness when made into a syrup, sweetened with sugar."

Dr. Bagley points out that summer savory "helps colds, stomach, and asthma, by promoting an expectoration of thick viscid matter, which stuffs up the lungs." The doctor reminds his readers that Alexandria senna was used first as a medicine by the Arabians.

"The herb" (life everlasting) "has a pleasant odor, and aromatic smell, and is slightly tart. The infusion taken in warm draughts produces perspiration, and is useful in colds, fevers and influenza."

A number of medicinal uses for herbs are included in the *American Frugal Housewife* (1833). "Sage is very useful both as a medicine, for the headache—when made into tea —and for all kinds of stuffing, when dried and rubbed into powder." Summer-savory

Plate 13. *Nineteenth century advertisement.*

is suggested for colic-relief, and "pennyroyal and tansy are good for the same medicinal purpose." An important "first-aid" ingredient seems to be green wormwood which when "bruised is excellent for a fresh wound of any kind. In winter, when wormwood is dry, it is necessary to soften it in warm vinegar, or spirit, before it is bruised, and applied to the wound."

The American Frugal Housewife cites, also, a number of medicinal teas. For example, "Hyssop tea is good for sudden colds, and disorders on the lungs. It is necessary to be very careful about exposure after taking it; it is peculiarly opening to the pores." A cough remedy is one made from colt's-foot and flaxseed tea, sweetened with honey. "Consumptions have been prevented by it. It should be drank when going to bed; though it does good to drink it at any time. Hoarhound is useful in consumptive complaints."

A natural "tranquilizer" seems to be motherwort tea, which is "very quieting to

Blue Flag

the nerves. Students, and people troubled with wakefulness, find it useful."

Thoroughwort is suggested by the *American Frugal Housewife* as being "excellent for dyspepsy, and every disorder occasioned by indigestion. If the stomach be foul, it operates like a gentle emetic." For a feverish state, sweet-balm tea is said to be cooling. To prevent a threatened fever, "catnip, particularly the blossoms, made into tea, is good. It produces a fine perspiration. It should be taken in bed, and the patient kept warm."

Various virtues of burdock and horseradish are mentioned. "Housekeepers should always dry leaves of the burdock and horseradish. Burdocks warmed in vinegar, with the hard, stalky parts cut out, are very soothing, applied to the feet; they produce a sweet and gentle perspiration. Horseradish is more powerful. It is excellent in cases of the ague, placed on the part affected. Warmed in vinegar, and clapped."

Succory is described as a valuable herb, which when sweetened with molasses, is "a gentle and healthy physic, a preventive of dyspepsy, humors, inflammation, and all the evils resulting from a restricted state of the system."

As for elder-blow tea, "it is cool and soothing, and peculiarly efficacious either for babes or grown people, when the digestive powers are out of order."

Another "certain cure" for a cough is "lungwort, maiden-hair, hyssop, elecampane and hoarhound steeped together. . . . A wine-glass full to be taken when going to bed."

Dr. Bagley writes the following poem at the conclusion of his essay, "On the Nature and Cause of Diseases":

AN INVOCATION

That nice machine the human frame,
O God, inspire my mind
That I may understand the same,
No more to Nature blind.
To thee, great God, to thee we look,
For naught there is but thine;
A lesson teach—'tis Nature's book—
To read it then incline.
All mortals here ope wide your eyes,
And view all Nature's ways;
Thou art the great Physician wise,
To thee be all the praise.

In the past century medical science has advanced so greatly that today even the geometric pattern of many sorts of viruses has been defined. The story of the progress of science is not unlike that of technology, where agricultural and industrial implements have changed more in the past century than in thousands of years.

From examining the remedies of the day, one discovers the ailments according to their contemporary designations. Those which were usual are as follows: ague, asthma, burns, cancer sores, colic, consumption, corns, coughs, diarrhea, dropsy, dyspepsy, dysentery, felons, fever, headache, hysterics, impure blood, itch, jaundice, kidney obstructions, palsy, piles, rheumatism, sore throat, sunburn, tetter or ringworm, toothache, typhus, ulcers, and warts.

Before examining the various ways in which these maladies and discomforts were treated, one might find useful an explanation of various terms used in classifying medicines which Dr. W. Beach included in *The Amer-*

Burdock

ican Practice Abridged, or the Family Physician (1846), along with his "Classification of Articles Composing Materia Medica" and his advice concerning the "Season of Collecting Vegetable Medicines."

GLOSSARY OF OLD MEDICINAL TERMS

Narcotics are substances which diminish the actions and powers of the system, without occasioning any sensible evacuation. They have the effect of producing sleep.

Anti-spasmodics are medicines which have the power of allaying irritation and spasms.

Tonics are those articles which increase the tone of the animal fibre, by which strength is given to the system.

Astringents are articles which have the power of binding or contracting the fibres of the body.

Emetics are medicines which excite vomiting, independent of any effect arising from the mere quantity of matter introduced into the stomach.

Purgatives or Cathartics are medicines which increase

Boneset

the peristaltic motion of the intestines, and thereby produce a preternatural discharge.

Emmenagogues are those medicines which are capable of promoting the menstrual discharge.

Diuretics are those medicines which increase the urinary discharge.

Diaphoretics are those medicines which increase the natural exhalation by the skin, or promote moderate perspiration.

Sudorifics are those medicines which produce copious exhalations or sweating.

Expectorants are those medicines which increase the discharge of mucus from the lungs.

Sialagogues are those medicines which excite a preternatural flow of saliva.

Errhines are those medicines which increase the secretion from the head, and excite sneezing.

Epispastics or Blisters are those substances which, when applied to the surface of the body, produce a serous or puriform discharge, by exciting a previous state of inflammation.

Rubefacients are substances which, when applied to the skin, stimulate, redden, or inflame it.

Refrigerants, medicines which allay the heat of the body or of the blood.

Antacids, remedies which obviate acidity in the stomach.

Lithontryptics, medicines which are supposed to have the power of dissolving urinary concretions in the bladder.

Escharotics or Caustics, substances which corrode or dissolve the animal solids.

Anthelmintics, medicines which have the effect of expelling worms from the intestines.

Demulcents, medicines which obviate and prevent the action of stimulating and acrid substances, by involving them in a mild and viscid matter, which prevents their action on the body.

Diluents, those medicines which increase the fluidity of the blood.

Emollients, substances which soothe and relax the living fibre.

Alteratives. This term is applied to substances which are found to promote a change in the system favorable to recovery from disease, but not with certainty referable to any other class.

Counter-irritants, agents applied to the surface, which excite an eruption or an inflammation, and thus divert the humors from internal to external parts.

The American Practice, 1846

MATERIA MEDICA
CLASSIFICATION

The various articles composing the materia medica may be classed or divided as follows:

1st.	Medicinal Plants.	
2d.	,,	Roots.
3d.	,,	Flowers.
4th.	,,	Seeds.
5th.	,,	Extracts.
6th.	,,	Barks.
7th.	,,	Gums.
8th.	,,	Oils and Balsams.
9th.	,,	Salts.
10th.	,,	Minerals.
11th.	,,	Earthy Substances.

The American Practice, 1846

COLLECTING OF
MATERIA MEDICA

1st. Roots.—Roots must be collected in the spring, before the sap begins to rise, or in the fall after the top is dead.

2d. Barks.—Barks may be stripped from the tree or shrub any time when the sap prevents it from adhering to the wood. The exterior portion must be shaved off; the bark then cut thin, and dried in the shade.

3d. Medicinal Plants.—Medicinal plants should be collected while in blossom, and also dried in the shade; their virtues, however, are not essentially diminished any time before frost appears.

4th. Flowers and Seeds.—Flowers and seeds should be collected when they are fully ripe, and likewise dried in the shade. All vegetables, after having been dried, should be kept from the air, and preserved airtight, or in a dry place. In this way they may be preserved for many years, without losing any of their medicinal properties.

Preparations.—1st. Extracts.—The best method to obtain all the strength and virtues of a plant or vegetable is, to mash them, to which add a little alcohol if necessary, press out the juice, and evaporate in the sun to the consistence of honey; then put it in jars, and cover tight with bladder or skin. This is the inspissated juice, and is much superior to extracts made by boiling.

Infusions or Teas.—Put a handful of the herb into a tea-pot, add one pint of boiling water, and let it stand fifteen or twenty minutes: dose, a full draught three or four times a day, unless differently prescribed. To promote perspiration, take it warm.

Decoctions.—Make the same as infusion; but continue the boiling till all the strength is extracted.

Component parts. . . —Plants are chymical compounds, prepared by the hand of nature; and, although despised by the foolish as simple, they are more ingenious than can be made by the greatest chymist in the world. Nor will his productions bear any comparison with them as regards *beauty* or *medical properties;* and the reason is, because one is made by man, therefore imperfect; the other by the Creator, and therefore absolutely perfect.

The American Practice, 1846

Camphor Tree

RECIPES FOR REMEDIES

The nature of flowers, dame Physic doth shew;
She teacheth them all, to be known to a few,
To set or to sow, or else sown to remove,
How that should be practised, learn if ye love.
THOMAS TUSSER, 1573

AGUE: The flowers (of Medesweet, Queen of the Meadow or Lady of the Meadow) boiled in wine and drunke, do take away the fits of a quarantine ague, and maketh the hart merrie.

The Herball or Generall Histoire of Plantes, 1597

APOPLEXY: The wine (of the lilies-of-the-valley) is more precious than gold, for if any one that is troubled with apoplexy drink thereof with 6 grains of Pepper and a little Lavender water they shall not need to fear it that moneth. *Complete Herbal,* 1652

APOPLEXY, ANOTHER: It (lilies-of-the-valley) cureth Apoplexy by Signature; for as that disease is caused by the dropping of humours into the principall Ventricles of the brain: so the flowers of this Lilly hanging on the plants as if they were drops, are of wonderful use herein, if they be distilled with Wine, and the quantity of a spoonful thereof drunk, and so it restoreth speech to them that have the dumb Palsy. *Adam in Eden,* 1657

ASTHMA: Taken in meat it (saffron) causeth a long and easie breathing, and helpeth the Asthma.

Gardeners Labyrinth, 1577

ASTHMA. ELIXIR ASTHMATIC: Take liquorice root, (pounded pretty fine,) one pound; common honey, one pound; Benzoic acid, or flowers, half an ounce; gum opium, (good,) half an ounce; gum camphor, a third of an ounce; oil of annise, two drachms; common pearlash, half an ounce; best old spirits, eight pints. To the liquorice, pounded pretty fine, add the other ingredients, taking care to pulverize the *opium.* When prepared, it should be kept in a warm place ten or twelve days, and decanted clear. The remaining liquor must be squeezed from the roots, and filtered through a piece of unsized paper.

A New Family Encyclopedia, 1833

ASTHMA. ESSENCE OF PEPPERMINT: By means of a little white sugar, readily mixed with water, and, in the proportion of thirty drops to a pint, makes a pleasanter and better simple water than that distilled from the recent herb; which, from not retaining its flavour in perfection long, is seldom to be procured good in the winter season. The spirituous peppermint-water may be made, by employing brandy in lieu of water, which will prove less pernicious to the organs of digestion than that sold under the name of peppermint cordial, made with spirit of wine. Essence of peppermint is chiefly employed to correct the griping quality of purgatives, and render nauseous medicines more palatable and pleasant to the stomach. It is, however, often taken alone on sugar, or in a little brandy or water, for flatulence, colicky pains in the stomach and intestines, and fits of spasmodic asthma, in which it generally affords speedy but temporary relief.

Medical Guide, 1808

BITTERS FOR STOMACH: One ounce of gentian

Capsicum

root sliced, one ounce of fresh rind of lemon, two drams of cardamom seeds bruised, three drams of Seville orange peel; pour a pint and a half of boiling water over the ingredients, let it stand an hour, then decant the clear liquor, and take a wine glass full two or three times a day.

It should be kept closely covered after the water is put in the ingredients.

Family Receipt Book, 1819

BLEEDING: The leaves, flowers and seedes stamped (of St. John's Wort), and put into a glass with oile olive, and set in the hot sunne for certaine weekes together and then strained from those herbes, and the like quantitie of new put in, and sunned in like manner, doth make an oile of the colour of blood, which is a most pretious remedy for deep wounds.

The Herball or Generall Histoire of Plantes, 1597

BLOOD PURIFIER: Honduras sarsaparilla 12 ozs.; guaiacum shavings 6 ozs.; winter green leaf 4 ozs.; sassafras-root bark 4 ozs.; elder flower 4 ozs.; yellow dock 3 ozs.; burdock-root 4 ozs.; dandelion-root 6 ozs.; bittersweet-root 2 ozs.; all bruised. Place these ingredients in a suitable vessel and add alcohol 1 pt., with water sufficient to cover handsomely, set them in a moderately warm place for 3 or 4 days, pour off 1 pt. of the tincture and set it aside until you add water to the ingredients and boil to obtain the strength, pour off and add more water and boil again, then boil the two waters down to 1 qt.; strain, and add the liquor first poured off, and add 2½ lbs. crushed or coffee sugar, and simmer to form a syrup; when cool, bottle and seal up for use. Dose—One to 2 tablespoons according to the age and strength of the patient, ½ hour before meals and at bed time.

This, or any other alterative, when given, should be followed up for weeks or months, according to the disease for which it is prescribed, as scrofula, and for every disease depending upon an impure condition of the blood. It ought to be used in sore eyes of long standing, old ulcers, saltrheum & c. I would not give this for Jayne's Alterative, nor Swain's, Townsend's or Ayer's Sarsaparillas, because I know it is good, andwe also know what it is made of.

Dr. Chase's Recipes, 1869

ANOTHER BLOOD PURIFIER (VERY STRONG):

Poke, mandrake, yellow dock, sassafras, blue flag, roots, and bark of the roots, guaiac wood raspings, and sweet elder flowers, of each 4 ozs.; caraway seed 3 ozs.; bruise the roots, and put to the whole, alcohol 1 qt., and water to cover all handsomely; let stand 3 or 4 days in a warm place as the last recipe above, making every way the same except to pour off 1 qt., instead of 1 pt., as in the first, of spirit; then boil the waters to 1 qt., adding 4 lbs. of sugar with the qt. of spirit tincture. The dose being only 1 table-spoon 4 times daily as above.

But if that amount should make the bowels too loose, reduce the quantity; and if that amount does not act upon the bowels at all, increase the dose to keep the bowels solvent. This may be used in the most inveterate diseases of long standing, syphilis not excepted.   *Dr. Chase's Recipes*, 1869

BLOOD PURIFIER:
> *Now leeks are in season for pottage ful good*
> *And spareth the milch cow, and purgeth the blood*
> *These having with peason, for pottage for Lent*
> *Thou spareth both oatmeal and bread to be spent.*
>   *Five Hundred Points of Good Husbandry*, 1573

BURNS AND ULCERS. PRIMROSE OINTMENT FOR BURNS AND ULCERS: Bruise one pound of the leaves of this well-known plant in a mortar, along with half a pound of the flowers; simmer these in an equal quantity of hog's lard, without salt, until the primroses become crisp; after which, the ointment, whilst fluid, must be strained through a coarse sieve. This is an excellent application for obstinate ulcers or burns.   *Practical Housewife*, 1860

CANCERS: Half a pint of the juice of the leaves, (Bean, Common) when the plant is in the blossom, boiled gently with a pint of new cream, and half a pound of the best honey, in an unglazed earthen pipkin, till half is consumed, is recommended for the cure of a cancer, or any other tumour, if applied thrice in a day. Vid, Father Abraham's Almanack, published at Philadelphia for 1795.
                          American Herbal, 1801

A Mrs. Loomis, in Connecticut, informed me, that an Indian cured a cancer, by the internal and external use of the juice of white-ash, that issued out of the ends of the wood, as it was burning.
                          American Herbal, 1801

Medicine Chests

CAREFULLY PREPARED

FOR ALL CLIMATES,

WITH

DIRECTIONS

FOR

USING THE MEDICINES.

AND

TREATMENT OF DISEASES

INCIDENT TO SEAMEN,

BY GREGG & HOLLIS,

No. 20, Union-St.........Boston.

BOSTON:
PRINTED BY MOORE AND PROWSE,
No. 62, Washington-Street.
1826.

Plate 14. *Title page of an 1826 book by Gregg & Hollis. The Hollis Drug Store of Boston supplied medical sea-chests for seamen. (Courtesy Shelburne Museum, Inc.)*

CANKER. VIOLET TEA: The common dark-blue violet makes a slimy tea, which is excellent for the canker. Leaves and blossoms are both good. Those who have families should take some pains to dry these flowers.   *American Frugal Housewife*, 1833

CONSUMPTION. REMEDY FOR THE CONSUMPTION: The following medicine has been found effectual in curing a gentleman, who was far gone with the consumption and had been given over as incurable; take hysop, colt's foot, and agrimony, of each one handful, of rue two ounces, of bruised aniseseed, figs sliced, and raisins stoned, of

Castor Bean

the consumption had reduced to a mere skeleton, and was considered to be incurable.

A New and Complete American Medical Family Herbal,
1814

CONSUMPTION: (Conserve and the candied flowers of borage for) those that have been long sicke and feeble or in a Consumption, to comfort the heart and spirits and thereby good for those that are troubled with often swooning or passion of the heart.
Theatrum Botanium, c. 1640

CONSUMPTION, ANOTHER: (The Syrup and conserve of violets are) good for inflammation of the Lungs, the Pleurisie, Coughs and Agues.
Countrie Farme, 1616

CORNS. RED SPURGE USED FOR CORNS, TOOTHACHE ETC.: Warts or corns anointed with the juice of this plant, (red spurge), presently disappear. A drop of it put into the hollow of a decayed and *aching tooth,* destroys the nerve, and consequently

each four ounces, shavings of hartshorn two ounces, and of the dry leaves of fox-glove half an ounce: put all the ingredients in a new earthen pot, pour four quarts of water on them, and add two ounces of liquorice root pulverized, six ounces of sugar candy, and two quarts of pure honey: cover the pot and set it near the fire, frequently putting hot ashes around it, shake the pot every now and then, and after a week's infusion strain the balsam, and put it in bottles for use, as follows: first give the patient a dose of Bowman's ipecacuanha (vide American ipecacuanha) the next morning give him a tablespoonful of the balsam, continuing it every two hours through the day, and a teacup, four times a day, of the following tea: take skunk cabbage and cross-wort, of each an handful, pour four quarts of boiling water on them, and sweeten it with honey when you give it. Let the patient apply to his breast a warm plaster of burgundy pitch, and ride out every pleasant day.

With similar medicine I was instrumental, under God, of restoring to health a poor blacksmith, who

Catnip

removes the pain. Some people rub it behind the ears that it may blister, and by that means give relief.

Family Receipt Book, 1819

COUGH SYRUP: Take of poplar bark and bethroot, each 1 lb; water, 9 quarts; boil gently in a covered vessel 15 or 20 minutes; strain through a coarse cloth; add 7 lbs. loaf sugar, and simmer till the scum ceases to rise. *Family Hand Book, c.* 1855

CURE-ALL: Take the flowers (of rosemary) and put them in a lynen clothe, and so boyle them in fayre cleane water to the halfe and cole (cool) it, and drynke it for it is much worth against all evyls in the body.

A Lytel Herball, 1550

CUTS. LOBELIA AND CAYENNE LINIMENT: Take a quart bottle and put into it ¼ oz. of cayenne, pulverized, then put in 2 ozs. of lobelia herb, and fill up the bottle with whiskey; in two weeks it is ready for use, and applicable for cuts, bruises, strains, sprains, & c.; and it will heal cork cuts in the feet of oxen or horses, without stopping them from labor, and with but very little soreness, by applying 2 or 3 times daily.

I know a gentleman who had a gash cut in his scalp, four inches in length, and to the scull in depth, by a falling limb, which by the use of this liniment only, as strange as it may appear, it healed without pain or soreness. But some may object to it as a whisky liniment. I admit it to be such, but by knowing how to make it yourselves, you get it for a whisky price, and if it be not found as good as one-half of the two-shilling-a-bottle liniments, then you may tell me that I do not know when I have a good thing.

Dr. Chase's Recipes, 1869

CUTS: (Bruised flowering tops of St. John's Wort) are good for wounds and bruises, they stop bleeding and serve as a balsam for one, and take off blackness in the other. *The Family Herball,* 1812

DENTIFRICE: (Juice of marigold petals mixed with vinegar to be rubbed on gums and teeth becomes) a soveraigne remedy for the assuaging of the grievous pain of the teeth. *Gardeners Labyrinth,* 1577

DIARRHEA SYRUP: (For Cases brought on by Long-Continued Use of Calomel) Boxwood, black

Celadine

cherry and prickly ash bark, with dandelion root, of each 2 ozs.; butternut bark 1 oz.; boil thoroughly, strain and boil down to 1 qt.; then add loaf sugar 2 lbs., and alcohol 1 gill, or brandy ½ pt. Dose—A wine glass from 3 to 5 times daily, according to circumstances.

This regulates the bowels and tones up the system at the same time, no matter whether loose or costive. In one case of costiveness it brought a man around all right who had been sewed up tight for twelve days. On the other hand, it has regulated the system after months of calomel-Diarrhea.

Dr. Chase's Recipes, 1869

DIURETIC DECOCTION: Queen of the meadow, dwarf-elder, yellow dock and poke-roots, of each 1 oz.; dandelion, burdock, American Sarsaparilla, and blue flag roots, of each ½ oz.; grind or pound all up, and thoroughly mix. Dose—Take up a pinch with the ends of the fingers and thumb of one hand, say ¼ to ½ oz., and pour upon it 1 pt. of boiling water, steeping awhile; when cool, take a swallow or two sufficiently often to use up the pt. in the course of the day.

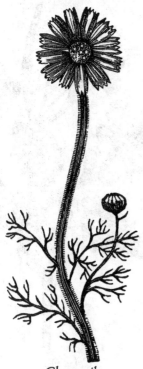

Chamomile

Follow this plan two or three days, or as may be necessary, resuming the course once in ten or twelve days. It may be used in all obstructions of the kidneys, where the urine is high colored or scanty.

Dr. Chase's Recipes, 1869

DROPSY: Parsley is good for dropsy, gravel, and obstructions of the liver and kidneys.

Thomsonian Materia Medica, 1814

DYSENTERY: Blackberries are extremely useful in cases of dysentery. To eat the berries is very healthy; tea made of the roots and leaves is beneficial; and a syrup made of the berries is still better. Blackberries have sometimes effected a cure when physicians despaired.

American Frugal Housewife, 1833

ECLECTIC EMETIC: Which is composed of lobelia, and ipecacuanha, equal parts, and blood root half as much as of either of the others, each pulverized separately, and mix thoroughly. Dose—Half a common tea-spoon every 15 or 20 minutes in some of the warm teas, for instance, camomile-flowers, pennyroyal, or boneset—drinking freely between doses of the same tea in which you take it; continue until you get a free and full evacuation of the contents of the stomach.

Dr. Chase's Recipes, 1869

EMPYEMA (pus in the pleural cavity). COMPOUND SPIRIT OF JUNIPER: Take of: Juniper berries, well bruised, one pound, Caraway seeds, Sweet Fennel seeds, each bruised, one ounce and a half, Diluted alcohol, nine pounds, Water, sufficient to prevent empyreuma. Macerate two days, and draw off nine pounds by distillation. It is unnecessary to make particular observations on each of these simple spirits, as their virtues are the same with those of the substances from which they are extracted, united to the stimulus of the alcohol.

American New Dispensatory, 1813

EYES: Take ooze of this same wort (celandine) or the blossoms wrung out, and mixed with honey; mingle them gently hot ashes thereto, and seethe together in a brazen vessell; this is a special leechdom for dimness of eyes.

Herbarium, 5th Century

EYES: (Cornflowers are) Styptick, and good to Take away Redness, and Inflammation of the Eyes and pains thereof: they cool in fevers, resist Poison, help in Dropsie.

Botanologia, 1710

EYES: The distilled water of the (meadowsweet) flowers dropped into the eies, taketh away the burning and itching thereof and cleareth the sight.

The Herball or Generall Histoire of Plantes, 1597

FELONS. TO CURE FELONS IN SIX HOURS: Venice turpentine 1 oz., and put into it half a teaspoon of water, and stir with a rough stick until the mass looks like candied honey, then spread a good coat on a cloth and wrap around the finger. If the case is only recent, it will remove the pain in 6 hours.

Dr. Chase's Recipes, 1869

FEVER AND AGUE MIXTURE: Take of the best brandy, one pint; camphor, one oz. dissolve: cloves and jalap, each ½ oz., Peruvian bark, 2 oz., Virginia Snake Root, 1 oz., water, one pint; boil the cloves and root with the water, to one half; strain and mix the

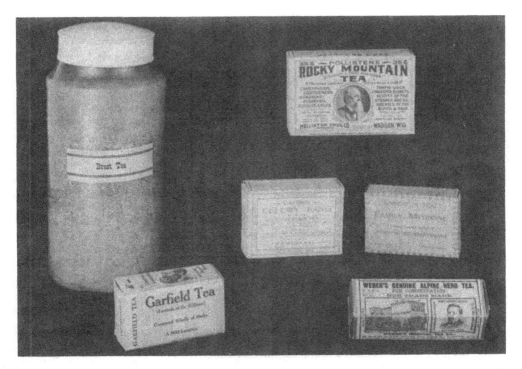

Plate 15. *A collection of various herb teas, including "Rocky Mountain Tea" from Madison, Wisconsin; "Lane's (A Tea) Family Medicine;" "Weber's Genuine Alpine Herb Tea" made in Brooklyn; "Bacon's Celery King," a product of Wells and Company, New York; "Garfield Tea (Formula of Dr. Stillman);" and "Brest Tea," probably made by the German population that migrated from there. (Courtesy Shelburne Museum, Inc.)*

others in powder, with the above. Dose.—A table-spoonful three times a day, in the absence of the fever.

Family Hand-Book, 1855

FEVER. TINCTURE OF BARK, OR HUXHAM'S TINCTURE: Take of Peruvian bark in powder, two ounces; orange peal, dried, half an ounce; Virginia snake root, bruised, three drachms: saffron, one drachm; proof spirits, (rum), two pounds; steep fourteen days and strain. Good preparation of the bark, taken as a bitter, a teaspoonful to a glass of wine before eating; useful in low fevers.

A New Family Encyclopedia, 1833

GARGLE: Mention is made of the value of the flowers of marshmallow, boiled in water and sweetened with a small amount of honey, as being an effective gargle.

Adam in Eden, 1657

GARGLE: It is good to garble (gargle) the mouth with the decoction of the flowers (of lavender), against the paines of the teeth. Two spoonfuls of the distilled water of the flowers taken, doth helpe those that have lost their speech or voyce, restoring it them again.

Theatrum Botanium, 1640

GERMICIDE. BALSAMIC AND ANTI-PUTRID VINEGAR: Take rue, sage, mint, rosemary, and lavender, fresh gathered, of each a handful, cut them small, and put them into a stone jar, pour upon the herbs a pint of the best white-wine vinegar; cover the jar close, and let it stand 8 days in the sun, or near a fire; then strain it off, and dissolve in it an ounce of camphor. This liquid, sprinkled about the sick chamber, or fumigated, will much revive the patient, and prevent the attendants from receiving infection.

Mackenzie's 5,000 Receipts, 1829

GOUT: The flowers of May Lillies (Lillies-of-the-Valley) put into a glasse, and set in a hill of antes close stopped for the space of a moneth, and then taken out, therein you shall finde a liquor, that appeaseth the paine and griefe of the goute, being outwardly applied; which is commended to be most excellent.
The Herball or Generall Histoire of Plantes, 1597

GOUT: That woorthie Prince of famous memorie Henerie the eight King of England, was woont to drinke the distilled water of Broome flowers against surfets and diseases thereof arising.
The Herball or Generall Histoire of Plantes, 1597

GOUT: The (Broome) flowers also bruised and mixed with Hon(e)y and Roses or the white of an egge beaten together and applyed, consume the hard Swellins of the Kings Evil.   *Adam in Eden,* 1657

GUNSHOT WOUNDS: Chamomile was an important ingredient of an Ambroise Pare remedy for gunshot wounds. It has remarkable sedative effects.
HEADACHE: The flowers (of chamomile) boiled in lee, are good to wash the head and comfort both it and the brain.   *Complete Herbal,* 1652

Cicuta

HEADACHE: (Clove Gilliflowers) are cordial, and good for disorders of the head; they may be dried, and taken in powder or in form of tea, but the best form is the syrup. This is made by pouring five pints of boiling water upon three pounds of the flowers picked from the husks, and with the white heels cut off; after they have stood twelve hours, straining off the clear liquor without pressing, and dissolving in it two pounds of the finest sugar to every pint. This makes the most beautiful and pleasant of all syrups.
The Family Herball, 1812

HEADACHE. ROSEMARY. Prop. Odor fragrant, grateful; taste aromatic, warm, bitterish; depending on an essential oil, combined with camphor.
Oper. Tonic, stimulant, emmenagogue, resolvent.
Use. In nervous headaches, and in chlorosis, under the form of infusion; but it is now scarcely ever used, unless as an adjunct, to give odor to sternutatory powders.
Dose. Of the powders, gr. x. to 3 ss.
Thomson's Conspectus, 1844

HEADACHE: If a peece of Red Rose Cake (a mixture of roses and sugar candied) moistened therewith (with vinegar of roses) be cut fit for the Head and heated between a double folded Cloth, with a little beaten Nutmeg and Poppy Seed, strewed on the side that must lie next to the Forehead and Temples and bound so thereto for all night.
Adam in Eden, 1657

HEART: Gather the yellow (saffron) (for they shape much like Lillies) dry, and after dry them, they be precious, expelling diseases from the heart and stomacke.   *Country Housewife's Garden,* 1617

HEART: A conserve made of the (marigold) flowers and sugar taken in the morning fasting cureth the trembling of the hart; and is also given in time of plague or pestilence, or corruption of the aire.
The Herball or Generall Histoire of Plantes, 1597
HEART INFECTION: Take of Burrage, Langdebeef (bugloss) and Calamint, of each a good handful, of Hart's-Tongue, Red Mint, Violets, and Marygolds, of each half a handful, boyle them in White-Wine, or fair running water, then add a pennyworth of the best Saffron, and as much Sugar, and boyle them over

again well, then strain it into an earthen pot, and drink thereof morning and evening to the quantity of seven spoonfuls.   *Countrie Farme, 1600*

HICCOUGH: (Dill will) stay the hiccough being boiled in wine, and but smelled unto, being tied in a cloth. The seed is of more use than the leaves ... and in used in medicines that serve to expel wind.
Complete Herbal, 1652

HOT DROPS: Take of myrrh 4 lbs.; bayberry bark 1 lb.; balmony 12 oz.; scull cap ½ lb.; cayenne 5 oz.; good brandy 5 gallons.   *Family Hand-Book, 1855*

HULL'S COLIC PILLS: Take cinnamon, cloves, mace, myrrh, saffron, ginger, castile soap, of each, one drachm, socotorine aloes one ounce, essence of peppermint sufficient to moisten it. Make common sized pills and take them till they operate.
A New Family Encyclopedia, 1833

HYSTERICS. CARAWAY SEEDS FOR PREVENTING HYSTERICS: Caraway seeds, finely pounded, with a small proportion of ginger and salt, spread upon bread and butter, and eaten every day, especially early in the morning, and at night, before going to bed, are successfully used in Germany, as a domestic remedy against hysterics.
Family Receipt Book, 1819

HYSTERICS: Dr. Joseph Orne, of Massachusetts, relates that a woman was cured of a hysterical complaint, and two men and a young woman of the epilepsy, with the remedy (cow parsnip); which removed flatulence, the vertigo, giddiness, trembling, anxiety, distress, and want of appetite.
    Dose of the root in powder ... A strong infusion of the leaves and tops is also to be taken at bed time.
American Herbal, 1801

INDIGESTION. WHORTLEBERRIES: commonly called huckleberries, dried, are a useful medicine for children. Made into tea, and sweetened with molasses, they are very beneficial, when the system is in a restricted state, and the digestive powers out of order.
American Frugal Housewife, 1833

INDIGESTION. SAFFRON, ETC. BEVERAGE: Elixir proprietatis is a useful family medicine for all

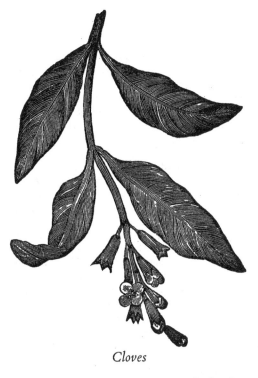

Cloves

cases when the digestive powers are out of order. One ounce of saffron, one ounce of myrrh, and one ounce of aloes. Pulverize them; let the myrrh steep in half a pint of brandy, or N.E. rum, for four days; then add the saffron and aloes; let it stand in the sunshine, or in some warm place, for a fortnight; taking care to shake it well twice a day. At the end of the fortnight, fill up the bottle (a common sized one) with brandy, or N.E. rum, and let it stand a month. It costs six times as much to buy it in small quantities, as it does to make it.   *American Frugal Housewife, 1833*

INSOMNIA: Take drie rose leaves keep them in a glasse which will keep them sweet and then take powder of mynte, powder of cloves in a grosse powder, and putte the same to the Rose leves thanne putte all these together in a bagge and Take that to bedde with you and it wyll cause you to sleepe and it is goode to smelle unto at other tymes.
Little Dodoen, 1606

INTESTINAL DISTRESS: Carminatives are medicines which allay intestinal pain, arrest or prevent griping caused by cathartics and exert a general soothing effect. They are aromatic, and to a certain extent, stimulant. *Anise-seed.* Anise is a pleasant, aromatic carminative, and is used in flatulent colic. Dose—Of the powdered seed, ten to fifteen grains; of the infusion (a teaspoonful of seed to a gill of water), sweetened, may be given freely; of the oil, five to ten drops on sugar. *Fennel-seed.* This is one of our most grateful aromatics, and is sometimes employed to modify the action of senna and rhubarb. Dose—Same as that of anise-seed. *Ginger.* The root is the part used. This is a grateful stimulant and carminative. Dose— Of the powder, ten to twenty grains; of the infusion, one teaspoonful in a gill of water; of the tincture, twenty to thirty drops; of the essence, ten to fifteen drops; of the syrup, one teaspoonful. *Wintergreen.* The leaves are used. This plant possesses stimulant, aromatic, and astringent properties. The essence of Wintergreen is carminative, and is used in colics. Dose—Of the essence, one-half to one teaspoonful in sweetened water; of the oil, three to five drops on sugar. *Peppermint.* Peppermint is a powerful stimulant, carminative, and antispasmodic. It is used in the treatment of spasms, colic, and hysteria. Dose—The infusion may be used freely. The essence may be taken in doses of fifteen to thirty drops in sweetened warm water; of the oil, one to five drops on sugar. *The People's Common Sense Medical Adviser,* 1875

Cohosh

IRRITATING PLASTER (Extensively Used by Eclectics): Tar 1 lb.; burgundy pitch ½ oz.; white pine turpentine 1 oz.; rosin 2 ozs. Boil the tar, rosin and gum together a short time, remove from the fire, and stir in finely pulverized mandrake root, blood root, poke root, and Indian turnip, of each 1 oz.

This plaster is used extensively in all cases where counter irritation or revulsives are indicated; as in chronic affections of the liver and lungs, or diseased joints, & c. It is applied by spreading it on cloth and over the seat of pain, renewing it every day, wiping off any matter which may be on it, and also wiping the sore produced by it with a dry cloth, until relief is obtained, or as long as the patient can bear it. Always avoid wetting the sore, as it will cause inflammation, and you will be obliged to heal it up immediately, instead of which the design is to keep a running sore as long as may be necessary, using at the same time constitutional remedies as the case may require.

Dr. Chase's Recipes, 1869

JAUNDICE: Black cherry-tree bark, barberry bark, mustard-seed, petty morrel-root, and horseradish, well steeped in cider, are excellent for the jaundice.
American Frugal Housewife, 1833

MUSCLE ACHE: Though Mugwort be an Herb noted amongst the Vulgar for preventing weariness upon sore Travell (the gentry, of course, did not travel on foot.), . . . yet I find Ladies Bedstraw (also called Cheese Rennet) more celebrated for that purpose amongst Authors who say that the Decoction of the Herbe and Flowers being yet warme, is of admirable use to bath the Feet of Travellers, and others who are surbated by long Journeys in hot weather, and for Lackies and such like, where running long causeth not onely wearinesse, but stiffenesse in the Sinews and Joynts, to both which this herb is so friendly, that it maketh them to become as lissome, as if they had never been abroad.

Adam in Eden, 1657

NAUSEA: Of the red Roses are usually made many compositions all serving to sundry good uses. . . . To entreate of them all exactly I doe not entend for so a pretty volume of itselfe might be composed, I will therefore only give you a hint. . . . Rose leaves and Mints heated and applyed outwardly to the stomacke stayeth castings and strengthneth a weake stomache very much.   *Theatrum Botanicum,* 1640

56

Comfrey

NERVE TONIC: (A conserve of sage flowers) eaten to warme and comfort the Brain and Nerves, to help and restore the memory, quicken the Senses, . . .
Botanologia, the English Herbal, 1710

NERVE TONIC: A tea made of them (lily-of-the-valley flowers) and drank for a constancy, is excellent against all nervous complaints, it will cure nervous headaches, and trembling of the limbs: a great deal too much has been said of this plant, for people call it a remedy for apoplexies and the dead palsies, but though all this is not true, enough is, to give the plant a reputation and bring it again into use.
The Family Herball, 1812

NOSEBLEED: The bruised flowers of Ladies' Bedstraw pushed up the nostrils, stayeth their bleeding. *Complete Herbal, 1652*

OILS OF FLOWERS: To make oyle of Roses or Violets. Take the flowers of Roses or Violets, and break them small, and put them into Sallet oyle, and let them stand in the same ten or twelve dayes and then presse it. (This recipe could be used for making oils of any flowers. Typical oils of flowers used in medicines included arnica, chamomile, fleabane,

57

lavender, marjoram, orange flowers, pennyroyal, rosemary, thyme.)
English Housewife, 1615

OINTMENT FOR PALSYE: Take the flowers of stickades (stoechas lavender), the flowers of ye right spike, the flowers of french, the flowers and cropps of rosemary, ye flowers and cropps of Isop; ye flowers and cropps of maudeline, and a handfull of kowslipp flowers, ye crops of sage, of each of them a handfull, and of Camomill-flowers, three handfuls: put them all into a sallet oile, and make it as you make oile of Roses. *Fairfax Family's Still-Room Book, 17th. C.*

OINTMENT FOR SUNBURN AND WRINKLES: An oyntment made of the leaves (of cowslips) and Hogs grease, healeth wounds; and taketh away Spots, Wrinkles, and Sunburnings, and so doth the distilled water of the flowers; As divers Ladies, Gentlewomen and she Citizens whether wives or widdows know well enough.
Adam in Eden, 1657

OINTMENT FOR WRINKLES AND BLEMISHES: (The juice of cowslip flowers is suggested for clearing away blemishes and says that they will) take

Common Elder

away the wrinkles thereof and cause the skinne to become smooth and faire.   *Paradisi in Sole,* 1629

PALSY. COMPOUND SPIRIT OF LAVENDER: Was first introduced into the practice of medicine under the name of Palsy Drops. It may be conveniently taken upon sugar, or in a glass of wine, from forty to eighty drops, in cases of langour, weakness of the nerves, decay of age, lowness of spirits, and fainting fits.

It is chiefly employed by apothecaries to cover the ill flavour of nauseous drugs, as well as to colour their medicines.   *Medical Guide,* 1808

PHYSIC: In a Garden there be Turneps and Carrets which serve for sauce, and if meat be wanting, for that too. Neither doth it afford us Aliment only, but Physic . . . But besides this inestimable profit, there is another not much inferior to it, and that is the wholesome exercise a man may use in it.
    The Art of Simpling, 1656

PHYSIC: The red or Clove Gilliflower is most used in Physicke in our Apothecaries shops, none of the other being accepted of or used (and yet I doubt not, but all of them might serve, and to good purpose, although not to give so gallant a tincture to a Syrupe as the ordinary red will doe) and is accounted to be very Cordiall.   *Paradisi in Sole,* 1629

PILES: Tea made of slippery elm is good for the piles, and for humors in the blood; to be drank plentifully.
    American Frugal Housewife, 1833

PLAGUE AND POISON FROM INSECTS (Scorpion and Spider Poison): We in these dayes doe chiefly use them (cornflowers) as a cooling Cordiall and commended by some to be a remedy not onely against the plague and pestilential diseases, but against the poison of Scorpions and Spiders.
    Theatrum Botanium, 1640

RHEUMATISM WINTER EVERGREEN—ALSO CALLED RHEUMATISM-WEED-TEA: Winter evergreen is considered good for all humors, particularly scrofula. Some call it rheumatism-weed; because a tea made from it is supposed to check that painful disorder.
    American Frugal Housewife, 1833

RING-WORM. NARROW-LEAVED DOCK ROOT FOR RING-WORM: Narrow-leaved (yellow) dock root, sliced and soaked in good vinegar, used as a wash, is highly recommended as a cure for tetter, or ring-worm.   *Dr. Chase's Recipes,* 1869

SAGE: Sage is a perennial garden plant, from twelve to twenty inches high; its flowering summit and leaves have a strong fragrant odor, and a warm, bitter, aromatic, and somewhat astringent taste. It possesses a volatile oil which may be procured by distillation with water, and contains considerable camphor.

Medical Uses. There are combined in sage a considerable degree of tonic and astringent 'powers, which are common to most aromatic plants. In form of a gargle, when combined with alum or borax, in vinegar, with cayenne and honey, it is an excellent remedy for inflammation of the throat and relaxation of the uvula. In the Thomsonian practice, sage in connection with senna, has been used with good results. While the writer was in practice on the island of Nantucket, in 1822, the *typhus fever* was epidemic during the winter, and proved fatal to the greater part of those who were attended by the regular physicians. One family in particular, lost three of its members, all of whom were under a high state of mental

Copaiba

derangement, from the first or second day after the attack. The symptoms were pain in the head, back and limbs, with sore throat, and great anxiety and nervous excitability. The first lived seven days, the second four, and the third eleven. The unremitted attention of two or three physicians could afford no relief. After the decease of the last child, the father remarked, that should another member of his family be attacked, he should employ the botanic physician. In a few days, the eldest daughter was taken with precisely the same symptoms as the others, and much against her inclination, we were called. As it was highly important for the safety of the patient that she should possess her mental faculties during her sickness, in order that we might know from herself the situation of her system, and as she was already inclining to derangement, our first object was to quiet the

Dandelion

nervous irritability of the body, and relieve the distress in the head. To effect which, we took half an ounce of sage, half an ounce of senna, (cassia marilandica) and put the two articles into half a pint of boiling water, to which we added one teaspoonful of ginger. The articles were simmered together about twenty minutes; then half the quantity was poured off and administered at a time, when cool enough to drink. We also applied to the neck an adhesive stimulating plaster, and put a bottle of hot water to the feet. The medicine operated, and in about three hours, the pain in the head was entirely gone, the nervous excitement was much reduced, and the patient felt quite comfortable. Tonics were next given, and in a few days she was restored to health without at any time losing her senses. The same winter we attended five patients in that family, three of the typhus fever, and the case above mentioned is a fair account of the others. They all recovered to the great satisfaction of

Devils' Bit

their parents. I occasionally gave a light emetic, and sometimes ordered an injection of milk, in which were cayenne and castor oil: this would entirely remove the stricture of the bowels. Cathartics and astringents were given in such proportions as to produce just a healthy motion of the bowels, consequently the head was clear, easy and comfortable. When these two opposite medicines were given, in just proportions to correct the action, I found no danger of mortification, or of any other injury resulting from the physic.

In putrid difficulties, sage tea may be used with great advantage, as an *antiseptic;* and if an aperient were to be used, it should be of oil and milk. This creates an agreeable sensation, and renders the patient comfortable. In all cases of violent diseases, attended with insanity, the bowels are generally the seat of disease, attended with cold feet and pressure of the blood to the head. In such cases, after using the proper remedies for the bowels as laxatives, bathe the feet in hot water, and thus you will much assist the favorable operation of the medicine. Powerful physic should never be given.

The Thomsonian Materia Medica, 1841

SORE THROAT. ROSEMARY FOR SORE THROAT: Take rosemary tops, about a handful, put them into a basin, and pour a pint of boiling hot ver-juice upon it; then cover it over with a tin funnel, the broad side downwards, and the steam will come through the nozzle of the funnel; then hold your mouth over the steam till it is gone down your throat.

N.B. Be very careful that you do not put your mouth too close to the funnel, as it may scald it, but let the steam go down your throat as much as possible, and repeat it as often as necessary.

Family Receipt Book, 1819

SPIRIT OF CARAWAY: Take of Caraway seeds bruised, half a pound, Diluted alcohol, nine pounds. Macerate two days in a close vessel; then pour on as much water as will prevent empyreuma, and draw off by distillation nine pounds. In the same manner is prepared the same quantity of spirit from:

One pound of Bark of cinnamon, bruised . . . . . *Spirit of cinnamon.*

One pound and a half of Peppermint in flower . . . . *Spirit of peppermint.*

One pound and a half of Spearmint in flower . . . . . *Spirit of spearmint.*

Two ounces of Nutmeg, well bruised . . . . . *Spirit of nutmeg.*

Half a pound of The fruit of pimento bruised . . . . . *Spirit of pimento, or allspice.*

American New Dispensatory, 1813

SPLINTERS, THORNS: It is found by good experience, that if Cloathes and Spunges be wet in the said water and applyed to any place whereinto thornes, Splinters etc. have entered and be there abiding, it will notably draw forth, so that the thorn gives a medicine for its own pricking. (Reference, here, is to the distilled water of the hawthorn flowers.)

Adam in Eden, 1657

STEAM BATHS. HERBS FOR STEAM BATHS. People in general think they must go abroad for vapor-baths; but a very simple one can be made at home. Place *strong* sticks across a tub of water, at the boiling point, and sit upon them, entirely enveloped in a blanket, feet and all. The steam from the water will be a vapor-bath. Some people put *herbs* into the water. Steam-baths are excellent for severe colds, and for some disorders in the bowels. They should not be taken without the advice of an experienced nurse, or physician. Great care should be taken not to renew the cold after; it would be doubly dangerous.

American Frugal Housewife, 1833

STIMULANT APERIENT PILLS: Take Extract of Bitter apple, 20 grains; Aloes, 20 grains; Flowers fo Benzamin, 20 grains; Salt of Amber, 20 grains; Myrrh, 20 grains; Castor, 30 grains; Calomel prepared, 30 grains; Camphor, 10 grains; Salt of Hartshorn, 10 grains; Balsam of Peru, sufficient to form pills. Dose: One dram.

Art of Preventing Diseases, 1794

SUNBURN. ELDER-FLOWER OINTMENT: This is the mildest, blandest, and most cooling ointment, as the old women term it, which can be used, and is very suitable for anointing the face or neck when sun-burnt. It is made of fresh elder-flowers stripped from the stalks, two pounds of which are simmered in an equal quantity of hog's lard till they become crisp, after which the ointment, whilst fluid, si strained through a coarse sieve.

Practical Housewife, 1860

TINCTURES: In making any of the tinctures in common use, or in making any of the medicines called for in this work, or in works generally, it is not only expected, but absolutely necessary, that the roots, leaves, barks, & c., should be dry unless otherwise directed; then:

Take the root, herb, bark, leaf or gum called for, 2 ozs.; and bruise it, then pour boiling water $\frac{1}{2}$ pt., upon it, and when cold add best alcohol $\frac{1}{2}$ pt., keeping warm for from 4 to 6 days, or letting it stand 10 or 12 days without warmth, shaking once or twice daily; then filter or strain; or it may stand upon the dregs and be carefully poured off as needed.

With any person of common judgment, the foregoing directions are just as good as to take up forty times as much space by saying—take lobelia, herb and seed, 2 ozs.; alcohol $\frac{1}{2}$ pt.; boiling water $\frac{1}{2}$ pt.,—then do the same thing, over and over again, with every tincture which may be called for; or at least those who cannot go ahead with the foregoing instructions, are not fit to handle medicines, at all; so I leave the subject with those for whom the given information is sufficient.

In making compound tinctures, you can combine the simple tinctures, or make them by putting the different articles into a bottle together, then use the alcohol and water it would require if you was making each tincture separately.

Dr. Chase's Recipes, 1869

Dwarf Elder

Elecampane

TONIC. MEDICATED WINE OR BEER: Take of Gentian, Lemon Peel, Mint, Juniper Berries, of each 4 ounces. Cinnamon, 2 ounces. Rust of Iron, 1 ounce.

Infuse these in a Gallon of Wine, or Ale, for fourteen days.

Dose: Of the Ale half a pint, of the Wine three or four ounces.

Art of Preventing Diseases, and Restoring Health, 1794

TONIC. A MEDICINE WHICH WILL INVIGORATE THE SYSTEM, ETC.: Take the juice of sage one gill, powdered cinnamon and ginger of each one ounce, bruised fresh angelica root one ounce, fresh spikenard root cut small two ounces, saffron two ounces, galangal root two ounces, and one ounce of cloves: put all the ingredients in a brass kettle, and boil them in six quarts of mountain Malaga, or Madeira wine for an hour: strain the wine through a piece of fine muslin, put it in bottles well corked, and keep it in a cool cellar for use. In all debility, lowness of spirits, and dejection of mind, the patient may take half a wine glass, every morning and before dinner, increasing the dose after a week to a wine glass twice a day, until it has answered the effect: then omit the

medicine for a week or two, when he may proceed again to use it for a week or so, alternately.

In case of costiveness, the patient may drink frequently the following laxative: pour a pint of boiling water on an ounce of cream of tartar, and when cool take a tea-cup full frequently, which will keep the body soluble without weakening the patient. Use the salt water bath twice a week in the warm months, and ride about in good weather.

A New and Complete American Medical Family Herbal, 1814

VENEREAL DISEASE: Dr. Tracy of Connecticut, informed me that a decoction of the root (Common Flag) cured a woman of the lues venerea, when mercurials failed. . . .   *American Herbal,* 1801

WARTS. USE OF CELANDINE TO CURE WARTS, ITCH, ETC.: The juice of this plant (celandine) cures tetters and ring-worms, destroys warts, and cures the itch.

Family Receipt Book, 1819

WOUNDS. LAVENDER, ETC.: Take the best white wine vinegar, a handful of lavender leaves and flowers, the same quantity of sage leaves and flowers, hysop, thyme, balm, savory; a good handful of salt, and two heads of garlic; infuse these in the vinegar a fortnight or three weeks; the longer the better; and then it is found to be an excellent remedy for wounds.

Family Receipt Book, 1819

Euphorbia

LISTS OF DISEASES AND REMEDIAL HERBS

The writer found the scope and comprehensiveness of the following list so interesting that it is included. The source of this list of "Diseases; Also the Name of the Plant, Herb, or Root, Useful to Cure, or Alleviate the Same" is Joseph Taylor's *Nature the best Physician; or, a Complete Domestic Herbal*, 1818.

ague
  betony
  hemp agrimony
  mustard
  St. John's wort
  wormwood
  foxglove
asthma
  burdock
  coltsfoot
  horehound
  hyssop
  lovage
  mallows
  marjoram
  nettles
  scurvy grass
  valerian
  speedwell
  hogs fennel
  stramonium
apoplexy
  lavender
  sage

appetite
  mint
  little Centaury
blood, sweetener of
  balm
blood, purifier of
  brooklime
blood, spitting of
  groundsel
  nettles
  shepherd's purse
  mullein
  plantain
blood, coolers of
  lettuce
blood, coagulated
  spear mint
  St. John's wort
bruises
  briony
bilious humours
  endive
bilious humours, fevers
  endive

boils
  onions
brain, to strengthen
  rosemary
  thyme
brain, disorders of
  sage
body, to cool
  strawberrys
breath, shortness of
  thyme
breasts, swelled
  turnips
breasts, sore
  comfry
cancers
  goose grass
consumption
  coltsfoot
  pimpernell
  chickweed
  stramonium
cholic
  ground ivy

lovage
spearmint
parsley
anise
speedwell
cough
  mallows
  horehound
  marjoram
  nettles
  penny royal
  horse raddish
  saffron
  turnips
  vervain
  liquorice
  comfry
  mullein
  elecampane
  stramonium
catarrh
  lavender
convulsions
  mother wort

valerian
piony dwarf
cold
turnip
common violet
costiveness
common violet
corns
houseleck
dropsy
agrimony
betony
blackberry
brooklime
butcher's broom
chervil
garlic
parsley
horse raddish
tansey
wormwood
crowfoot
liquorice
speedwell
buckbean
butter wort
toad flax
foxglove
digestion, to help
hyssop
lovage
marjoram
horse raddish
sage
thyme
centaury
diuretic
leeks
dysentery
strawberry
mullein
diarrhoeas
horse bean
throatwort
diabetes
horse bean
eye-sight
fennel
rue

trefoil
houseleek
eyes
eyebright
toad flax
celandine
expectoration
hyssop
nettles
liquorice
epilepsy
rosemary
sage
valerian
foxglove
evil
figwort
emetic
foxglove
fevers
agrimony
sorrel
strawberry
shepherd's purse
houseleek
germander
feet, swelled
agrimony
flux
spear mint
dead nettle
celandine
fits
mother wort
fits, fainting
saffron
flatulency
thyme
coriander
anise
garden clary
face, spots on
horse bean
gravel
butcher's broom
ground ivy
mallows
nettles
parsley

penny royal
garden raddish
horse raddish
strawberry
common violet
asparagus
dandelion
dittander
cuckoo-point
gout
burdock
nettles
St. John's wort
crowfoot
buck bean
ground pine
green sickness
horehound
scurvy grass
tansey
gums, sore
scurvy grass
heartburn
camomile
heart, palpitation of
saffron
valerian
humours, to cleanse
coltsfoot
cresses
lovage
oats
rosemary
succory
turnips
hoarseness
mallows
horse raddish
common violet
hysteric affections
mother wort
penny royal
rue
St. John's wort
valerian
southernwood
mugwort
hypochondria
mustard

viper grass
head-ache
primroses
sage
savory
sneezewort
valerian
vervain
cowslip
crowfoot
thyme
lilly of the valley
garden clary
piony dwarf
hog's fennel
haemorrhage
yarrow
celandine
intestines
mallows
indigestion
anise
garden clary
itch
speedwell
figwort
jaundice
agrimony
brooklime
burdock
groundsel
agrimony
lovage
nettles
penny royal
rosemary
St. John's wort
strawberry
succory
vervain
pile wort
speedwell
centaury
buckbean
toad flax
eryngo
kidneys
horse raddish
lethargy

lavender
lungs
  mallows
  onions
  horse raddish
  turnips
  speedwell
  mullein
  eryngo
  elecampane
limbs, trembling of
  lavender
  rosemary
liver complaints
  succory
  piony dwarf
looseness
  yarrow
  shepherd's purse
  comfry
  plantain
low spirits
  garden clary
menses, to promote
  brooklime
  horehound
  mother wort
  penny royal
  rue
  St. John's wort
  valerian
  yarrow
  shepherd's purse
menses, discharge of
  mullein
  plantain
  ground pine
memory, to strengthen
  rosemary
melancholy
  St. John's wort
madness
  St. John's wort
mouth, disorders of
  scurvy grass
  throat wort
night mare
  primroses

rue
thyme
piony dwarf
nervous disorders
  rosemary
  sage
  savory
  thyme
  valerian
  vervain
  cowslip
  thyme
  lilly of the valley
  garden clary
  piony dwarf
  ground pine
obstructions
  cresses
  dandelion
  agrimony
  hops
  mother wort
  rosemary
  rue
  savory
  scurvy grass
  viper's grass
  crowfoot
  asparagus
  germander
  dandelion
  piony dwarf
  centaury
  celandine
  hog's fennel
  eryngo
  mugwort
piles
  brooklime
  pilewort
  figwort
  mullein
  toad flax
palsey
  lavender
  rosemary
  sage
pleurisy

nettles
perspiration, to promote
  rue
  viper's grass
  pimpernell
palpitation of heart
  valerian
purging
  shepherd's purse
  butter wort
  toad flax
paralytic cases
  cuckoo-point
ring-worms
  blackberry
rheumatism
  horse-raddish
  buckbean
  cuckoo-point
stomach
  angelica
  camomile
  mustard
  penny royal
  horehound
  hyssop
  lovage
  spear mint
  horse raddish
  sage
  tansey
  thyme
  viper's grass
  centaury
scurvy
  brooklime
  goose grass
  cresses
  dandelion
  garden raddish
  endive
  agrimony
  lettuce
  horse raddish
  scurvy grass
  sorrel
  succory
  turnips

water-dock
crowfoot
figwort
buck bean
dittander
scrophula
  briony
sleepy disorders
  mustard
sores and ulcers
  carrots
stone
  nettles
scalds
  onions
spasms
  lavender
spleen
  mother wort
stone
  betony
spirits, to refresh
  rue
  garden clary
swellings of wounds
  sage
swellings
  crowfoot
stranguary
  strawberry
sciatica
  dittander
skin, eruptions on
  figwort
spleen
  vervain
sore throat
  strawberry
throat, inflamed
  groundsel
tumours
  mallows
trembling of limbs
  sage
tooth-ache
  dittander
teeth, tartar, to remove
  strawberry

ulcers of kidnies	toad flax	wounds	St. John's wort
agrimony	Uvala, falling of	brooklime	tansey
ulcers of legs	throatwort	ground ivy	wormwood
blackberry	vertigo	St. John's wort	germander
ulcers and sores	lavender	wind	dittany
carrots	vomitings	camomile	centaury
ground ivy...	spear mint	lovage	whites
urine, acrimonious	vapours	marjoram	rosemary
St. John's wort	valerian	worms	warts
asparagus	venomous bites	mother wort	crowfoot
dandelion	dittany	groundsel	horse bean

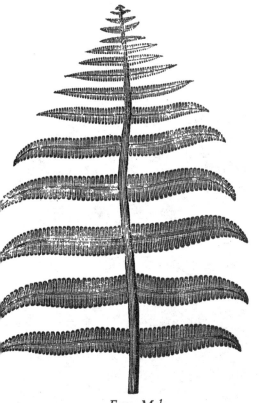

Fern, Male

Flowering Ash

Plate 16. *The cover from a copy of Peterson's Magazine published in 1864.*

Plate 17. *An 1864 engraving entitled "The Damask Rose" that appeared in Peterson's Magazine.*

CHAPTER THREE

Toiletries
Perfumes
Pomatum

They that smell least, smell best.
New Help to Discourse, 1669

HISTORICAL BACKGROUND

SINCE THE EARLIEST of times, woman has displayed an avid interest in being beautiful even if her beauty had to be attained by artificial means. The women living in colonial America were no exception.

Among the early Dutch, for example, some ladies powdered their hair, painted their faces, darkened their eyebrows, and daubed powder under their eyes often so skillfully that one could hardly detect make-up.

Good grooming was also essential among the men, especially those of the wealthy class. But all classes of men in America wore wigs throughout the seventeenth century. Even the Negro slaves displayed white horse-hair wigs, goat's hair bobbed wigs,

natural wigs, the plainer wigs, and many of the costlier sorts, if they were given to them as half-worn and second-hand.

These wigs required a great deal of care; their dressing was costly and they wore out quickly. One account mentions how barbers cared for them by the month or year. Two pounds a year was an approximate sum necessary for the care of a single wig. "On Saturday afternoons, the barber's boys were seen flying through the narrow streets, wig-box in hand, hurrying to deliver all the dressed wigs ere sunset came."

In these days before chemical insecticides, one is a little apprehensive over the pomatum used by the early Dutch. Really, it was an orange butter, a Dutch marmalade. An account in the *Closet of Rarities* (1706) discloses the recipe for making this orange butter. "Take new cream two gallons, beat it up to a thickness, then add half a pint of orange-flower-water, and as much red wine, and so being become the thicknesse of butter, it has both the colour and smell of an orange."

In the recipes for various herb pomades which follow, one finds the grease ingredient of the pomatum provided by using beef marrow, hog's lard, or mutton suet, but there is the pleasant addition of lavender or rosemary for scent.

There were many ladies who wished to keep their complexion soft and fair. The Southern lady considered a flawless complexion extremely important, for this was one way one could differentiate between a lady and a woman whose leathery, reddish complexion would disclose her exposure to the kitchen fire and the weather. The following 1709 recipe for curing a red face was considered an effective one even though it did not contain herbs. "Take of Spring-water a pint, Oil of Tartar, and Oil of Bitter Almonds, each a quarter of an ounce, mix them and wash your face Night and Morning. Another, take one pound of Lime, put it into two quarts of Spring-water, let it stand till it be clear, then take off the top of it, and wash your Face with the Water Morning and Night."

At times, guests might even help with the gathering of some of the ingredients. A letter written by a woman in New Jersey mentions having been elegantly entertained at the Clarks'. "By way of amusement after dinner we all went into the garden to pick roses. We gathered a large basketfull, and prepared them for distilling. As I had never seen Rosewater made, Mrs. Clark got her still and set it going, and made several bottles while we were there. They were extremely civil, and begged us whenever we rode that way in the evening to stop and take a syllabub with them."

Just how rose water was made is explained in the following 1709 recipe: "Take Damask Roses when just blown, before they open too much, and lose their Fragrancy in the Air, gather them when the Sun has dried off the Dew or Moisture; and having picked the Leaves from the Stalks, without suffering any Seeds to scatter among them, spread them on a clean Carpet free from Dust, till they are almost free from any moisture; then put them into a Pewter Still, and make a Fire

Foxglove

under them gently by degrees, and fasten your Bottle or Receiver, to the Nose of the Still, tying Paper or Linnen about it, to keep in the Scent; and so Corking them up, when full of the Water, within an Inch of the Cork, set them in the Sun two or three days, and then in a warm place especially, lest the Frost take them and either break the Bottle, or spoil the Scent of the Water."

As for the syllabub Mrs. Clark offered her guest, early recipes indicate that a sprig of rosemary was an important ingredient along with wine, raspberry juice, nutmeg, lemon, sugar, and cream.

There were peddlers as early as the 1600's. In 1699, Edward Ward said of Boston, "in the chief or High Street there are stately Edifices, some of which have cost the owners two or three Thousand Pounds the raising. ... For the Fathers of these Men were Tinkers and Peddlers."

In colonial times, the New England peddler carried a rather limited stock. By 1750, James Duncan, one of the first settlers of Londonderry, Vermont, started out at a young age "with a small pack of goods as a peddler." Later, he became a well-to-do merchant.

By 1830, the peddlers carried all sorts of merchandise. Timothy Dwight, president of Yale, wrote in his *Travels in New England and New York* (1823), that "many of these young men employed in this business, part at an early period with both modesty and principle. Their sobriety is exchanged for cunning, and their decent behaviors for coarse impudence."

Hawthorne in his *American Notes* describes one type of Yankee Peddler, the essence peddler. "His essences were of aniseed, cloves, red cedar, wormwood, together with opodeldoc, and an oil for the hair. ... Cologne water is among the essences manufactured, tho' the bottles have foreign labels on them. ... This man was a peddler in quite a small way, and carrying no more than an open basket full of essences, but some go out with wagon loads."

This sort of peddler for a few dollars could fill his tin trunk with wintergreen, peppermint, and bergamot and have a successful sales trip through the backwoods territory.

As will be noted from the following recipes, in the pre-Revolutionary era and even for some time later, these flavors were mixed with various homemade beverages.

Let us examine the early methods of concocting cologne water, room scenters, lotion, perfume and pomade as well as shaving materials, soap, tooth powder, and homemade "vegetable tooth brushes."

Garden Nightshade

COLOGNE RECIPES

If odours, or if taste may worke satisfaction, they are both so soveraigne in plants, and so comfortable, that no confection of the Apothecaries can equall their excellent vertue. But these delights are in the outward senses: the principall delight is in the minde, singularly enriched with the knowledge of these visible things, setting foorth to us the invisible workmanship of almightie God.

Preface to the Herbal, 1597

COLOGNE WATER: Of alcohol, one gallon; oil of lavender, twelve drachms; oil of rosemary, four drachms; essence of lemon, twelve drachms; oil of bergamot, twelve drachms; oil of cinnamon, twelve drops. *Young Housekeeper's Friend, 1846*

COLOGNE WATER: Turn a quart of alcohol gradually on to the following oils; a couple of drachms of the oil of rosemary, two of the oil of lemon, or orange-flower water, one drachm of lavender, ten drops of oil of cinnamon, ten of cloves, and a teaspoonful of rosewater. Keep the whole stopped tight in a bottle —shake it up well. It will do to use as soon as made, but it is much improved by age. *Kitchen Directory, 1846*

COLOGNE WATER (ROSEMARY, LAVENDER, ETC.): Take of oil rosemary and lemon each 60 drops; oil (of) garden lavender, 90 drops; otto of rose, and oil nevoli each 20 drops; rectified oil of amber, 30 drops; extract of vanilla, 20 drops; alcohol, one quart. Be sure that the oils are fresh and pure.

Family Hand-Book, c. 1855

EAU DE COLOGNE: Rectified spirits of wine, four pints; oil of bergamot, one ounce; oil of lemon, half an ounce; oil of rosemary, half a drachm; oil of neroli, three-quarters of a drachm; oil of English lavender, one drachm, oil of oranges, one drachm. Mix well and then filter. If these proportions are too large, smaller ones may be used.

Practical Housewife, 1860

EAU DE MELISSE DE CARMES: Take of dried balm leaves, 4 oz., dried lemon-peel, 2 do., nutmegs and coriander seeds, each, 1 oz., cloves, cinnamon, and dried angelica roots, each, 4 dr., spirit of wine, 2 lbs., brandy, 2 ditto. Steep and distil in balneum mariae, re-distil, and keep for some time in a cold cellar.

Mackenzie's 5,000 Receipts, 1829

DEODERIZER RECIPES

INCENSE PERFUME: Take equal quantities of lignum rhodium, and anise, in powder, with a little powder of dried Seville orange peel, and the same of gum benzoin, or benjamin, and beat all together in a marble mortar. Then, adding some gum dragon, or tragacanth, dissolved in rose water, put in a little civet; beat the whole again together, make up this mixture into small cakes, and place them on paper to dry. One of these cakes being burnt in the largest apartment, will diffuse a most agreeable odour through the whole room.

Family Receipt Book, 1819

SWEET JARS: Take a china jar, and put into it three handfuls of fresh damask rose-leaves; three of sweet pinks, three of wall-flowers, and stock gilly-flowers, and equal proportions of any other fragrant flowers that you can procure. Place them in layers; strewing fine salt thickly between each layer, and mixing with them an ounce of sliced orris root.

You may fill another jar with equal quantities of lavender, knotted marjoram, rosemary, lemon thyme, balm of Gilead, lemon-peel, and smaller quantities of laurel leaves and mint; and some sliced orris root. You may mix with the herbs, (which must all be chopped), cloves, cinnamon, and sliced nutmeg; strewing salt between the layers.

Flowers, herbs, and spice may all be mixed in the same jar; adding always some orris root. Every thing that is put in should be perfectly free from damp.

The jar should be kept closely covered, except when the cover is occasionally removed for the purpose of diffusing the scent through the room.

Miss Leslie's Directions for Cookery, 1839

VINEGAR OF THE FOUR THIEVES: Take lavender, rosemary, sage, wormwood, rue, and mint, of each a large handful; put them in a pot of earthenware, pour on them four quarts of very strong vinegar, cover the pot closely, and put a board on the top; keep it in the hottest sun two weeks, then strain and bottle it, putting in each bottle a clove of garlic. When it has settled in the bottle and become clear, pour it off gently; do this until you get it all free from sediment. The proper time to make it is when the herbs are in full vigour, in June. This vinegar is very refreshing in crowded rooms, in the apartments of the sick; and is peculiarly grateful when sprinkled about the house in damp weather.

Virginia Housewife, 1856

HAIR TONIC RECIPES

ERASMAS WILSON'S LOTION TO PROMOTE THE GROWTH OF HAIR: Eau de Cologne, two ounces; tincture of cantharides, two drachms; oil of rosemary and oil of lavender, of each ten drops.

Practical Housewife, 1860

MACASSAR OIL TO MAKE THE HAIR GROW AND CURL: Olive oil, one pound; oil of origanum, one drachm; oil of rosemary, one drachm and a quarter. Mix.

Practical Housewife, 1860

TO PROMOTE THE GROWTH OF HAIR: Mix equal parts of olive oil and spirits of rosemary, and add a few drops of oil of nutmeg. If the hair be rubbed every night with a little of this liniment, and the proportion be very gradually augmented, it will answer every purpose of increasing the growth of hair, much more effectually than can be attained by any of the boasting empirical preparations which are imposed on the credulous purchaser.

Family Receipt Book, 1819

PERFUME RECIPES

ORRIS PERFUME: Take best dried and scraped orris roots, free from mould. Bruise or grind them: the latter is best, as being very tough, they require great labour to pound. Sift the powder through a fine hair sieve, and put the remainder in a baker's oven, to dry the moisture. A violent heat will turn the roots

yellow. When dry, grind again, and sift; and repeat the same until the whole has passed through the sieve; mix nothing with it, as it would mould and spoil it.

Mackenzie's 5,000 Receipts, 1829

PERFUMED BAGS FOR DRAWERS: Cut, slice and mix well together, in the state of very gross powder, the following ingredients: 2 oz. of yellow saunders, 2 oz. of coriander seeds, 2 oz. of cinnamon bark, 2 oz. of dried rose-leaves, 2 oz. of lavender flowers, and 1 lb. of oak shavings. When properly mixed, stuff the above into small linen bags, which place in drawers, wardrobes, & c., which are musty or liable to become so.

Mackenzie's 5,000 Receipts, 1829

TO PERFUME LINEN: Rose leaves dried in the shade, cloves beat to a powder, and mace scraped: mix them together, and put the composition into little bags.

Family Receipt Book, 1819

PLEASANT PERFUME, AND ALSO PREVENTIVE AGAINST MOTHS: Take of cloves, caraway seeds, nutmegs, mace, cinnamon, and Tonquin beans, of each one ounce; then add as much Florentine orris-root as will equal the other ingredients put together. Grind the whole well to powder, and then put it in little bags, among your clothes & c.

Practical Housewife, 1860

TO PERFUME HAIR POWDER: Take one drachm of musk, four ounces of lavender blossoms, one and a half drachm of civet, and half a drachm of ambergris; pound the whole together, and pass it through a sieve. Preserve this mixture in well-stopped bottles, and add more or less thereof, as agreeable, in your hair powder.

Family Receipt Book, 1819

TO PERFUME LINEN: Rose-leaves dried in the shade, or at about four feet from a stove, one pound; cloves, carraway-seeds, and allspice, of each one ounce; pound in a mortar, or grind in a mill; dried salt, a quarter of a pound. Mix all these together, and put the compound into little bags.

Practical Housewife, 1860

PERFUME: (Costmary flower sprays are) tyed up with small bundels of lavender Toppes, these being put in the middle of them to lye upon the toppes of

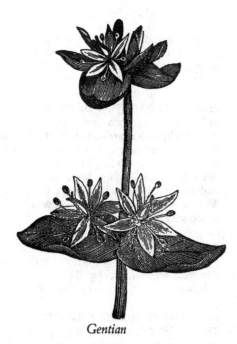

Gentian

beds, presses, etc. for the sweet sent and savour it casteth.   *Paradisi in Sole, 1629*

PERFUME: Sweet perfumes work immediately upon the spirits for their refreshing, sweet and healthful ayres are special preservatives to health and therefore much to be prised.
Treatise of Fruit-Trees, 1653
PERFUMED WASHING WATERS: The ordinary Basill is in a manner wholly spent to make sweet, or washing waters, among other sweet herbes, yet sometimes it is put into nosegayes. The Physicall (medicinal) properties are, to procure a cheerefull and merry heart, whereunto the seede is chiefly used to that, and to no other purpose.   *Paradisi in Sole, 1629*

PERFUMED SCENT: Rosemary is so well known through all our Land, being in every woman's garden, that it were sufficient but to name it as an ornament among other sweete herbes and flowers in our Garden, seeing everyone can describe it . . . the whole plant as well leaves as flowers, smelleth exceeding sweete.   *Paradisi in Sole, 1629*

POT POURRI: Take of orris-root, flag-root,

bruised, each four ounces; yellow sandal-wood, three ounces; sweet cedar-wood, one ounce; gum benzoin, storax, of each one ounce; cloves, half an ounce; nutmegs, one ounce; patchouli leaves, one ounce. The above should be all coarsely powdered, and well mixed. Then add—bay salt, one pound; rose leaves, three ounces; essence of lemon, half a drachm; millefleurs, one drachm; oil of lavender (English) twenty drops; musk, ten grains. The above may be used for *saquets,* if the bay salt and rose leaves are omitted, substituting for the latter ten drops of otto of roses. The above forms a grateful perfume, and will retain its scent for a considerable time. It may be relied upon as excellent.—W.G.G.
Practical Housewife, 1860

POMADE RECIPES

POMADE DIVINE: According to Dr. Beddoes, this composition is as follows, viz. beef marrow, twelve ounces steeped in water ten days, and afterwards in rose water twenty-four hours; flowers of benjamin, pounded storax, and Florentine orris, of each half an ounce; cinnamon, a quarter of an ounce; clove and mutmeg a quarter of an ounce. The whole to be put in an earthen vessel, closely covered down, to keep in the fumes, and being suspended in water made to boil three hours; after which, the whole is to be strained and put into bottle.   *Family Receipt Book, 1819*

POMATUM RARE: Take a pound of Lambs-suet shred small, and put it in a coarse Cloth, bear it till it be in a Cake, then shred it small again, and put it in a Glass or Pot; with it, put three ounces of White Lilly-Roots cut, two ounces of Sperma-Ceti, and tye up the Vessel close; set it in Warm Water till it is all melted, strain it thro' a fine Holland Cloth, and put it in a Bason, and put to it a dram and half of Camphire, dissolved with a little spirit of Wine, and stir it till it be cold, the longer you stir it the better it will be; but three hours is the least you can bestow upon it.
The Family Dictionary: or, Household Companion, 1710

ROSEMARY POMATUM: Strip from the stems two large handfuls of recently gathered rosemary. Boil these in a well-tinned saucepan, with half a pound of hog's lard, till reduced to four ounces. Strain

Plate 18. *Containers for "Elixir Dentrifice," "Wyeth's Solution, Sage and Sulphur" (for coloring grey and faded hair), "Indian Herb Tablets," "Shaker Society" sugared flagroot, and "Genuine Bears Oil." (Courtesy Shelburne Museum, Inc.)*

it, and put it into a pomatum pot. Oils for the hair may be made by simply stirring any essential oils into oil of ben, oil of almonds, olive oil, or castor oil. The pink and red oils are coloured by being heated to the boiling point, and poured upon alkanet root. But such preparation is bad, because heating the oil to the point necessary to make it act upon the dye of the alkanet root, gives it a tendency to become rancid. Coloured oils should therefore be avoided, if it be for this reason only; but for ladies who wear caps, there is still stronger —coloured oils always stain these caps.

Practical Housewife, 1860

SOFT POMATUM: Take 25 pounds of hog's lard, 8 pounds of mutton suet, 6 ounces of oil of Bergamot, 4 ounces of essence of lemons, half an ounce of oil of lavender, and a quarter of an ounce of oil of rose-

mary. These ingredients are to be combined in the same manner as those for the hard pomatum. This pomatum is to be put up in pots, in the usual way.

Mackenzie's 5,000 Receipts, 1829

SHAVING MATERIAL: Mix one pint and a half of clear lime water, two ounces of gum arabic, half an ounce of isinglass, an eighth of an ounce of cochineal, a quarter of an ounce of tumeric root (made into powder), an eighth of an ounce of salt of tartar, and an eighth of an ounce of cream of tartar, together; boil them for one hour at least (stirring up the mixture during the whole time of boiling, and be careful not to let it boil over) clear it through a sieve; then add two pounds and a half of pumice-stone, finely pulverized; mix the whole together, with the hands, into one cake, by the assistance of the white of two eggs, well stirred up. Then divide the cake, so made, into twelve smaller cakes; dry them in the open air for three days; put them into an oven of moderate heat, for twenty-four hours, when they will be completely dry and fit for use. Apply them with a gentle friction to the beard, and they will produce the complete effect of shaving, by rubbing off the hair.

Family Receipt Book, 1819

SOAP RECIPES

JAMAICA VEGETABLE SOAP: This soap is prepared from the great American aloe, in the following manner:—The large succulent leaves being cut, are passed between the rollers of a mill, with their point foremost, and the juice being conducted into wide, shallow receivers, through a coarse cloth or strainer, lies exposed to a hot sun, till it is reduced to a thick consistence. It is then made up into balls, with ley ashes, to prevent it from sticking to the fingers; after which it may be kept for years, and serve for use, as well as Castile soap, in washing linen; but has the superior quality of mixing and forming a lather with salt water as well as fresh.

Another method of preparing this soap is, by cutting the leaves in pieces, pounding them in a large wooden mortar, and then expressing the juice, which is brought afterwards to a consistence, either by the sun or by boiling. One gallon of this juice, thus prepared, will yield about one pound, avoirdupois, of a soft extract. It will answer prepared in either of these ways, provided the juice, before exposure to the sun or fire, be very carefully strained from the bruised fibres, and other membrane of the leaves. The extract must never be compounded with tallow, or any other unctuous materials, for such mixtures destroy its effect.

The leaves are used for scouring pewter and other kitchen utensils, and also for floors.

Family Receipt Book, 1819

SUBSTITUTE FOR SOAP: Collect, before the time of seeding, thistles, nettles, fern, and such other weeds as usually infest the borders of high roads and hedges, and burn them in a large heap, gradually, till the whole are consumed, and carefully preserve the ashes in a dry place, ready to make the ley wanted for the purpose of making a substitute for soap.

The requisite materials and utensils should be prepared, which are but few in number. They consist, 1st, of a small tub of white-wood, nine inches in width, and as many in height. This tub should be perforated near the bottom; its use is for mixing the leys. (Were it made of oak, it would colour the leys.) 2nd, A small copper basin, with a round bottom, a foot in diameter, and seven or eight inches in depth; or where this cannot be procured, an iron pot, or earthen vessel, that can bear the fire, may be used. This vessel is intended for boiling the mixture. 3d. For this small manufacture are finally required a skimmer, a spatula of white wood, and two earthen pans. The materials necessary are: 1, some good ashes; 2, lime; and 3, oil, tallow, or kitchen fat.

Family Receipt Book, 1819

SUBSTITUE FOR SOAP: (Burn ferns until they become) blewish, which being then layd by will dissolve into powder of itself like unto lime. (It was suggested that a few of these fern balls dissolved in water would be excellent for cleaning a whole basket of clothes).

Paradisi in Sole, 1629

Golden Seal

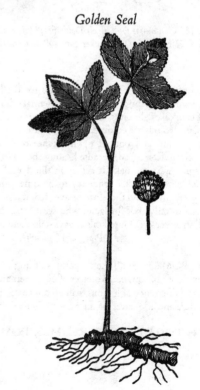

WINDSOR AND CASTILE SOAP: To make the celebrated Windsor soap, nothing more is necessary than to slice the best white soap as thin as possible, and melt it over a slow fire. Take it from the fire when melted. And when it is just lukewarm, add enough of the oil of caraway to scent it. If any other fragrant oil is liked better, it may be substituted. Turn it into molds and let it remain in a dry situation for five or six days.

To make Castile soap, boil common soft soap in lamp oil three hours and a half.

Kitchen Directory, 1846

TOILET WATER RECIPES

COLOGNE WATER: Take two drachms of oil of rosemary, two of the oil of lemon, one of lavender, ten of cinnamon, one tea-spoonful of rose-water. Pour on these one quart of alcohol; put all in a glass bottle, and shake it up well; to have it very clear, put some cotton in a tunnel, and place a piece of clean tissue or printing paper over it, and strain the contents through it.

Another way—One pint of alcohol, sixty drops lavender, sixty of bergamot, sixty of essence of lemon, sixty of orange-water. To be corked up, and well shaken. It is better for considerable age.

American Economical Housekeeper, 1850

HUNGARY WATER: Take a quantity of the flowers of rosemary, put them into a glass retort, and pour in as much spirit of wine as the flowers can imbibe; dilute the retort well, and let the flowers macerate for six days, then distil it in a sand heat.

Family Receipt Book, 1819

LAVENDER WATER: Turn a pint of alcohol slowly on to an ounce and a half of the oil of lavender, two drachms of ambergris. Keep the lavender water in a tight-corked bottle—it should be shook up well when first put in. *Kitchen Directory*, 1846

LAVENDER WATER: Put two pounds of lavender pips into two quarts of water, put them into a cold still, and make a slow fire under it; distil it off very slowly, and put it into a pot till you have distilled all your water; then clean your still well out, put your lavender water into it, and distil it off slowly again; put it into bottles, and cork it well.

Family Receipt Book, 1819

LAVENDER WATER: Take a quart of highly-rectified spirits of wine, essential oil of lavender two ounces, essence of ambergris five drachms; put it all in a bottle, and shake it till perfectly incorporated. Or, —Put two pounds of lavender-blossoms into half a gallon of water, and set them in a still over a slow fire; distil it off gently till the water is all exhausted; repeat the process a second time, then cork it closely down in bottles.

American Economical Housekeeper, 1850

ROSE-WATER: When the roses are in full blossom, pick the leaves carefully off, and to every quart of water put a peck of them. Put them in a cold still over a slow fire, and distil very gradually; then bottle the water, let it stand in the bottle three days, and then cork it close.

American Economical Housekeeper, 1850

TOOTH BRUSHES AND POWDERS

VEGETABLE TOOTH BRUSHES: Take marine marsh-mallow roots, cut them into lengths of 5 or 6 inches, and of the thickness of a middling rattan cane. Dry them in the shade, but not so as to make them shrivel.

Next finely pulverize two ounces of good dragon's blood, put it into a flat bottomed glazed pan, with four ounces of highly rectified spirit, and half an oz. of fresh conserve of roses. Set it over a gentle charcoal fire, and stir it until the dragon's blood is dissolved; then put in about thirty of the marsh-mallow sticks; stir them about, and carefully turn them, that all parts may absorb the dye alike. Continue this until the bottom of the pan be quite dry, and shake and stir it over the fire, until the sticks are perfectly dry and hard.

Both ends of each root or stick should, previous to immersion in the pan, be bruised gently by a hammer, for half an inch downwards, so as to open its fibres, and thereby form a brush.

They are generally used by dipping one of the ends in the powder or opiate, and then, by rubbing them against the teeth, which they cleanse and whiten admirably. *Mackenzie's 5,000 Receipts, 1829*

TOOTH POWDER: Powdered orris-root, half an ounce; powdered charcoal, two ounces; powdered Peruvian bark, one ounce; prepared chalk, half an ounce; oil of bergamot or lavender, twenty drops. These ingredients must be well worked up in a mortar, until thoroughly incorporated. This celebrated tooth-powder possesses three essential virtues, giving an odorous breath, cleansing and purifying the gums, and preserving the enamel; the last rarely found in popular toothpowders.—C. *Practical Housewife, 1860*

TOOTH POWDER (ORRIS ROOT, ETC.): Take of cuttle fish bone, 2 ounces; fresh orris root, 4 ounces, cream of tartar, 1 ounce; drop lake, 2 drachms; oil of cloves, 16 drops. Powder, mix, and sift. *Family Hand-Book, 1854*

TURKISH ROUGE, TO GIVE A BEAUTIFUL COMPLEXION: Get three cents worth of alkanet chips at any druggist's; tie them in a gauze bag, and suspend it in a glass vessel containing a half pint of alcohol. When it comes to the right color, take out the alkanet. This is a superior rouge; it will not rub off, and is in no ways injurious to the face. *The American Family Keepsake, 1849*

Plate 19. *Mrs. Daisy Williams preparing herbs for sifting in the Shaker hair sieve, seated before the hearth of the Little Stone Cottage (1840) at the Shelburne Museum. An Herb cutter hand forged from an old file can be seen on the table, in front of which there is a branch of hops. The Shaker basket at the right contains hops and various other dried herbs. (Courtesy Shelburne Museum, Inc.)*

CHAPTER FOUR

Culinary Uses of Herbs

Things three, no more; but three are needful.
The one is clothing, to save thee from chill,
The one is meat, for thy health's sake,
The third is drink when thou driest.

WILLIAM LANGLAND,
Piers Plowman, Pt. ii

THE DIET OF the colonists was quite similar in many respects to our own, except that food was much more available in the immediate vicinity of the home. Not too much attention was paid to variety, however, and various sorts of meats were a major portion of most meals.

Goodrich in his *Universal Traveler* (1847) notes that "In New England, in the country towns, breakfast is usually made at an early hour, and often at sunrise or before. In a farmer's family, it consists of little less than ham, beef, sausages, pork, bread, butter, boiled potatoes, pies, coffee, and cider. The use of coffee in the morning and of tea at night is almost universal."

Breakfast was even more elaborate at public eating places. Goodrich adds that "At

hotels and boarding-houses, breakfast is of beef, mutton, ham, broiled chickens, sausages, tripe, various kinds of fish, tongue, bread, butter, coffee, and cider."

Meat was served in abundance in the South, as well. One traveler who was lost in North Carolina in 1760 mentioned that he was warmly received at the home of a planter, where he discovered "a large table loaded with fat roast turkies, geese and ducks, boiled fowls, large hams, hung-beef, barbecued pig . . . enough for five and twenty men."

The Compleat Housewife, one of several "bookes of cookery" used in the colonies, suggests the following menu for a winter dinner: First course: giblet pie, gravy soup and chicken, and roast beef with horseradish and pickles; second course: a tansy with orange, woodcocks on toast, rabbit with savory pudding, roasted turkey, and butter apple pie.

Beef, pork, and other meats were usually available "on the place"; otherwise, they could be purchased very reasonably as can be

Guaiacum

noted in the early account or "day" books. The year round, huge quantities of both fresh and salt meat were consumed. Wild game was always abundant.

In the South, in North Carolina, it was said if the farmer "could raise enough corn and pork for subsistence, he cared for nothing more." William Byrd II reported once that he "made a North Caronlina Dinner upon Fresh Pork," while a French traveller in the colonies in 1765, stopped at a "poor farmer's house" where he "dined on fat Bacon, greens, and Indian bread and had good sider to Drink." Every New England farmer prepared his "pork barrel" for the winter months.

But not everyone was so fortunate to have such an array of food upon which to dine. Some even stole what they could to survive. A story is told of such a theft from Thomas Hooker of Hartford, in the 1630's or '40's.' It was late in Autumn when one night Mr.

Hooker was awakened by a noise in the cellar. "He immediately arose, dressed himself, and went silently to the foot of the cellar stairs. There he saw a man, with a candle in his hand, taking pork out of the barrel. When he had taken out the last piece, Mr. Hooker said pleasantly, 'Neighbor, you act unfairly; you ought to leave a part for me.' Thunderstruck at being detected, especially at being detected by so awful a witness, the culprit fell at his feet; condemned himself for his wickedness, and implored his pardon. Mr. Hooker cheerfully forgave him, and concealed his crime; but forced him to carry half the pork to his own house."

As one early writer expressed the problem: "Most of the first planters were poor; and as many of them had numerous families of small children, the burden of providing food for them was heavy, and discouraging. Some relief they found, at times, in the game, with which the forests were formerly replenished. But supplies from that source were always precarious; and could never be relied on with safety. . . . In desperate cases the old settlements, though frequently distant, were always in possession of abundance; and, in the mode, either of commerce, or of charity, would certainly prevent them, and theirs, from perishing with hunger."

Dwight reemphasizes the use of pickled pork in New England. He writes, "Pork, except the hams, shoulders, and cheeks, is never converted into bacon. I do not know that I ever saw a flitch of bacon, cured in New-England, in my life."

Goodrich mentions that in the Western States, "The two great articles of food are bacon and Indian corn."

From the following recipes, one detects the importance of herbs for seasoning the various meat concoctions. Again, both familiar and unusual ingredients are included or directions different from those found in modern cook books can be detected. Take, for example, hashed Calf's Feet or Calf's Head, from which the brains are removed and parboiled separately in a sauce-pan and then mixed with herbs, bread crumbs, lemon peel, nutmeg, and egg to be fried in lard and butter mixed. (Recipe on page 82)

One wonders if the meat was inclined to "run away," for in several recipes it is suggested that a stone be put on it until it is quite cold. In these days before refrigeration, some of it was probably "strong" enough to do just that.

The ingredients for making Head Cheese, for example, are boiled, put in an earthen pan, seasoned with herbs and spices, and then one is told to put it "into a coarse cloth, twist it up, and lay a stone upon it." (See page 84)

There is even reference to attempting to find good use for the water in which the pieces of head cheese were boiled. One idea suggested is the possibility of making isinglass from pig's feet, "as it is made from calves' feet." (Recipe on page 84)

A synonym for a rolling pin appears to be a "meat beetle," for this is the term mentioned in the flattening of mutton steaks.

These were the days when it was customary to stuff a whole pig, like a turkey, with bread, salt pork, and cold meat stuffing.

As early as 1839, there is warning against "under-done" pork: "If it is the least red inside, return it to the gridiron."

These early housewives had their own equivalent of today's waxed paper: "butter some half sheets of white paper and put cutlets into them, securing paper with pins or strings." Later, when they were ready to serve at the table, these "envelopes" were to be removed, as they "make a very bad appearance." See the recipe for Mutton Cutlets on page 84.

"First Watch," a stew described on page 83, is reminiscent of the days of the old sailing vessels. Many of the ingredients would likely have been available for such a "hotch-potch" on board ship.

As for commercially available meats, especially for those living in the larger communities, one might consider the first markets of New Amsterdam which were open spaces with a stall for the butcher; thus, he could be protected from bad weather conditions at one side.

After the British took over in the area of what is now New York, the stalls and open-

Henbane

air markets were replaced by substantial buildings. One such structure built on the shore of the East River toward the end of the 1600's lasted until after 1800.

Around 1738, a market was founded on Broadway. By this time the street was lined with a long, low, rambling market building stocked with quarters of beef and large shining fish. This was the Oswego Market the success of which attracted many more stores along Broadway. When traffic conditions became so overcrowded because of these busy markets, it was decided in 1771 by the city authorities to clear Broadway of all business enterprises. When the Oswego Market was demolished, a new one was built at Meiser's Dock on the shore of the Hudson River.

According to the record, "the first meat sold in this new market was the flesh of a bear that had been killed close by as it clambered up the river bank after swimming from the Jersey shore." From this incident the new market was popularly acclaimed, Bear Market, "and was so called until the year 1814."

An unknown author of a manuscript, *The Selkirk Grace*, written about 1650, made this comment about meat:

> Some have meat but cannot eat;
> Some could eat but have no meat;
> We have meat and can all eat;
> Blest, therefore, be God for our meat.

William Penn wrote in 1693 in his *Fruits of Solitude*, "If thou rise with an appetite, thou art sure never to sit down without one." Thomas Hood certainly referred to someone with an appetite, when in his *Review of*

Arthur Coningsby (1838) he wrote, "There are wholesale eaters who can devour a leg of mutton and trimmings at a sitting."

Anyone wishing to try the recipes for Fricassee of Rabbit (page 87) or Roast Rabbit (page 87) which follow should remember a statement attributed to Dr. Hill which appeared in a 1747 cook book: "To make a ragout, first catch your hare."

As the following recipes are tried, many of which have French titles, it will be interesting to see whether or not one agrees with Hawthorne, who wrote in his *Journals*, January 6, 1858: "I doubt whether English cookery, for the very reason that it is so gross, is not better for man's moral and spiritual nature than French. In the former case, you know that you are gratifying your animal needs and propensities, and are duly ashamed of it; but, in dealing with these French delicacies, you delude yourself into the idea that you are cultivating your taste while filling your belly."

MEAT RECIPES

This dish of meat is too good for any but anglers, or very honest men. ISAAC WALTON

BEEF ALAMODE: Choose a piece of thick flank of a fine heifer, or ox. Cut into long slices some fat bacon, but quite free from yellow. Let each bit be near an inch thick, and dip them in vinegar, and then in a seasoning ready prepared of salt, black and Jamaica peppers, and a clove in finest powder, with parsley, chives, thyme, savory and knotted marjoram, shred as small as possible, and well mixed. With a sharp knife make holes deep enough to let in the larding; then rub the beef over with the seasoning, and bind it up tight with tape. Set it in a well tinned pot over a fire or rather stove. Three or four onions must be fried brown and put to the beef, with two or three carrots, one turnip, and a head or two of celery, and a small quantity of water. Let it simmer gently ten or twelve hours, or till extremely tender, turning the meat twice.

Put the gravy in a pan, remove the fat, keep the beef covered, then put them together, and add a glass of port wine. Remove the tape, and serve with the vegetables: or you may strain them off, and send up fresh, cut in dice for garnish. Onions roasted, and then stewed with the gravy, are a great improvement. A teacup full of vinegar should be stewed with the beef.   *A New System of Domestic Cookery,* 1807

BEEF A-LA-DAUBE: Get a round of beef, lard it well, and put it in a Dutch oven; cut the meat from a shin of beef, or any coarse piece in thin slices, put round the sides and over the top some slices of bacon, salt, pepper, onion, thyme, parsley, cellery tops, or seed pounded, and some carrots cut small, strew the pieces of beef over, cover it with water, let it stew very gently till perfectly done, take out the round, strain the gravy, let it stand to be cold, take off the grease carefully, beat the whites of four eggs, mix a little water with them, put them to the gravy, let it boil till it looks clear, strain it, and when cold, put it over the beef.   *Virginia Housewife,* 1856

BEEF BOUILLI: Take part of a round of fresh beef (or if you prefer it a piece of the flank or brisket) and rub it with salt. Place skewers in the bottom of the stew-pot, and lay the meat upon them with barely water enough to cover it. To enrich the gravy you may add the necks and other trimmings of whatever poultry you may happen to have; also the root of a tongue, if convenient. Cover the pot, and set it over a quick fire. When it boils and the scum has risen, skim it well, and then diminish the fire so that the meat shall only simmer; or you may set the pot on hot coals. Then put in four or five carrots sliced thin, a head of celery cut up, and four or five sliced turnips. Add a bunch of sweet herbs, and a small table-spoonful of black peppercorns tied in a thin muslin rag. Let it stew slowly for four or five hours, and then add a dozen very small onions roasted and peeled, and a large table-spoonful of capers or nasturtians. You may, if you choose, stick a clove in each onion. Simmer it half an hour longer, then take up the meat, and place it in a dish, laying the vegetables round it. Skim and

Plate 20. *Frontispiece from* The London Complete Art of Cookery *published by William Lane in 1797.*

strain the gravy; season it with catchup, and made mustard, and serve it up in a boat.

Mutton may be cooked in this manner.
          Miss Leslie's Directions for Cookery, 1839

BEEF COLLARED: Choose the thin end of the flank of fine mellow beef, but not too fat. Lay it in a dish with salt, and saltpetre. Turn and rub it every day for a week, and keep it cool. Then take out every bone and gristle; remove the skin of the inside part, and cover it thick with the following seasoning cut small: a large handful of parsley, the same of sage, some thyme, marjorum, pennyroyal, pepper, salt and

Hops

pimento. Roll the meat up as tight as possible, and bind it; then boil it gently for seven or eight hours. A cloth must be put round before the tape. Put the beef under a good weight while hot, without undoing it; the shape will then be oval. Part of a breast of veal, rolled in with the beef, looks and eats very well.

A New System of Domestic Cookery, 1807

BEEF STEAK, STUFFED: Take a thick and tender slice of rump, of about three pounds' weight; make two gills of stuffing, of crumbs of bread, pepper, salt, and powdered clove, or sweet marjoram, as you choose; *roll the stuffing up in the steak, wind a piece of twine around it, taking care to secure the ends of the roll, so that the stuffing will not come out. Have ready a kettle, or deep stew-pan, with a slice or two of pork fried crisp. Take out the pork and lay in the steak, and turn it on every side, until it is brown. Then put in two gills of hot water, and half a gill of tomato catsup; sprinkle in a little salt, cover close, and stew steadily an hour and a half. Add more water after a while, if it becomes too dry. Some persons like the addition of chopped onion. There should, however, be very little; half of a small one is enough. When you take up the meat, unwind the string carefully so as not to unroll it. Lay it in a fricassee dish, thicken the gravy, if not thick enough already, with

a little flour pour it over the meat. Cut the meat in slices through the roll.

*Stuffing is much better, for most purposes, made without eggs. It is rendered hard and close by the use of them. *Young Housekeeper's Friend, 1846*

BEEF STEW: Take very good Beef, and slice it very thin; and beat it with the back of a Knife; Put it to the gravy of some meat, and some wine or strong broth, sweet-herbs a quantity, let it stew till it be very tender; season it to your liking; and varnish (garnish) your dish with Marygold-flowers or Barberries.

The Closet Opened, 1669

BLACK PUDDINGS: Catch the blood as it runs from the hog, stir it continually till cold to prevent its coagulating; when cold thicken it with boiled rice or oatmeal, add leaf fat chopped small, pepper, salt, and any herbs that are liked, fill the skins and smoke them two or three days; they must be boiled before they are hung up, and prick them with a fork to keep them from bursting. *Virginia Housewife, 1856*

BOLOGNA SAUSAGES: Take equal quantities of bacon, fat and lean, beef, veal, pork, and beef suet; chop them small, season with pepper, salt, & c., sweet herbs, and sage rubbed fine. Have a well-washed intestine, fill, and prick it; boil gently for an hour, and lay on straw to dry. They may be smoked the same as hams. *Practical Housewife, 1860*

CALF'S FEET, TO FRY: Having first boiled them till tender, cut them in two, and (having taken out the large bones) season the feet with pepper and salt, and dredge them well with flour. Strew some chopped parsley or sweet marjoram over them, and fry them of a light brown in lard or butter. Serve them up with parsley-sauce.

Miss Leslie's Directions for Cookery, 1839

CALF'S HEAD, HASHED: Take a calf's head and a set of feet, and boil them until tender, having first removed the brains. Then cut the flesh off the head and feet in slices from the bone, and put both meat and bones into a stew-pan with a bunch of sweet herbs, some sliced onions, and pepper and salt to your taste; also a large piece of butter rolled in flour, and a little water. After it has stewed awhile slowly till the flavour is well extracted from the herbs and onions, take out the meat, season it a little with cayenne pepper, and lay it in a dish. Strain the gravy in which it was stewed, and stir into it two glasses of madeira, and the juice and grated peel of a lemon. Having poured some of the gravy over the meat, lay a piece of butter on the top, set it in an oven and bake it brown.

In the mean time, having cleaned and washed the brains (skinning them and removing the strings) par-boil them in a sauce-pan, and then make them into balls with chopped sweet herbs, grated bread-crumbs, grated lemon-peel, nutmeg, and beaten yolk of egg. Fry them in lard and butter mixed; and send them to table laid round the meat (which should have the tongue placed on the top) and garnish with sliced lemon. Warm the remaining gravy in a small sauce-pan on hot coals, and stir into it the beaten yolk of an egg a minute before you take it from the fire. Send it to table in a boat.

Miss Leslie's Directions for Cookery, 1839

CALF'S HEAD, TO ROAST: Wash and pick the head very nicely; having taken out the brains and tongue, prepare a good quantity of forced meat, with veal and suet well seasoned; fill the hole of the head with this forced meat, skewer and tie it together upon the spit, and roast it for an hour and a half. Beat up the

Horehound

brains with a little sage and parsley shred fine, a little salt, and the yelks of two or three eggs; boil the tongue, peel, and cut it into large dice, fry that with the brains, also some of the forced meat made up into balls, and slices of bacon. Let the sauce be strong gravy, with oysters, mushrooms, capers, and a little white wine thickened.   *Virginia Housewife*, 1856

CALF'S LIVER, ROASTED: Wash and wipe it: then cut a long hole in it, and stuff it with crumbs of bread, chopped anchovy, herbs, a good deal of fat bacon, onion, salt, pepper, a bit of butter, and an egg. Sew the liver up; then lard or wrap it in a veal caul, and roast it. Serve with a good brown gravy, and currant jelly.

A New System of Domestic Cookery, 1807

DUCKS, (WILD), TO STEW: Having prepared the fowls, rub the insides with salt, pepper, and a little powdered cloves; put a shallot or two with a lump of butter in the body of each, then lay them in a pan that will just hold them, putting butter under and over them, with vinegar and water, and add pepper, salt, lemon peel, and a bunch of sweet herbs; then cover the pan close, and let them stew till done—pass the liquor through a sieve, pour it over the ducks, and serve them up hot, with a garnish of lemon sliced, and raspings of bread fried. The same way may teal & c. be dressed.   *Virginia Housewife*, 1856

FIRST-WATCH STEW: Cut pieces of salt beef and pork into dice, put them into a stewpan with six whole peppercorns, two blades of mace, a few cloves, a tea-spoonful of celery seeds, and a faggot of dried sweet herbs; cover with water, and stew gently for an hour; then add fragments of carrots, turnips, parsley, or any other vegetables at hand, with two sliced onions, and some vinegar to flavour; thicken with flour, or rice, remove the herbs, and pour into the dish with toasted bread, or freshly baked biscuit broken small, and serve hot. When they can be procured, a few potatoes improve it very much.

Practical Housewife, 1860

HAMS, TONGUES, ETC., GLAZING FOR: Boil a shin of beef twelve hours in eight or ten quarts of water; draw the gravy from a knuckle of veal in the same manner; put the same herbs and spices as if for soup, and add the whole to the shin of beef. It must be boiled till reduced to a quart. It will keep good for a year; and when wanted for use, warm a little, and spread over the ham, tongue, & c., with a feather.

Practical Housewife, 1860

HAM DUMPLINGS: Chop some cold ham, the fat and lean in equal proportions. Season it with pepper and minced sage. Make a crust, allowing half a pound of chopped suet, or half a pound of butter to a pound of flour. Roll it out thick, and divide it into equal portions. Put some minced ham into each, and close up the crust. Have ready a pot of boiling water, and put in the dumplings. Boil them about three quarters of an hour.

Miss Leslie's Directions for Cookery, 1839

HEAD CHEESE: Boil in salted water the ears, skin, and feet of pigs till the meat drops from the bones; chop it like sausage meat. Season the liquor with pepper, salt, cloves, nutmeg, and cinnamon, or with pepper, salt, and sweet herbs, mix the meat with it, and while hot tie it in a strong bag and keep a heavy stone upon it until quite cold.

Beecher's Domestic Receipt Book, 1857

HEAD CHEESE: Take the head, feet, ears and tail of a hog, and boil them until every bone falls out. Then take all the meat, both fat and lean, and put into an earthen pan. Season it with salt, pepper, sage, cloves

Indian Turnip

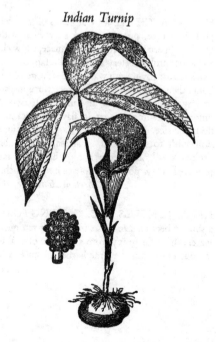

and summer savory, or any spice and herbs you may prefer. Put it into a coarse cloth, twist it up, and lay a stone upon it. This is a favorite article of food in some parts of the country, and certainly is very good. Great care is necessary in cleaning such giblets of pork.

I am unable to say how the water may be used in which the pieces were boiled; but the recent improvements in making isinglass from pigs' feet, as it is made from calves' feet, shows that it might be put to some good use. *Young Housekeeper's Friend,* 1846

LAMB, SHOULDER OF, GRILLED. The shoulder of lamb is good roasted plain, but is better cooked in the following manner. Score it in checkers, about an inch long, rub it over with a little butter, and the yelk of an egg; then dip it into finely pounded bread crumbs; sprinkle on salt, pepper, and sweet herbs; roast it till of a light brown. This is good with plain gravy, but better with a sauce, made in the following manner. Take a quarter of a pint of the drippings from the meat, mix it with the same quantity of water, set it on the fire; when it boils up, thicken it with a little flour and water mixed, put in a table spoonful of tomato catsup, the juice and grated rind of a lemon, season it with salt and pepper.

Kitchen Directory, 1846

LAMB, STUFFED: Pick off all the fat from a nice leg of lamb, or small leg of mutton. Cut off the shank, make deep incisions in various parts of the inside of the leg; fill them with stuffing made of crumbs of bread, salt pork, sweet marjoram and pepper; stuff it very full. Put hardly water enough into the pot to cover the leg. Throw in a dozen or two of cloves, half an onion sliced or chopped very fine, and a little salt. A half a teacup of catsup or a few tomatoes improve it very much. Let it simmer, steadily, three hours.

When you take up the leg, thicken the gravy, if it is not thick enough. Put a few spoonfuls over the meat, and the rest in a gravy tureen.

Young Housekeeper's Friend, 1846

MUTTON CUTLETS À LA MAINTENON: Cut a neck of mutton into steaks with a bone in each; trim them nicely, and scrape clean the end of the bone. Flatten them with a rolling pin, or a meat beetle, and lay them in oiled butter. Make a seasoning of hard-boiled yolk of egg and sweet-herbs minced small, grated bread, pepper, salt, and nutmeg; and, if you choose, a little minced onion. Take the chops out of the butter, and cover them with the seasoning. Butter some half sheets of white paper, and put the cutlets into them, so as to be entirely covered, securing the paper with the pins or strings; and twisting them nicely round the bone. Heat your gridiron over some bright lively coals. Lay the cutlets on it, and broil them about twenty minutes. The custom of sending them to table in the papers had best be omitted, as (unless managed by a French cook) these envelopes, after being on the gridiron, make a very bad appearance.

Serve them up hot, with mushroom sauce in a boat, or with a brown gravy, flavoured with red wine. You may make the gravy of the bones and trimmings, stewed in a little water, skimmed well, and strained when sufficiently stewed. Thicken it with flour browned in a Dutch oven, and add a glass of red wine.

You may bake these cutlets in a Dutch oven without the papers. Moisten them frequently with a little oiled butter.

Miss Leslie's Directions for Cookery, 1839

MUTTON HARICO: Take a neck of mutton, cut it into chops, and fry them brown. Then put them into a stew-pan with a bunch of sweet herbs; two or three cloves, a little mace, and pepper and salt to your taste. Cover them with boiling water, and let them stew slowly for about an hour. Then cut some carrots and turnips into dice; slice some onions, and cut up a head of celery; put them all into the stew-pan, and keep it closely covered except when you are skimming off the fat. Let the whole stew gently for an hour longer, and then send it to table in a deep dish, with the gravy about it.

You may make a similar harico of veal steaks, or of beef cut very thin.

Miss Leslie's Directions for Cookery, 1839

MUTTON AND LAMB, ROAST: Six or seven pounds of mutton will roast in an hour and a half. Lamb one hour. Mutton is apt to taste strong; this may be helped by soaking the meat in a little salt and water for an hour before cooking. However, unless meat is very sweet, it is best to corn it, and boil it.

Fresh meat should never be put in to cook till the

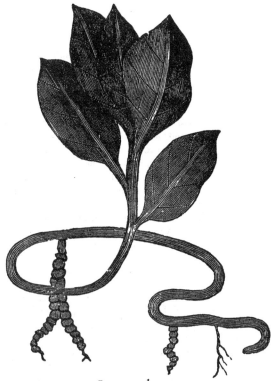

Ipecacuanha

water boils; and it should be boiled in as little water as possible; otherwise the flavor is injured. Mutton enough for a family of five or six should boil an hour and a half. A leg of lamb should boil an hour, or little more than an hour, perhaps. Put a little thickening into boiling water; strain it nicely; and put sweet butter in it for sauce. If your family like broth, throw in some clear rice when you put in the meat. The rice should be in proportion to the quantity of broth you mean to make. A large table spoonful is enough for three pints of water. Seasoned with a very little pepper and salt. Summer-savory, or sage, rubbed through a sieve, thrown in.

American Frugal Housewife, 1833

MUTTON, SHOULDER OF: Bone the larger half of your shoulder, lard the inside with well seasoned larding, tie it up in the shape of a baloon, lay some slips of bacon in your pan, on them your meat, with three or four carrots, five onions, three cloves, two bay leaves, thyme, and the bones that have been taken out, moisten with bouillon, set all on the fire and simmer for three hours and a half; garnish with small onions. *Mackenzie's 5,000 Receipts*, 1829

MUTTON CHOPS, STEWED: Cut a loin or neck of mutton into chops, and trim away the fat and bones. Beat and flatten them. Season them with pepper and salt, and put them into a stew-pan with barely sufficient water to cover them, and some sliced carrots, turnips, onions, potatoes, and a bunch of sweet herbs, or a few tomatas. Let the whole stew slowly about three hours, or till everything is tender. Keep the pan closely covered, except when you are skimming it. Send it to table with sippets or three-cornered pieces of toasted bread, laid all round the dish.
Miss Leslie's Directions for Cookery, 1839

OXFORD SAUSAGES Take 1 lb. of young pork, fat and lean, without skin or gristle, 1 lb. of beef suet, chopped fine together; put in ½ lb. of grated bread, half the peel of a lemon shred, a nutmeg grated, 6 sage leaves chopped fine, a teaspoonful of pepper, and 2 of salt, some thyme, savory, and marjoram, shred fine. Mix well together and put it close down in a pan till used. Roll them out the size of common sausages, and fry them in fresh butter of a fine brown, or broil them over a clear fire, and send them to table hot.
Mackenzie's 5,000 Receipts, 1829

PIG, BAKED OR ROASTED: Take a pig that weighs from seven to twelve pounds, and as much as five weeks old. Wash it thoroughly outside and inside. Take any fresh cold meat, say one pound, and a quarter of a pound of salt pork, and twice as much bread as you have meat.

Chop the bread by itself, and chop the meat and pork fine and mix all together, adding sweet herbs, pepper and salt, half a tea-cup of butter, and one egg. Stuff the pig with it, and sew it up tight. Take off the legs at the middle joint. Put it into a dripping-pan with cross-bars or a grate to hold it up, and with the legs tied, and pour into the pan a pint of water and set it in the oven. As soon as it begins to cook, swab it with salt and water, and then in fifteen minutes do it again. If it blisters it is cooking too fast; swab it, and diminish the heat. It must bake, if weighing twelve pounds, three hours. When nearly done, rub it with butter. When taken out set it for three minutes in the cold, to make it crisp.
Beecher's Domestic Receipt Book, 1857

PORK, COLLARED: A leg of fresh pork, not large. Two tablespoonfuls of powdered sage. Two tablespoonfuls of sweet-marjoram (powdered). One tablespoonful of sweet-basil (powdered). A quarter of an ounce of mace (powdered). Half an ounce of cloves (powdered). Two nutmegs (powdered). A bunch of pot-herbs, chopped small. A sixpenny loaf of stale bread. Half a pound of butter, cut up in the grated bread. Two eggs. A table-spoonful of salt. A table-spoonful of black pepper.

Grate the bread, and having softened the crust in water, mix it with the crumbs. Prepare all the other ingredients, and mix them well with the grated bread and egg.

Take the bone out of a leg of pork, and rub the meat well on both sides with salt. Spread the seasoning thick all over the meat. Then roll it up very tightly and tie it round with tape.

Put it into a deep dish with a little water, and bake it two hours. If eaten hot, put an egg and some wine into the gravy. When cold, cut it down into round slices. *Seventy-five Receipts*, 1838

PORK: PORTUGUESE METHOD OF DRESSING A LOIN: Steep it during an entire week in red wine, (claret in preference) with a strong infusion of garlic and a little spice; then sprinkle it with fine herbs, envelope it in bay leaves, and bake it along with Seville oranges.
Mackenzie's 5,000 Receipts, 1829

PORK STEAKS: Pork steaks or chops should be taken from the neck, or the loin. Cut them about half an inch thick, remove the skin, trim them neatly, and beat them. Season them with pepper, salt, and powdered sage-leaves or sweet marjoram, and broil them over a clear fire till quite done all through, turning them once. They require much longer broiling than beefsteaks or mutton chops. When you think they are nearly done, take up one on a plate and try it. If it is the least red inside, return it to the gridiron. Have ready a gravy made of the trimmings, or any coarse pieces of pork stewed in a little water with chopped onions and sage, and skimmed carefully. When all the essence is extracted, take out the bits of meat, & c., and serve up the gravy in a boat to eat with the steaks. They should be accompanied with apple-sauce. *Miss Leslie's Directions for Cookery*, 1839

RABBIT, FRICASSEE OF: Wash and cut a young rabbit into joints, put them in a stewpan, with a quarter of a pound of streaky bacon cut small, an onion stuck with cloves, a faggot of herbs, a blade of mace, and some salt; cover the whole with water, and let it simmer twenty minutes, keeping it well skimmed; pass the liquor through a sieve. Into another stewpan put two ounces of butter, a table-spoonful of flour, and a little of the liquor; set on the fire; stir well until it boils; add the rabbit and bacon, with a dozen and a half of small onions; let the whole simmer until the onions are done; skim well; then pour in a wine-glassful of white wine, mixed with the yolks of two eggs, and a little grated nutmeg; leave it to thicken, remove the rabbit, pile it on sippets, sauce over, garnish with sliced lemon, and serve hot.

Practical Housewife, 1860

RABBITS, ROAST: When you have cased the rabbits, skewer their heads with their mouths upon their backs, stick their forelegs into their ribs, skewer the hind-legs doubled, then make a pudding for them of the crumb of half a loaf of bread, a little parsley, sweet marjoram and thyme, all shred fine, nutmeg, salt and pepper to your taste, mix them into a light stuffing, with a quarter of a pound of butter, a little good

Juniper

cream, and two eggs; put it into the body, and sew them up; dredge and baste them well with lard, roast them near an hour, serve them up with parsley and butter for sauce, chop the livers, and lay them in lumps round the edge of the dish.

Virginia Housewife, 1856

SAUSAGES, FINE: Take some fresh pork, (the leg is best), and clear it from the skin, sinews, and gristle. Allow two pounds of fat to three pounds of lean. Mince it all very fine, and season it with two ounces and a half of salt, half an ounce of pepper, thirty cloves, and a dozen blades of mace powdered, three grated nutmegs, six table-spoonfuls of powdered sage, and two tea-spoonfuls of powdered rosemary. Mix all well together.Put it into a stone jar, and press it down very hard. Cover it closely, and keep it in a dry cool place. When you use this sausage-meat, mix with it some beaten yolk of egg, and make it into balls or cakes. Dredge them with flour, and dry them in butter.

Miss Leslie's Directions for Cookery, 1839

SAUSAGES, TO MAKE: Take the tender pieces of fresh pork, chop them exceedingly fine—chop some of the leaf fat, and put them together in the proportion of three pounds of pork to one of fat, season it very high with pepper and salt, add a small quantity of dried sage rubbed to a powder, have the skins nicely prepared, fill them and hang them in a dry

Jalap

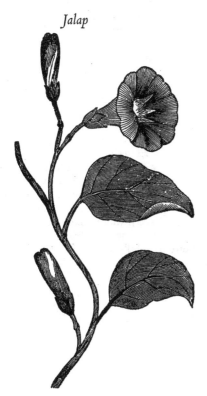

Ladies Slipper

place. Sausages are excellent made into cakes and fried, but will not keep so well as in skins.

Virginia Housewife, 1856

TRIPE, PEPPER POT: Boil two or three pounds of tripe, cut it in pieces, and put it on the fire with a knuckle of veal, and a sufficient quantity of water; part of a pot of pepper, a little spice, sweet herbs according to your taste, salt, and some dumplins; stew it till tender, and thicken the gravy with butter and flour. *Virginia Housewife*, 1856

VEAL À LA MAINTENON: Cut slices of veal into pieces three quarters of an inch thick, and of a moderate size, beat well with a rolling-pin, and egg over both sides, then dip them into a mixture of bread crumbs, pepper, salt, grated nutmeg, thyme, and parsley, and put into white papers folded down at the sides. Broil and serve with melted butter and mushroom ketchup in a sauceboat.

Practical Housewife, 1860

VEAL, BREAST OF: Before roasted, if large, the two ends may be taken off and fried to stew, or the whole may be roasted. Butter should be poured over it.

If any be left, cut the pieces in handsome sizes, and putting them into a stewpan, pour some broth over it; or if you have none, a little water will do. Add a bunch of herbs, a blade or two of mace, some pepper, and an anchovy. Stew till the meat is tender: thicken with butter and flour, and add a little catsup; or the whole breast may be stewed, after cutting off the two ends.

The sweetbread is to be served up whole in the middle; and if you have a few mushrooms, truffles, and morels, stew them with it, and serve.

Boiled breast of veal, smothered with onion sauce, is an excellent dish, if not old, or too fat.

A New System of Domestic Cookery, 1807

VEAL OR MUTTON, TO BOIL A LEG OF: Make a stuffing of bread, and a quarter as much of salt pork, chopped fine and seasoned with sweet herbs, pepper and salt. Make deep gashes, or what is better, take out the bone with a carving knife, and fill up with stuffing, and sew up the opening with strong thread. When there is a flap of flesh, lap it over the opening and sew it down.

Put it into a large pot and fill it with water, putting in a table-spoonful of salt, and let it simmer slowly three hours. If it is needful to add water, pour in *boiling* water. When it is done take it up, and save the broth for next day's dinner.

Beecher's Domestic Receipt Book, 1857

VEAL, SAVORY DISH OF: Cut some large scollops from a leg of veal, spread them on a dresser, dip them in rich egg batter; season them with cloves, mace, nutmeg, and pepper beaten fine; make force-meat with some of the veal, some beef suet, oysters chopped, sweet herbs shred fine; strew all these over the scollops, roll and tie them up, put them on skewers and roast them. To the rest of the force-meat, add two raw eggs, roll them in balls and fry them. Put them into the dish with the meat when roasted: and make the sauce with strong broth, an anchovy or a shalot, a little white wine and some spice. Let it stew, and thicken it with a piece of butter rolled in flour. Pour the sauce into the dish, lay the meat in with the force-meat balls, and garnish with lemon.

Mackenzie's 5,000 Receipts, 1829

VEAL, SHOULDER EN GALANTINE: Bone a

fat, fleshy shoulder of veal, cut off the ragged pieces to make your stuffing, viz. one pound of veal to one pound of salt pork minced extremely fine, well seasoned with salt, pepper, spices, and mixed with three eggs, spread a layer of this stuffing well minced over the whole shoulder to the depth of an inch, over this, mushrooms, slips of bacon, slices of tongue, and carrots in threads, cover this with stuffing as before, then another layer of mushrooms, bacon, tongue, & c. when all your stuffing is used, roll up your shoulder lengthways, tie it with a thread, cover it with slips of larding and tie it up in a clean white cloth: put into a pot the bones of the shoulder, two calves' feet, slips of bacon, six carrots, ten onions, one stuck with four cloves, four bay leaves, thyme, and a large faggot of parsley and shallots, moisten the whole with bouillon; put in your meat in the cloth and boil steadily for three hours. Try if it is done with the larding needle; if so, take it up, press all the liquor from it, and set it by to grow cold; pass your jelly through a napkin, put two eggs in a pan, whip them well and pour the strained liquor on them, mixing both together, add peppercorns, a little of the four spices, a bay leaf, thyme, parsley; let all boil gently for an hour, strain it through a napkin, put your shoulder on its dish, pour the jelly over and serve cold.

Mackenzie's 5,000 Receipts, 1829

VEAL, STEWED BREAST OF: Cut it into handsome pieces and fry it brown, either in lard or the fat fried out of salt pork. Be careful to brown all parts thoroughly; then pour in hot water enough barely to cover it. Add lemon peel cut fine and sweet marjoram. Cover it close as possible and stew it gently two hours; then pour off the liquor into a sauce-pan, and thicken it with browned flour. Take up the veal into a hot fricassee dish, and pour the gravy over it.

Always allow half an hour for frying veal brown. No other meat requires as much time.

Young Housekeeper's Friend, 1846

VEAL, TO STUFF A SHOULDER OF: Take off the shoulder blade from the ribs beneath, and with a sharp knife remove the bone on the inside; make a stuffing of crumbs of bread, chopped pork and sweet herbs, as for a fillet; fill the space where the bone was removed with stuffing, and spread it also over the inner surface; then roll it up and wind a tape round it, flour it, and roast in the stove. It will require between

Liquorice

an hour and a half and two hours' roasting. To serve it, unwind the tape, lay the roll upon a hot dish, and pour over it the gravy from the dripping-pan, having put into it some water, or some of the stock, a small bit of butter, and some flour.

It is not necessary to pour gravy from the dripping-pan into a sauce-pan in order to boil it. Such a pan as is used in a stove may be set upon coals in the front of the stove, and the necessary ingredients stirred in quickly. It will boil up in an instant.

Young Housekeeper's Friend, 1846

GRAVY AND SAUCE RECIPES

My more-having would be a sauce
To make me hunger more.

SHAKESPEARE, *Macbeth*

OBVIOUSLY, THE JUICE that came from the meat in cooking was used to make gravies and sauces for the meat, potatoes, and other dishes. In 1664, Sir Balthazar Gerbier concluded in his *Counsel:* "Every cook commends his own sauce."

It has already been pointed out that during the seventeenth and eighteenth centuries, some American housewives were fortunate in possessing an English cook book. It was not until the 1800's that American publications offering culinary directions were widely sold.

One British book of "receipts" was *The London Complete Art of Cookery* printed for William Lane, at the Minerva Press, Leadenhall-Street, 1797. It offers among other items directions for "Different sorts of Sauce for a Pig": "Some do not love any sage in the pig, only a crust of bread; but then you should have a little dried sage rubbed and mixed with the gravy and butter. Some love bread sauce, in a bason, made thus—take a pint of water, put in a good piece of crumb of bread, a blade of mace, and a little whole pepper, boil it for about five or six minutes and then pour the water off, take out the spice, and beat up the bread with a good piece of butter, and a little milk or cream. Some love a few currants boiled in it, a glass of wine and a little sugar; but that you must do just as you like it. Others take half a pint of good beef gravy, and the gravy that comes out of the pig, with a piece of butter rolled in flour, two spoonfuls of catchup, and boil them all together; then take the brains of the pig, and bruise them fine; put all these together, with the sage in the pig, and pour into your dish. It is a very good sauce. When you have not gravy enough comes out of your pig, with the butter, for sauce, take about half a pint of veal gravy and add to it; or stew

the pettitoes and take as much of that liquor as will do for sauce, mixed with the other. Some like the sauce sent in in a boat or bason."

The above mentioned use of butter for a sauce agrees with the observations of Marquis Caraccioli, a Neapolitan ambassador, who wrote, "There are in England sixty different religions and only one *gravy,* melted butter." Upon examination of the American sauces and gravies which follow, one will find many varieties.

As for a "Sauce for a Goose or Duck", the *London Complete Art of Cookery* recommends, "As to geese or ducks, you should have sage and onions shred fine, with pepper and salt put into the belly. Put only pepper and salt into wild ducks, easterlings, wigeons, teal, and all other sorts of wild fowl, with gravy in the dish, or some like sage and onion in one."

Later, this same book refers "To make Sauce for Fowls": "Boil any bones or bits of veal, with a small bunch of sweet herbs, an

Loverwort

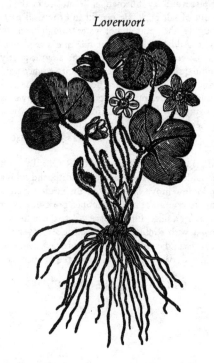

onion, a slice of lemon, a few white pepper-corns, and a little celery; strain it; there should be near half a pint; put to it some good cream, with a little flour mixed smooth in it, a good piece of butter, a little pounded mace, and some salt; keep it stirring, add mushrooms, or a little lemon juice."

Other sauces suggested in this same early source include Aspic Sauce for which chervil, tarragon, burnet, garden cress, and a little mint are infused for about half an hour, sifted. A spoonful of "garlick-vinegar," salt, and pepper are added.

Fennel Sauce is made from boiling a bunch of fennel and parsley, chopping it fine, and stirring the mixture into melted butter.

The juice of sorrel is added to some "cod-dled gooseberries," a little ginger, and melted butter to make Gooseberry Sauce.

Ham Cullis calls for a "nosegay of thyme and parsley" to be mixed with half a laurel-leaf, one clove of garlic, a few mushrooms and shalots to be added to slices of veal-fillet, bits of ham, "all sorts of roots, a saltless broth and a glass of white wine."

Poor Man's Sauce consists of nothing more than some young onions and chopped parsley. "It is very good with roasted mutton."

Among the recipes which follow there are directions for making "gravy cakes" by pouring the gravy liquor resulting from stewing two legs of beef for a day and a night and adding herbs, spices, and onions. The liquid is strained into a milk-pan; later, after it has cooled, the fat is skimmed off and put into a saucepan and seasoned. "Simmer it on a slow fire till reduced to about twelve saucers two-thirds full, put them in an airy

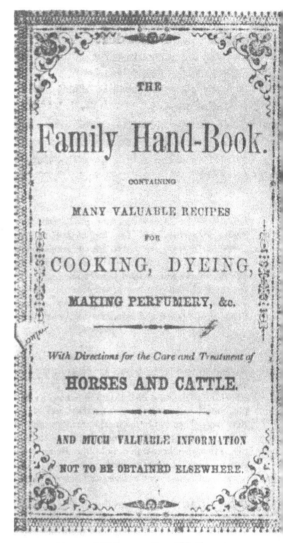

Plate 21. *Title page of an old book.*

place till as dry as leather, put them in paper bags, and keep in a dry place." This is a method used by an 1829 housewife to prepare for mealtimes when she needed "instant gravy."

The General's Sauce for which the warn-

ing is given that "it must be used in moderation" is a curious one for it is stipulated that
to make this sauce properly, infuse all the
ingredients for twenty-four hours on "ashes
in an earthen pot, if possible, which must be
very well stopped."

Let us examine some of the gravy and
sauce recipes used to add a special zest to the
various meat and fish or poultry dishes of
early days.

CLEAR GRAVY: Slice beef thin: broil a part of it,
over a very clear quick fire, just enough to give
colour to the gravy, but not to dress it: put that, and
the raw (beef) into a very nicely tinned stewpan, with
two onions, a clove, or two Jamaica and black peppers, and a bunch of sweet herbs: cover it with hot
water; give it one boil, and skim it well·two or three
times: then cover it and simmer till quite strong.
A New System of Domestic Cookery, 1807

GRAVY: Cut thin lean beef: put it in a fryingpan
without any butter: set it on a fire covered, but take
care it does not burn: let it stay till all the gravy that
comes out of the meat be dried up into it again; then
put as much water as will cover the meat, and let that
stew away. Then put to the meat a small quantity of
water, herbs, onions, spice, a bit of lean ham: simmer
till it is rich, then keep it in a cool place. Remove the
fat only when going to be used.
A New System of Domestic Cookery, 1807

GRAVY CAKES: Chop two legs of beef in pieces,
put them into a pot of water, stew it over a slow fire
a day and a night; then add onions, herbs and spices
as for gravy; continue stewing it till the meat is off the
bones, and the gravy quite out; then strain the liquor
into a milk-pan, to which quantity it should be reduced; when cold, take off the fat, put it into a sauce-
pan, and add whatever is required to flavour it; simmer it on a slow fire till reduced to about twelve
saucers two-thirds full, put them in an airy place till
as dry as leather, put them in paper bags, and keep in
a dry place.
Mackenzie's 5000 Receipts, 1829

Lobelia

RICH GRAVY: Cut beef in thin slices, according to
the quantity wanted: slice onions thin, and flour both:
fry them of a light pale brown, but on no account
suffer them to go black: put them into a stewpan, and
pouring boiling water on the browning in the frying-
pan, boil it up, and pour on the meat. Put to it a bunch
of parsley, thyme, savory, and a small bit of knotted
marjorum, and the same of tarragon, some mace,
Jamaica and black peppers, a clove or two, and a bit of
ham or gammon. Simmer till you have all the juices
of the meat; and be sure to skim the moment it boils,
and frequently after. If for a hare, or stewed fish,
anchovy should be added.

The shank bones of mutton are a great improvement to the richness of the gravy; being first well
soaked, and scoured clean.
A New System of Domestic Cookery, 1807

VEAL GRAVY: Make as directed for the cullis,
leaving out the spice, herbs, and flour. It should be
drawn very slowly: and if for white dishes, do not let
the meat brown.
A New System of Domestic Cookery, 1807

CULLIS, OR BROWN SAUCE: Lay as much lean veal over the bottom of a stewpan as will cover it an inch thick: then cover the veal with thin slices of undressed gammon, two or three onions, two or three bayleaves, some sweet herbs, two blades of mace, and three cloves. Cover the stewpan, and set it over a slow fire. When the juices come out, let the fire be a little quicker. When the meat is of a fine brown, fill the pan with good beef broth, boil and skim it, then simmer an hour: add a little water, mixed with as much flour as will make it properly thick: boil it half an hour, and strain it. This will keep a week. *A New System of Domestic Cookery,* 1807

FISH SAUCE A-LA-CRASTER: Thicken a quarter of a pound of butter with flour, and brown it; then put to it a pound of the best anchovies, cut small, six blades of pounded mace, ten cloves, forty black and Jamaica peppers, a few small onions, a faggot of sweet herbs; namely, savory, thyme, basil, and knotted marjoram; a little parsley, and sliced horseradish. On these pour half a pint of the best sherry wine, and a pint and a half of strong gravy: simmer all gently for twenty minutes; then strain it through a sieve, and bottle it for use: the way of which, is to boil some of it in the butter, as melting.
A New System of Domestic Cookery, 1807

GENERAL'S SAUCE: To make this sauce properly, infuse all the following ingredients for twenty-four hours, on ashes in an earthen pot, if possible, which must be very well stopped; viz. split six shallots, a clove of garlic, two laurel leaves, thyme and basil in proportion, truffles, tarragon leaves, half an ounce of mustard seed, bruised, six small pieces of Seville orange peel, a quarter of an ounce of cloves, as much mace, half an ounce of long pepper, two ounces of salt; squeeze in a whole lemon, and add half a glass of verjuice, five spoonsful of vinegar, and a pint of white wine; let it settle, and sift it very clear. This may be kept, bottled, a long time, and it will serve for all sorts of meat and fish—but it must be used in moderation. *Mackenzie's 5,000 Receipts,* 1829

ROAST LAMB SAUCE: The following is a very excellent sauce for roast lamb. Pick, wash, and shred fine, some fresh mint, put on it a tablespoonful of sugar, and four tablespoonfuls of vinegar: or chop some hard pickles to the size of capers, and put them to half a pint of melted butter, and a teaspoonful of vinegar. *Beecher's Domestic Receipt Book,* 1857

SAUCE FOR BOILED RABBITS: Boil the livers, and shred them very small, chop two eggs not boiled very hard, a large spoonful of grated white bread, some broth, sweet herbs, two spoonsful of white wine, one of vinegar, a little salt, and some butter; stir all together, and take care the butter does not oil. *Virginia Housewife,* 1856

SAUCE ITALIENNE: Put a piece of butter into a stew-pan, with mushrooms, onion, parsley, and the half of a laurel leaf, all cut fine; turn the whole over the fire some time, and shake in a little flour; moisten it with a glass of white wine, and as much good broth; add salt, pepper, and a little mace; beat all fine. Let it boil half an hour: then skim away the fat, and serve it up. A fine flavour may be given to it whilst boiling, by putting in a bunch of sweet herbs, which take out before the dish is served up.
Mackenzie's 5,000 Receipts, 1829

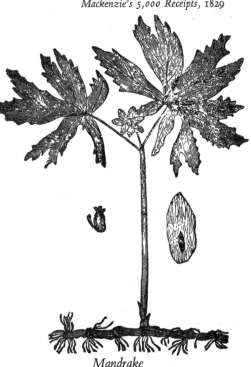

Mandrake

SAUCE PIQUANTE: Put a bit of butter with two sliced onions into a stew-pan, with a carrot, a parsnip, a little thyme, laurel, basil, two cloves, two shallots, a clove of garlic, and some parsley; turn the whole over the fire until it be well coloured; then shake in some flour, and moisten it with some broth, and a spoonful of vinegar. Let it boil over a slow fire: skim, and strain it through a sieve. Season it with salt and pepper, and serve it with any dish required to be heightened.   *Mackenzie's 5,000 Receipts, 1829*

SAUCE FOR TURTLE, OR CALF'S HEAD: To half a pint of hot melted butter, or beef gravy, put the juice and grated rined of half a lemon, a little sage, basil, or sweet marjorum, a little cayenne, or black pepper, and salt. Add a wine glass of white wine just before you take it up.   *Kitchen Directory, 1846*

SOY SAUCE: One pound of salt, two pounds of sugar, fried half an hour over a slow fire, then add three pints of boiling water, half a pint of essence of anchovies, a dozen cloves, and some sweet herbs. Boil till the salt dissolves, then strain and bottle it.
      Beecher's Domestic Receipt Book, 1857

TO MAKE WHITE SAUCE FOR FOWLS: Take a scrag of veal, the necks of fowls, or any bits of mutton or veal you have; put them in a sauce pan with a blade or two of mace, a few black pepper corns, one anchovy, a head of celery, a bunch of sweet herbs, a slice of the end of a lemon; put in a quart of water, cover it close, let it boil till it is reduced to half a pint, strain it, and thicken it with a quarter of a pound of butter mixed with flour, boil it five or six minutes, put in two spoonsful of pickled mushrooms, mix the yelks of two eggs with a tea cup full of good cream and a little nutmeg—put it in the sauce, keep shaking it over the fire, but don't let it boil.
      Virginia Housewife; 1856

TO MELT BUTTER: Nothing is more simple than this process, and nothing so generally done badly. Keep a quart tin sauce-pan, with a cover to it, exclusively for this purpose; weigh one quarter of a pound of good butter; rub into it two tea-spoonsful of flour; when well mixed, put it in the sauce-pan with one table-spoonful of water, and a little salt; cover it, and set the sauce-pan in a larger one of boil-ing water; shake it constantly till completely melted, and beginning to boil. If the pan containing the butter be set on coals, it will oil the butter and spoil it. This quantity is sufficient for one sauceboat. A great variety of delicious sauces can be made, by adding different herbs to melted butter, all of which are excellent to eat with fish, poultry, or boiled butchers' meat. To begin with parsley—wash a large bunch very clean, pick the leaves from the stems carefully, boil them ten minutes in salt and water, drain them perfectly dry, mince them exceedingly fine, and stir them in the butter when it begins to melt. When herbs are added to butter, you must put two spoonsful of water instead of one. Chervil, young fennel, burnet, tarragon, and cress, or pepper-grass, may all be used, and must be prepared in the same manner as the parsley.   *Virginia Housewife, 1856*

SOUP RECIPES

The soup precedes the coming feast,
As cards precede a ball.

THE PHRASE, "Pease-Porridge hot, pease-porridge cold" reminds us of childhood rhymes. But Dr. Salmon included in his 1690-edition, *Salmon's Herald,* a recipe for "Pease-Porridge, or Soop." For this, one took a leg of beef, or other fresh meat, and made of it a strong broth. Then, "take two or three quarts of Holl'd Pease, and boil them by themselves to a Pulp with a little piece of Bacon; then take Sorrel, Spear Mint and Parsley chopt, put it into the strong Broth, and stew it over some Coals, with a quarter of a pound of Butter; thicken it with the Pulp of the Pease, and stir it: when you put them together, put in some French Bread with a little Salt, Pepper and Butter when you eat it."

There are many other recipes, too, for "Soop Brown;" "Soop Good;" and "Soop

White." Soup was truly an integral part not only of meals in England and early America, but a century or two ago, the soup toureen occupied a position of great importance on nearly every table. Often, the traveller even carried "a portable soup" with him on long trips, for wayside stops were often few and far between. It was the herbs and seasonings, however, that gave these soups their unique flavor.

Thick stews, soups with chopped vegetables and meats, and similar dishes were especially popular, particularly among the many people who had poor, if any, teeth.

William M. Thackery, the famous nineteenth century English novelist who was born in India but later lived in England and travelled extensively on the Continent and in the United States, as a lecturer, wrote a *Ballad of Bouillabaisse* in which he said,

Plate 22. *Entrance to the Apothecary Shop at the Shelburne Museum at Shelburne, Vermont. (Courtesy Shelburne Museum, Inc.)*

> *This Bouillabaisse a noble dish is—*
> *A sort of soup or broth, or bew,*
> *Or hotchpotch of all sorts of fishes,*
> *That Greenwich never could outdo;*
> *Green herbs, red peppers, mussels, saffron,*
> *Soles, onions, garlic, roach, and dace;*
> *All these you eat at Terre's tavern,*
> *In that one dish of Bouillabaisse.*

Brillet-Savarin, a French lawyer, economist and gastronomist, wrote his famous *La Physiologie du Gout*, in 1825. This was published in English as *The Physiology of Taste*. In it, he remarked: "A rich soup; a small turbot; a saddle of venison; an apricot tart; this is a dinner fit for a king."

In the recipes which follow, one finds both the soups used quite generally in modern times and the more unusual. Among the

former might be included asparagus, beef, chicken or turkey, pea, oyster, and vegetable soups.

But let us consider for a moment Pigeon Soup. There were multitudinous numbers of wild pigeons in the early days. Tremendous nets used to be laid in which to gather them up, once they unknowingly settled there to feed or rest. They were a reliable source of food. In the soup recipe which follows, all but two of the requisite eight are left whole and are added to the stock along with fried bread and herbs.

One is likely to think of today's dried soup mix as a relatively new concoction. Yet, in 1857, there was a "soup powder," which is different from the modern mixes in that it consists really of dried herbs, lemon peel, and celery seeds which can be bottled and added later to a soup for flavor.

Marsh Mallows

Vegetable Soup", one relied on turnips, carrots, potatoes, onions, celery, and a bunch of sweet herbs; still an appetizing combination, nevertheless.

For Mock Turtle Soup, a calf's head was boiled until perfectly tender. For meat balls to be later added to the soup, the brains were mixed with chopped lean veal, a little salt pork, some herbs and spices, Part of this mixture was boiled in the soup; the rest was fried and served as a separate dish.

The recipe for Hessian Soup recalls the participation of the Hessian soldiers as mercenaries for the British during the American Revolution. For this, a half of an ox head was required.

Let us examine this and the other varieties of soup which are included.

In these days prior to the raising of all sorts of crops in the warmer regions of the country and the shipment of these to markets throughout the nation, one was limited to the vegetables available at that season of the year. There are, for example, separate recipes for "Spring Soup" and "Winter Vegetable Soup." It is learned from the following recipes that in the former, one would include green split peas, onions, turnips, celery, one leek, asparagus, cabbage, and various herbs including green mint. In the "Winter

GENERAL REMARKS: Soup is economical food, and by a little attention may be made good with very small materials. It should never be made of meat that has been kept too long. If meat is old, or has become tainted in the least, the defect cannot be disguised, and is peculiarly offensive in soup. All meat and bones for soup should be boiled a long time, and set aside until the next day, in order that the fat may be entirely removed. Then add the vegetables, rice and herbs, and boil it from an hour to an hour and a half. The water in which fresh meat is boiled should always be saved for soup and broth; and the bones of roast beef should never be thrown away without boiling, as they make excellent soup, and if not used for this purpose, should be boiled in order to save the fat which they contain.

Young Housekeeper's Friend, 1846

ASPARAGUS SOUP: Put a small boiled bone to $1\frac{1}{2}$ pints of peas, and water in proportion, a root of celery, a small bunch of sweet herbs, a large onion, Cayenne pepper, and salt to taste; boil it briskly for five hours, strain and pulp it; then add a little spinach juice, and asparagus boiled and cut into small pieces.

A teaspoonful of walnut soy, and a tea-spoonful of mushroom catsup, answers as well as the bone.
Mackenzie's 5,000 Receipts, 1829

ASPARAGUS: Cut half a pound of fat bacon into thin slices, place at the bottom of a stewpan, then add five pounds of lean beef cut into dice, and rolled in flour; cover the pan close, stirring occasionally until the gravy is drawn, then add two quarts of water, and half a pint of ale. Cover, stew gently for an hour, with some whole pepper and salt. Strain off the liquor, and skim off the fat. Add some spinach, cabbage-lettuce, white beet leaves, sorrel, a little mint, and powdered sweet marjoram; let these boil up in the liquor, then put in the green tops of asparagus cut small, boil till all is tender, and serve hot.
Practical Housewife, 1860

BEEF GRAVY SOUP: Cut slices of lean beef, according to the quantity wanted, which place in a stew-pan, upon sliced onions and roots, adding two spoonsful of fat broth; soak this on a slow fire for half an hour, stirring it well; when it catches a proper colour add thin broth made of suitable herbs, with a little salt over it.
Mackenzie's 5,000 Receipts, 1829

BEEF OR BLACK SOUP: The shank of beef is the best part for soup—cold roast beef bones, and beef steak, make very good soup. Boil the shank four or five hours in water, enough to cover it. Half an hour before the soup is put on the table, take up the meat, thicken the soup with scorched flour, mixed with cold water, season it with salt, pepper, cloves, mace, a little walnut, or tomato catsup improves it, put in sweet herbs or herb spirit if you like. Some cooks boil onions in the soup, but as they are very disagreeable to many persons, it is better to boil and serve them up in a dish by themselves. Make force meat balls of part of the beef and pork, season them with mace, cloves, pepper, and salt, and boil them in the soup fifteen minutes. *Kitchen Directory, 1846*

BRAWN: Boil a hock of beef, and any little pieces you may have besides, several hours. When the meat is ready to fall from the bones, take it out into an earthen pan, salt it, and season it with pepper, sage, and sweet marjoram. Put it into a coarse linen cloth or towel, twist it up tight and lay a stone upon it. A good

deal of fat will thus be pressed out. When it has lain twenty-four hours, take off the cloth, and cut thin slices for breakfast. It is very good, and will keep in a cool place several weeks. The water in which it was boiled will make excellent soup, or stock for gravies.
Young Housekeeper's Friend, 1846

BROTH OF BEEF, MUTTON, AND VEAL: Put two pounds of lean beef, two pounds of scrag of mutton, sweet herbs, and ten peppercorns, into a nice tin saucepan, with five quarts of water; simmer to three quarts; and clear from the fat when cold.
Note. That soup and broth made of different meats are more supporting, as well as better flavoured.
A New System of Domestic Cookery, 1807

BROTH: The Yellow leaves of the (marigold) flowers are dried and kept throughout Dutchland against winter to put into broths,..., in such quantity that in some Grocers or Spicesellers are to be found barrels filled with them and retailed by the penny or less, inasmuch that no broths are well made without dried Marigold. *Countrie Farme, 1600*

BROTH: The simple water of the Damask Roses is put into broth.s *Paradisi, 1629*

CHEAP SOUP—FOR THE POOR: Soak a quart of split peas for a day in cold water, and then put them into a boiler with two gallons and a half of water, and two pounds of cold boiled potatoes well bruised, a faggot of herbs, salt, pepper, and two onions sliced. Cover it very close, and boil *very gently* for five hours, or until only two gallons of soup remain.
Practical Housewife, 1860

CHICKEN OR TURKEY SOUP: The liquor that a turkey or chicken is boiled in, makes a good soup. If you do not like your soup fat, let the liquor remain till the day after the poultry has been boiled in it then skim off the fat, set it where it will boil. If there was not any rice boiled with the meat, put in half a tea cup full, when the liquor boils, or slice up a few potatoes and put in—season it with salt and pepper, sweet herbs, and a little celery boiled in it improves it. Toast bread or crackers, and put them in the soup when you take it up. *Kitchen Directory, 1846*

COMMON SOUP: Take the bones of beef, (ribs,

Mullein

Mustard

sirloin, & c.) break small, put into a digester or a large pan, cover with water, boil, and keep covered; then add a crust of bread toasted, a pound of pearl barley, two onions in slices, a faggot of sweet herbs, a bay-leaf, two carrots cut small, and other vegetables; fill up to a gallon with the liquor that corned beef, bacon, pork, or any other meat has been boiled in, and season with pepper and salt to taste.

Practical Housewife, 1860

FASTING-DAY SOOP: Take Spinnage, Sorrel, Chervil and Lettuce, and chop them a little; then brown some Butter, and put in your Herbs, keep them stirring that they do not burn; then have boiling Water over the fire, and put to it a very little Pepper, some Salt, a whole Onion stuck with Cloves, and a French roll cut in slices and dried very hard, and some Pistachia kernels blanched and shred fine, and let all boil together; then beat up the yolks of eight Eggs, with a little White-wine and the juice of a Lemon, and mix it with your Broth, and toast a whole French roll, and put in the middle of your dish, and pour your Soop over it; garnish your dish with ten or twelve poached Eggs and scalded Spinnage. *The Compleat Housewife,* 1728

FLEMISH SOUP: Scald half a dozen of turkey pinions, four sheeps' rumps, and $\frac{1}{2}$ a pound or more of pickled pork; then tie up each sort together, scald also a good savoy cut into quarters and tied; put them altogether into a pan with good broth, a faggot of sweet herbs, parsley, green shallots, 3 cloves, pepper and salt; boil slowly; when done, drain the meat; put it into the tureen, and serve a good gravy sauce with it. *Mackenzie's 5,000 Receipts,* 1829

GIBLET SOUP: Scald and clean three or four sets of goose or duck giblets; then set them on to stew with a scrag of mutton, or a pound of gravy beef, or bone of knuckle of veal, an oxtail, or some shankbones of mutton; three onions, a blade of mace, ten peppercorns, two cloves, a bunch of sweet herbs, and two quarts of water. Simmer till the gizzards are quite tender, which must be cut in three or four parts; then put in a little cream, a spoonful of flouer rubbed smooth with it and a spoonful of mushroom catsup; or two glasses of sherry or Madeira wine instead of cream, and some Cayenne.

A New System of Domestic Cookery, 1807

GIBLET SOUP (ANOTHER): Take the feet, neck, pinions, and giblets of two fowls, and add a pound and a half of veal, and a slice of lean ham. Pour on three quarts of cold water, and boil gently till the meat is very soft. Strain off the liquor, and, when cold, take off the fat. Cut the giblets and meat into half-inch pieces; add a tablepoonful of flour with one of butter, and some of the soup to thin it. Then put into the soup the butter and meat, with some sweet herbs tied in a bag, with salt to your taste. Boil it half an hour and it is done.

Beecher's Domestic Receipt-Book, 1857

GRAVY SOUP: Wash a leg of beef, break the bone, and set it over the fire with five quarts of water, a large bunch of herbs, two onions, sliced and fried, but not burnt, a blade or two of mace, three cloves, twenty Jamaica peppers, and forty black. Simmer till the soup be as rich as you choose; then strain off the meat, which will be fit for the servants' table. Next day take off the cake of fat, and that will warm with vegetables; or make a piecrust for the same. Have ready such vegetables as you choose to serve, cut in dice, carrot, and turnip, sliced, and simmer till tender. Celery should be stewed in it likewise; and before you serve, boil some vermicelli long enough to be tender, which it will be in fifteen minutes. Add a spoonful of soy, and one of mushroom catsup. Some people do not serve the vegetables, only boil for the flavour. A small roll should be made hot, and kept long enough in the saucepan to swell, and then be sent up in the tureen.

A New System of Domestic Cookery, 1807

GREEN PEA SOUP: Cut a knuckle of veal, and a pound of lean ham into thin slices; lay the ham at the bottom of a stewpan, then the veal; cut six small onions into slices, and put in two turnips, two carrots, a head of celery cut small, a faggot of sweet herbs, four cloves, and four blades of mace. Put a little water at the bottom, cover the pot close, stirring occasionally till the gravy is drawn; then add six quarts of boiling water, stew gently for four hours, and skim well. Take two quarts of green peas, stew in some of the broth till tender, strain, put in a marble mortar, and beat well, or mash with the spoon against the sides of the stewpan. Rub the peas through a hair sieve, or tamis, till thoroughly pulped, then put the soup into a clean pot, with a teacupful of spinach

juice, and boil for fiteeen minutes; season with pepper, salt, and a table-spoonful of brown sugar. If the soup is not thick enough, boil the crumb of a French roll in a little of the soup, and rub through the tamis; Then put in the soup and boil. Serve hot in the tureen, with dice of bread toasted very hard. (The celery must be omitted, until July, usingatable-spoonful of the seeds instead.) *Practical Housewife, 1860*

HARE OR RABBIT SOUP: Take a large newly killed hare, or two rabbits; cut them up and wash the pieces. Save all the blood, (which adds much to the flavour of the hare,) and strain it through a sieve. Put the pieces into a soup-pot with four whole onions stuck with a few cloves, four or five blades of mace, a head of celery cut small, and a bunch of parsley with a large sprig of sweet marjoram and one of sweet basil, all tied together. Salt and cayenne to your taste. Pour in three quarts of water, and stew it gently an hour and a half. Then put in the strained blood and simmer it for another hour, at least. Do not let it actually boil, as that will cause the blood to curdle. Then strain it, and pound half the meat in a mortar, and stir it into the soup to thicken it, and cut the remainder of the meat into small mouthfuls. Stir in, at the last, a jill or two glasses of red wine, and a large table-spoonful of currant jelly. Boil it slowly a few minutes longer, and then put it into your tureen. It will be much improved by the addition of about a dozen and a half small force-meat balls, about the size of a nutmeg. This soup willrequire cooking at least four hours.

Partridge, pheasant, or grouse soup may be made in a similar manner.

If you have any clear gravy soup, you may cut up the hare, season it as above, and put it into a jug or jar well covered, and set in boiling water till the meat is tender. Then put it into the gravy soup, add the wine, and let it come to a boil. Send it to table with the pieces of the hare in the soup.

When hare soup is made in this last manner, omit using the blood.

Miss Leslie's Directions for Cookery, 1839

HERB SOUP: Wash and cut small twelve cabbage lettuces, a handful of chervil, one of purslane, one of parsley, eight large green onions, and three handsful of sorrel; when peas are in season omit half the quantity of sorrel, and put a quart of young green peas;

put them all into a sauce-pan, with half a pound of butter and three carrots cut small, some salt and pepper; let them stew closely covered for half an hour, shaking them occasionally to prevent their adhering to the pan; fry in butter six cucumbers cut long-ways in four pieces; add them with four quarts of hot water, half a French roll, and a crust of bread toasted upon both sides; and let the whole boil till reduced to three quarts, then strain it through a sieve; beat up the yolks of four eggs with half a pint of cream, and stir it gently into the soup just before serving.

The Practice of Cookery, 1830

HESSIAN SOUP: Clean the root of a tongue very nicely, and half an ox head, with salt and water, and soak them afterwards in plain water; then stew them in five or six quarts of water till tolerably tender. Let the soup stand to be cold: take off the cake of fat, which will make good paste for hot meat pies, or serve to baste. Put to the soup a pint of split peas or a quart of whole, twelve carrots, six turnips, six potatoes, six large onions, a bunch of sweet herbs, and two heads of celery. Simmer them without the meat, till the vegetables are done enough to pulp with the peas through a sieve, when the soup will be about the consistence of cream. Season it with pepper, salt, mace, pimento, a clove or two, and a little Cayenne, all in the finest powder. If the peas are bad, the soup may not be thick enough; then boil in it a slice of roll, and put through the colander; or put a little rice flour, mixing it by degrees.

A New System of Domestic Cookery, 1807

HODGE-PODGE: Take either a brisket of beef, mutton, steaks, whole pigeons, rabbits cut in quarters, veal, or poultry; boil a long time over a slow fire in a short liquid, with some onions, carrots, parsnips, turnips, celery, a fagot of parsley, green shallots, one clove of garlic, 3 of spices, a laurel leaf, thyme, a little basil, large thick sausages, and thin broth or water; when done, drain the meat, and place it upon a dish intermixed with roots, sift and skim the sauce, reduce some of it to a glaze, if desired; glaze the meat with it, then add some gravy on the same stew-pan and broth sufficient to make sauce enough with pepper and salt: sift it in a sieve, and serve upon the meat. If brisket of beef is used, let it be half done before putting in the roots, which should be scalded first, as it makes the broth more palatable.

Mackenzie's 5,000 Receipts, 1829

MACARONI SOUP: Make a good stock with a knuckle of veal, a little sweet marjoram, parsley, some salt, white pepper, three blades of mace, and two or three onions; strain and boil it. Break in small bits a quarter of a pound of macaroni, and gently simmer it in milk and water till it be swelled and is tender; strain it, and add it to the soup, which thicken with two table-spoonsful of flour, mixed in half a pint of cream, and stirred gradually into the soup. Boil it a few minutes before serving.

The Practice of Cookery, 1830

MEG MERRILIES SOUP: Cut a hare in pieces, and save the blood, reserve some bits of the meat and the liver to make forcemeat balls of, and put the rest of the hare into a saucepan with six quarts of water; season with four onions, a bunch of sweet herbs, pepper, and salt, stew it gently for two hours; in another sauce-pan put the blood and the water the hare was washed in, stir in two heaped table-spoonsful of rice flour, to make it the consistence of gruel, and when it boils mix it with the stock. Take two partridges or moor-fowl, if they are fresh, or part of both, skin and cut each of them into four pieces, brown them in butter in a frying-pan, and add them to the soup, with about three pints of carrots and turnips neatly cut and parboiled. Make the forcemeat balls as follows:—Mince the liver and meat very finely with rather more than half its quantity of fat bacon or butter, one anchovy, a little lemon-peel and lemon thyme, pepper and salt, grated nutmeg, and crumbs of bread; make up the balls the size of a nutmeg, with a well-beaten egg, fry them of a light brown in clarified beef dripping, fresh lard, or butter, drain them before the fire, and add them to the soup half an hour before serving, and pick out all the loose bones of the hare.

The Practice of Cookery, 1830

MOCK TURTLE, OR CALF'S HEAD SOUP: Boil the head until perfectly tender—then take it out, strain the liquor, and set it away until the next day— then skim off the fat, cut up the meat, together with the lights, and put it into the liquor, put it on the fire, and season it with salt, pepper, cloves, and mace—add onions and sweet herbs, if you like—stew it gently for half an hour. Just before you take it up, add half a pint of white wine. For the balls, chop lean veal fine, with a little salt pork, add the brains, and season it with

salt, pepper, cloves, mace, sweet herbs or curry powder, make it up into balls about the size of half an
egg, boil part in the soup, and fry the remainder, and
put them in a dish by themselves.
Kitchen Directory, 1846

OYSTER SOUP: Three pints of large fresh oysters.
Two tablespoonfuls of butter, rolled in flour. A bunch
of sweet herbs. A saucer full of chopped celery. A
quart of rich milk. Pepper to your taste.

Take the liquor of three pints of oysters. Strain it,
and set it on the fire. Put into it, pepper to your taste,
two tablespoonfuls of butter rolled in flour, and a
bunch of sweet marjoram and other pot-herbs, with
a saucer full of chopped celery. When it boils, add a
quart of rich milk—and as soon as it boils again, take
out the herbs, and put in the oysters just before you
sent it to the table. Boiling then in the soup will
shrivel them and destroy their taste.

Toast several slices of bread. Cut them into small
squares, and put them into the soup before it goes to
the table.　　　　*Seventy-five Receipts, 1838*

PIGEON SOUP: Take eight good pigeons, cut up
two of the worst, and put them on with as much water
as will make a large tureen of soup, adding the pinions,
necks, gizzards, and livers of the others; boil well, and
strain. Season the whole pigeons within, with mixed
spices, and salt, and truss them with their legs into
their belly. Take a large handful of parsley, young
onions, and spinach, pick and wash them clean and
shread small; then take a handful of grated bread, put
a lump of butter about the size of a hen's egg in a
frying-pan, and when it boils throw in the bread,
stirring well until it becomes a fine brown colour.
Put on the stock to boil, add the whole pigeons,
herbs, and fried bread, and when the pigeons are done
enough, dish up with the soup.
Practical Housewife, 1860

POTTAGE: (Vegetable ingredients): Violet leaves
(petals), Succory, Strawberry leaves, Spinage, Langdebeef (a variety of bugloss), Marygold flowers,
Scallions, and a little Parsley, (with oatmeal added to
the kettle).　　　*English Housewife, 1615*

ROAST BEEF BONE SOUP: Boil the bones at least
three hours, or until every particle of meat is loose;
then take them out, scrape off the meat and throw
them into the oven to be burned the next time you

101 ✦ CULINARY USES OF HERBS

Oak

Olive Tree

bake; set aside the water in which the bones were boiled; the next day take from it every particle of fat, cut up an onion, two or three potatoes and a turnip, and put into it. Add also a spoonful of whole rice, a teaspoonful of cloves or powdered sweet marjoram, and some salt. Boil it an hour and a half.

Young Housekeeper's Friend, 1846

SOUP FOR THE POOR: Wash an ox head very clean; break the bones, and cut the meat in pieces; put it on in thirteen gallons of water, with a peck and a half of potatoes, half a peck of turnips, the same quantity of onions, and some carrots; peel and cut them all down. A handful of pot herbs, and two quarts of oatmeal; season with pepper and salt. Cover the pot closely, and let it stew till the next morning; add as much hot water as may have wasted in boiling, and let it stew for some hours longer, when it will be fit for use. This soup will be found very good for a family dinner.

The Practice of Cookery, 1830

Pennyroyal

SOUP CRESSY: Slice twelve large onions, and fry them pretty brown in a quarter of a pound of fresh butter; scrape and clean two dozen of good red carrots, boil them in four quarts of water till quite soft; pound them in a marble mortar, mix them with the onions and add the liquor in which the carrots were boiled, a bunch of sweet herbs, pepper, salt, a blade of mace, and two or three cloves; let them all boil about an hour, then rub them through a hair sieve; put it on again to boil rather quickly, till it be as thick as rich cream. Put a little dry boiled rice in the tureen, and pour the soup over it. If the carrots are large, one dozen will be found sufficient.

The Practice of Cookery, 1830

SOUP HERB SPIRIT: Those who like a variety of herbs in soup, will find it very convenient to have the following mixture. Take when in their prime, thyme, sweet marjoram, sweet basil, and summer savory. When thoroughly dried, pound and sift them. Steep them in brandy for a fortnight, the spirit will then be fit for use.

Kitchen Directory, 1846

SOUP MAIGRE: Take of veal, beef cut into small pieces, and scrag of mutton, 1 lb. each; put them into a saucepan, with 2 quarts of water; put into a clean cloth 1 oz. of barley, and onion, a small bundle of sweet herbs, 3 or 4 heads of celery cut small, a little mace, 2 or 3 cloves, 3 turnips pared and cut in two, a large carrot cut into small pieces, and a young lettuce. Cover the pot close, and let it stew very gently for six hours. Then take out the spice sweet herbs, and onion, and pour all into a soup dish, seasoned with salt.

Mackenzie's 5,000 Receipts, 1829

SOUP POWDER: The following is a very convenient article for soups. Dry, pound, and sift the following ingredients together. Take one ounce each, of lemon, thyme, basil, sweet marjoram, summer savory, and dried lemon peel, with two ounces of dried parsley, and a few dried celery seeds. Bottle it tight. Horseradish can be sliced thin, dried and pounded, and kept in a bottle for use. Mushrooms can be dried in a moderately warm oven, then powdered with a little mace and pepper, and kept to season soup or sauces.

Beecher's Domestic Receipt Book, 1857

SOUTHERN GUMBO: This is a favorite dish at the South and West, and is made in a variety of ways. The following is a very fine receipt, furnished by a lady, who has had an extensive opportunity for selection.

Fry one chicken, when cut up, to a light brown, and also two slices of bacon. Pour on to them three quarts of boiling water. Add one onion and some sweet herbs, tied in a rag. Simmer them gently three hours and a half. Strain off the liquor, take off the fat, and then put the ham and chicken, cut into small pieces, into the liquor. Add half a tea-cup of *ochre,* cut up; if dry, the same quantity; also half a tea-cup of rice. Boil all half an hour, and just before serving add a glass of wine and a dozen oysters, with their juice. Ochra is a fine vegetable, especially for soups, and is easily cultivated. It is sliced and dried for soups in winter. *Beecher's Domestic Receipt Book,* 1857

SPRING SOUP: Put on in four quarts of water a knuckle of veal cut down, and a quarter of a pound of lean ham, or a gammon of bacon; a quart of green split peas; cut small three or four onions, three turnips, a little parsley, thyme, celery, and one leek; stew them all together till the peas are very soft; take out the meat and press the remainder through a fine sieve; season the soup with pepper and salt. Cut small like peas a bunch of the tops of asparagus, the hearts of two or three cabbages, cutting off the top part and the outside leaves, and a little green mint, stew them till tender, keeping them of a good green, and add them to the soup a quarter of an hour before serving. If it should not be green enough, pound some spinach, squeeze the juice through a cloth, put about a quarter of a pint into the tureen, and pour in the soup. This is the best method to make green peas soup of a good colour. *The Practice of Cookery,* 1830

VEAL SOUP: Veal should boil about an hour, if a neck-piece; if the meat comes from a thicker, more solid part, it should boil longer. No directions about these things will supply the place of judgment and experience. Both mutton and veal are better for being boiled with a small piece of salt pork. Veal broth is very good. *American Frugal Housewife,* 1833

VEAL SOUP: The knuckle or leg of veal is the best for soup. Wash it and break up the bones. Put it into a pot with a pound of ham or bacon cut into pieces, and water enough to cover the meat. A set of calf's feet, cut in half, will greatly improve it. After it has stewed slowly, till all the meat drops to pieces, strain it, return it to the pot, and put in a head of celery cut small, three onions, a bunch of sweet marjoram, a carrot and a turnip cut into pieces, and two dozen black peppercorns, with salt to your taste. Add some small dumplings made of flour and butter. Simmer it another hour, or till all the vegetables are sufficiently done, and thus send it to the table.

You may thicken it with noodles, that is paste made of flour and beaten egg, and cut into long thin slips. Or with vermicelli, rice, or barley; or with green peas, or asparagus tops.

Miss Leslie's Directions for Cookery, 1839

VERMICELLI SOUP: Cut a knuckle of veal, or a neck of mutton into small pieces, and put them, with the bones broken up, into a large stew-pan. Add the

Peppermint

meat sliced from a hock or shank of ham, a quarter of a pound of butter, two large onions sliced, a bunch of sweet herbs, and a head of celery cut small. Cover the pan closely, and set it without any water over a slow fire for an hour or more, to extract the essence from the meat. Then skim it well, and pour in four quarts of boiling water, and let it boil gently till all the meat is reduced to rags. Strain it, set it again on the fire, and add a quarter of a pound of vermicelli, which has first been scalded in boiling water. Season it to your taste with salt and cayenne pepper, and let it boil five minutes. Lay a large slice of bread in the bottom of your tureen, and pour the soup upon it.

For veal or mutton you may substitute a pair of large fowls cut into pieces; always adding the ham or a few slices of bacon, without which it will be insipid. Old fowls that are fit for no other purpose will do very well for soup.

Miss Leslie's Direction for Cookery, 1839

WHITE SOUP: Boil in a small quantity of water a knuckle of veal, and scrag of mutton, mace, white pepper, two or three onions, and sweet herbs, the day before you want the soup. Next day take off the fat, and put the jelly into a saucepan, with a quarter of a pound of sweet almonds blanched, and beaten to a paste in a mortar with a little water to prevent oiling, and put to it a piece of stale white bread, or crumb of a roll, a bit of cold veal, or white of chicken. Beat these all to a paste with the almond paste, and boil it a few minutes with a pint of raw thick cream, a bit of fresh lemon peel, and half a blade of mace pounded; then add this thickening to the soup. Let it boil up and strain it into the tureen: if not salt enough then put it in. If macaroni or vermicelli be served, they should be boiled in the soup, and the thickening be strained after being mixed with a part. A small rasped roll may be put in.

Instead of the cream thickening, as above, ground rice, and a little cream may be used.

A New System of Domestic Cookery, 1807

WINTER VEGETABLE SOUP: To every gallon of water allow, when cut down small, a quart of the following vegetables; equal quantities of turnips, carrots, and potatoes, three onions, two heads of celery, and a bunch of sweet herbs; fry them brown in a quarter of a pound of butter, add the water with salt and pepper, and boil it till reduced to three quarts, and serve it with fried toasted bread.

The Practice of Cookery, 1830

FISH RECIPES

From ocean and lake, from river and brook,
We swim to thy bidding, oh capable cook.

FISH WERE AN IMPORTANT source of food for the early settlers. The sea, rivers, and lakes all abounded with many species. It seemed as if there was enough food, not only for this country, but for the whole world.

Europe wanted fish to eat, so large quantities were exported from this country, especially to the southern regions, bordering the Mediterranean. Also, there were demands for fish to feed the slaves in our South and in the West Indies. These locations were

Pine

markets for the poorer, inferior grades of fish.

In New England and New York, salted fish were as carefully prepared for home use as in England and Holland. The ling and herring, favorites in Europe, were replaced in this country by the cod, shad, and mackerel.

Lobsters were plentiful enough to prevent starvation. Early documents reveal that some caught in New York Bay were five and six feet long. One finds such dimensions difficult to imagine. Vanderdonk verified foot-long oysters seen by travelers and noted that these oysters roasted or stewed made a good bite.

Timothy Dwight, President of Yale and grandson of Jonathan Edwards, when on a trip to Newport through Westerly, wrote: "Pankatuc river . . . furnishes excellent

Pink-root

fisheries for bass, eels, blackfish, shad, and herrings. In the bay, . . . these kinds of fish are caught in as great abundance, as perhaps in any part of New England. Long and rounded clams, also, oysters, and a little farther out in the sound, lobsters are found in great numbers."

The following recipes particularly pertain to stewed black-fish, carp, perch, rock fish, sturgeon, and pike stuffed with a pudding.

BLACK FISH, STEWED: Flour a deep dish, and lay in the bottom a piece of butter rolled in flour. Then sprinkle it with a mixture of parsley, sweet marjoram, and green onion; all chopped fine. Take your black fish and rub it inside and outside with a mixture of cayenne, salt, and powdered cloves and mace. Place skewers across the dish, and lay the fish upon them. Then pour in a little wine, and sufficient water to stew the fish. Set the dish in a moderate oven, and let it cook slowly for an hour.

Shad or rock fish may be dressed in the same manner. *Miss Leslie's Directions for Cookery,* 1839

CARP, STEWED: Having cut off the head, tail, and fins, season the carp with salt, pepper, and powdered mace, both inside and out. Rub the seasoning on very well, and let them lay in it an hour. Then put them into a stew-pan with a little parsleg shred fine, a whole onion, a little sweet marjoram, a tea-cup of thick cream or very rich milk, and a lump of butter rolled in flour. Pour in sufficient water to cover the carp, and let it stew half an hour. Perch may be done in the same way. You may dress a piece of sturgeon in this manner, but you must first boil it for twenty minutes to extract the oil. Take off the skin before you proceed to stew the fish.
Miss Leslie's Directions for Cookery, 1839

CRABS, DRESSED: Choose a good heavy crab, boil for about half an hour in salt and water, remove the pot, let the crab get cold; take off the great shell without breaking it, extract the fish from the body and claws, and mince it well. Put some floured butter in a stewpan with six or eight small mushrooms, parsley, and green asparagus tops shred fine, fry a little, and put in the minced fish with half a wine-

Plantain

Pleurisy-root

glass of white wine and pepper, salt and sweet herbs to season; stew gently for fifteen minutes, thicken with flour, and flavour with lemon-juice. Fill the shell with this mixture, having previously removed the herbs, set in a baking-pan, or dish, strew stale bread crumbs over the top, set in an oven to brown, and then serve hot. Garnish with lemon, and parsley.

Practical Housewife, 1860

EEL PIE: Clean a pound or more of eels, cut them in lengths of two and three inches, season with pepper and salt, and put them in a dish with some lumps of butter, and a wine-glassful of water; cover with a light paste, and bake. Some add a couple of bay-leaves and a faggot of herbs, with a few cloves and an onion, and veal stock thickened with flour, instead of water. Cream added after the pie is done, instead of butter before, also improves it vastly.

Practical Housewife, 1860

MATELOTE OF ANY KIND OF FIRM FISH: Cut the fish in pieces six inches long, put it in a pot with onion, parsley, thyme, mushrooms, a little spice, pepper and salt—add red wine and water enough for gravy, set it on a quick fire and reduce it one-third, thicken with a spoonful of butter and two of flour; put it in a dish with bits of bread fried in butter, and pour the gravy over it.

Virginia Housewife, 1856

OYSTERS, PICKLED: After taking out the oysters, to each quart of liquor put a teaspoonful of pepper, two blades of mace, three tablespoonfuls of white wine, and four of vinegar, also a tablespoonful of salt. Simmer the oysters in this five minutes, then take them out and put in jars, then boil the pickle, skim it, and pour it over them.

Beecher's Domestic Receipt Book, 1857

PIKE, TO STEW: Take stale bread crumbs, finely-chopped sweet herbs and parsley, a little lemon-peel, three ounces of butter, mixed up with the yolks of two eggs, and seasoned with nutmeg, cayenne, common pepper, and salt, and form into a pudding to stuff the fish with. A few pickled or fresh oysters chopped fine and mixed with it improve the flavour considerably. Clean and wash the fish, stuff with the pudding, fix the tail in the mouth, and stew gently in the same manner as for carp, and garnish with sliced lemon. *Practical Housewife*, 1860

(TO DRESS ANY KIND OF) SALTED FISH: Take the quantity necessary for the dish, wash them, and lay them in fresh water for a night; then put them on the tin plate with holes, and place it in the fish kettle—sprinkle over it pounded cloves and pepper, with four cloves of garlic; put in a bundle of sweet herbs and parsley, a large spoonful of tarragon, and two of common vinegar, with a pint of wine; roll one quarter of a pound of butter in two spoonsful of flour, cut it in small pieces, and put it over the fish—cover it closely, and simmer it over a slow fire half an hour; take the fish out carefully, and lay it in the dish, set it over hot water, and cover it till the gravy has boiled a little longer—take out the garlic and herbs, pour it over the fish, and serve it up. It is very good when eaten cold with salad, garnished with parsley.
Virginia Housewife, 1856

SHAD, BAKED: Keep on the head and fins. Make a forcemeat or stuffing of grated bread crumbs, cold boiled ham or bacon minced fine, sweet marjoram, pepper, salt, and a little powdered mace or cloves. Moisten it with beaten yolk of egg. Stuff the inside of the fish with it, reserving a little to rub over the outside, having first rubbed the fish all over with yolk of egg. Lay the fish in a deep pan, putting its tail to its mouth. Pour into the bottom of the pan a little water, and add a jill of port wine, and a piece of butter rolled in flour. Bake it well, and when it is done, send it to table with the gravy poured round it. Garnish with slices of lemon.

Any fish may be baked in the same manner. A large fish of ten or twelve pounds weight, will require about two hours baking.
Miss Leslie's Directions for Cookery, 1839

FOWL RECIPES

SOME COUNTRY TAVERNS had the reputation of serving fowls "before the life had been an hour out of their bodies." To combat this, some travelers carried their own poultry with them on a trip. Such a person

was Judge Oliver Wendell when he drove from Boston to Pittsfield, a journey which in those days took four or five days. Often, he had a freshly killed chicken put under his carriage seat, "which at the end of twenty-four hours was delivered to the cook of the wayside inn, and another substituted to undergo a like seasoning."

In the autumn, the marshes were frequented by hunters in search of wild fowl, often of great flocks of wild pigeons. Early documents reveal that at times there were so many flocks of wild pigeons in the air that they literally blotted out the sunlight and gave one the impression it was a cloudy, dark day. Many homes owned their own huge pigeon nets; such a one can be viewed at the Stanley-Whitman House in Farmington, Connecticut.

Pheasant, partridge, woodcock, and quail were also often abundant. And there were many turkeys, which are described by early writers as coming in flocks of a hundred and weighing thirty or forty pounds.

As true to-day as when it was uttered in the 1600's is George Herbert's comment that, "The chicken is the country's, but the city eats it."

The following recipes reflect the many kinds of fowl whose preparation and flavor were enhanced by the use of herbs.

BIRDS, TO STEW: Wash and stuff them with bread crumbs, seasoned with pepper, salt, butter, or chopped salt pork, and fasten them tight. Line a stew-pan with slices of bacon, add a quart of water and a bit of butter the size of a goose egg, or else four slices of salt pork.

Add, if you like, sliced onions and sweet herbs, and mace. Stew till tender, then take them up and strain the gravy over them. Add boiling water if the liquor is too much reduced.

Beecher's Domestic Receipt Book, 1857

BOUDIN À LA RICHELIEU: Put the crumb of a good-sized stale roll into a basin, and cover it with milk, about as warm as when it comes from the cow; let it stand half an hour, then with a spoon take off all the milk, and put the bread into a sauce-pan, with a good bit of butter, one onion chopped very finely, and a little parsley and herbs. Keep stirring it on the fire till it become quite stiff, then take it off, and add the yolk of an egg, which must be well beaten into it; let it then cool before adding the meat, which may be of chicken, veal, or lamb, that has been already dressed. Half a pound of any of these meats, pounded or grated very fine, is the quantity required. Beat two eggs, whisking up well both yolks and whites; add them to the meat and bread, and beat them all together for some time; the more they are beaten, the lighter the boudin will be. Butter a shape, and fill it; tie the shape in a cloth, and put it on to boil for three hours. A rich sauce, thickened and seasoned, is to be poured over the boudin when it is dished.

The Practice of Cookery, 1830

CHICKEN—AU SOLEIL: Raise the thighs of as many large young fowls as you want, bone them, and have a large lump of butter melted in a frying pan, lay in your thighs with a little salt, pepper, a bay leaf, one onion, two cloves, and a bundle of shallots and parsley, put all over a quick fire till the meat is browned, then add a table-spoonful of flour, a ladle of hot bouillon, and a handful of buttered mushrooms; bubble for three quarters of an hour, carefully removing all the fat; take out your meat, throw away your onion, bay leaf, herbs, & c. beat and put in three yolks of eggs, pour the sauce over your fowl; when cold dip them well in the sauce, then in crumbs of bread, then in yolks of eggs beat and seasoned, more crumbs; fry them of a light brown in their sauce, drain, pile them in a circle, and fill the hollow with fried parsley.

Mackenzie's 5,000 Receipts, 1829

CHICKEN CROQUETS AND RISSOLES: Take some cold chicken, and having cut the flesh from the bones, mince it small with a little suet and parsley; adding sweet marjoram and grated lemon-peel.

Season it with pepper, salt and nutmeg, and having mixed the whole very well, pound it to a paste in a marble mortar, putting in a little at a time, and moistening it frequently with yolk of egg that has been previously beaten. Then divide it into equal portions, and having floured your hands, make it up in the shape of pears, sticking the head of a clove into the bottom of each to represent the blossom end, and the stalk of a clove into the top to look like the stem. Dip them into beaten yolk of egg, and then into breadcrumbs grated finely and sifted. Fry them in butter, and when you take them out of the pan, fry some parsley in it. Having drained the parsley, cover the bottom of a dish with it, and lay the croquets upon it. Send it to table as a side dish.

Croquets may be made of cold sweet-breads, or of cold veal mixed with ham or tongue.

Rissoles are made of the same ingredients, well mixed, and beaten smooth in a mortar. Make a fine paste, roll it out, and cut it into round cakes. Then lay some of the mixture on one half of the cake, and fold over the other upon it, in the shape of a half-moon. Close and crimp the edges nicely, and fry the rissoles in butter. They should be of a light brown on both sides. Drain them and send them to table dry.

Miss Leslie's Directions for Cookery, 1839

CHICKEN, FRICASSEE: Boil them rather more than half in a small quantity of water: let them cool; then cut them up, and put them to simmer in a little gravy, made of the liquor they were boiled in, and a bit of veal or mutton, onion, mace, lemonpeel, white pepper, and a bunch of sweet herbs. When quite tender, keep them hot while you thicken the sauce thus: strain off, and put it back into the saucepan, with a little salt, a scrape of nutmeg, a bit of flour and butter: give it one boil; and when you are going to serve, beat up the yelk of an egg, add half a pint of cream, and stir them over the fire, but do not let it boil. It will be equally good without the egg.

A New System of Domestic Cookery, 1807

CHICKEN PIE: Cut up two young fowls: season with white pepper, salt, a little mace, and nutmeg, all in the finest powder; likewise a little Cayenne. Put the chicken, slices of ham or gammon, forcemeat, and hard eggs, alternately. If to be in a dish, put a little water; if in a raised crust, none. Against the pie be baked, have ready a gravy of knuckle of veal, with a few shank bones, seasoned with herbs, onion, mace, and pepper. If in a dish, put in as much gravy as will fill it: if in crust, let it go cold; then open the lid, and put in the jelly.

A New System of Domestic Cookery, 1807

CHICKEN PUDDING, A FAVORITE VIRGINIA DISH: Beat ten eggs very light, add to them a quart of rich milk, with a quarter of a pound of butter melted, and some pepper and salt; stir in as much flour as will make a thin good batter; take four young chickens, and after cleaning them nicely, cut off the legs, wings, & c. Put them all in a sauce pan, with some salt and water, and a bundle of thyme and parsley, boil them till nearly done, then take the chicken from the water and put it in the batter, pour it in a deep dish, and bake it; send nice white gravy in a boat.   *Virginia Housewife,* 1856

DUCKS, NOTTINGHAM FASHION: Choose a pair of fine fat ducks, lard as usual, and then half-roast them. Remove from before the fire, place in a clean stewpan, and stew gently for half an hour with a pint of good gravy; then add half a pint of oysters nicely bearded (breaded), a dozen roasted and bruised chestnuts, a pint of red wine, and two small onions minced fine; three or four sprigs of thyme, a blade of mace, six peppercorns, the crumb of a French roll rubbed fine, and a pinch of cayenne pepper. When well flavoured, remove, and serve hot. It is necessary to cover the stewpan well during the time the ducks are cooking.   *Practical Housewife,* 1860

DUCK (TO STEW): Cut one or two ducks into quarters; fry them a light brown in butter; put them into a sauce-pan, with a pint of gravy, a tea-cupful of port wine, four onions whole, pepper and some salt, a bunch of parsley, two sage leaves, a sprig of winter savory, and sweet-marjoram. Cover the pan closely, and stew them till tender; take out the herbs and pepper; skim it; if the sauce be not sufficiently thick, mix with two table-spoonfuls of it a little flour, and stir it into the sauce-pan; boil it up, and garnish the dish with the four onions.

The Practice of Cookery, 1830

DUCK, STEWED: Half roast a large duck. Cut it up, and put it into a stew-pan with a pint of beef-

Poke

Polypody

gravy, or dripping of roast-beef. Have ready two boiled onions, half a handful of sage leaves, and two leaves of mint, all chopped very fine and seasoned with pepper and salt. Lay these ingredients over the duck. Stew it slowly for a quarter of an hour. Then put in a quart of young green peas. Cover it closely, and simmer it half an hour longer, till the peas are quite soft. Then add a piece of butter rolled in flour; quicken the fire, and give it one boil. Serve up all together.

A cold duck that has been under-done may be stewed in this manner.

Miss Leslie's Directions for Cookery, 1839

FOWL À LA CONDÉ: Draw the sinews of the legs of two fine white fowls, and take out the breast bones, truss them, and put into each a little lemon juice, and salt, mixed with a piece of butter, place them in a stew-pan, and cover them with thin slices of fat bacon, pour over them the following sauce: Cut into dice a pound of veal, the same quantity of fat bacon, and a little fat of ham, fry all this white in half a pound of butter, adding a bunch of parsley, a little thyme, half a bay leaf, a clove, some salt and pepper, and some boiling water; when sufficiently stewed, strain it over the fowls, and let them stew for three quarters of an hour upon a slow fire, but have a pretty brisk one upon the cover of the stew-pan; drain and serve them with a rich brown sauce, and a scarlet tongue placed between them in the dish.

The Practice of Cookery, 1830

GOOSE, TO ROAST: Chop a few sage leaves and two onions very fine, mix them with a good lump of butter, a tea-spoonful of pepper, and two of salt, put it in the goose, then spit it, lay it down, and dust it with flour; when it is thoroughly hot, baste it with nice lard; if it be a large one, it will require an hour and a half, before a good clear fire; when it is enough, dredge and baste it, pull out the spit, and pour in a little boiling water. *Virginia Housewife*, 1856

PHEASANT, LARDED AND ROASTED, SPORTSMAN'S FASHION: When the pheasant gives off a peculiar odour, and the skin of the breast changes colour a little, it should be plucked carefully, but not sooner. When plucked, lard it with some good fresh bacon very carefully, and then stuff with the following:—Take two woodcocks, and divide the flesh into one portion, and the tail and liver into another; mince and mix the meat with some good beef marrow, a little scraped bacon, salt, pepper, and lemon-thyme, or other herbs; add truffles sufficient to fill up the rest of the inside of the bird, then stuff it in and secure well, so that none of it may escape, which may be effectually done by placing a crust of bread over the opening, and sewing it up. Make a paste of the livers of the woodcocks, some truffles, grated bacon, an anchovy boned, and some fresh butter; cover the bird with this, put down to roast, and when done, serve upon a slice of toasted bread, surrounded with slices of orange, and some of the gravy round the bird. (This receipt was obtained from an old epicurean sportsman, who vouched for its being a first-rate way of cooking the bird, and further recommended that a table-spoonful of good champagne or burgundy should be poured over the bird, in addition to a good libation of the same wine during the time it is being partaken of.)

Practical Housewife, 1860

TURKEY, BONED: A large turkey. Three sixpenny loaves of stale bread. One pound of fresh butter. Four eggs. One bunch of pot-herbs, parsley, thyme, and little onions. Two bunches of sweet-marjoram. Two bunches of sweet-basil. Two nutmegs. Half an ounce of cloves, pounded fine. A quarter of an ounce of mace, pounded fine. A table-spoonful of salt. A table-spoonful of pepper.

(Skewers, tape, needle, and coarse thread will be wanted.)

Grate the bread, and put the crusts in water to soften. Then break them up small into the pan of crumbled bread. Cut up a pound of butter into the pan of bread. Rub the herbs to powder, and have two tablespoonfuls of sweet-marjoram and two of sweet basil, or more of each if the turkey is very large. Chop the pot-herbs, and pound the spice. Then add the salt and pepper, and mix all the ingredients well together. Beat slightly four eggs, and mix them with the seasoning and bread crumbs.

After the turkey is drawn, take a sharp knife and, beginning at the wings, carefully separate the flesh from the bone, scraping it down as you go; and avoid tearing or breaking the skin. Next, loosen the flesh from the breast and back, and then from the thighs.

It requires great care and patience to do it nicely. When all the flesh is thus loosened, take the turkey by the neck, give it a pull, and the skeleton will come out entire from the flesh, as easily as you draw your hand out of a glove. The flesh will then be a shapeless mass. With a needle and thread mend or sew up any holes that may be found in the skin.

Take up a handful of the seasoning, squeeze it hard and proceed to stuff the turkey with it, beginning at the wings, next to the body, and then the thighs.

If you stuff it properly, it will again assume its natural shape. Stuff it very hard. When all the stuffing is in, sew up the breast, and skewer the turkey into its proper form, so that it will look as if it had not been boned.

Tie it round with tape and bake it three hours or more. Make a gravy of the giblets chopped, and enrich it with some wine and an egg.

If the turkey is to be eaten cold, drop spoonfuls of red currant jelly all over it, and in the dish round it.

A large fowl may be boned and stuffed in the same manner.   *Seventy-five Receipts,* 1838

TURKEY (ROAST): A good sized turkey should be roasted two hours and a half, or three hours; very slowly at first. If you wish to make plain stuffing, pound a cracker, or crumble some bread very fine, chop some raw salt pork very fine, sift some sage, (and summer-savory, or sweet-marjoram, if you have them in the house, and fancy them,) and mould them all together, seasoned with a little pepper. An egg worked in makes the stuffing cut better; but it is not worth while when eggs are dear. About the same length of time is required for boiling and roasting.
American Frugal Housewife, 1833

VEGETABLE RECIPES

FRESH VEGETABLES and fruits were in scant supply except in season, for ice houses were relatively unknown until just before the American Revolution; even then, it was only the most luxurious homes which possessed one. In general, items considered

perishable were placed inside the well where they could remain cool.

Ann Capnerhurst is described in some early records as having been invited to a quilting frolic. One might guess that tea would be served, but not a whole meal such as she was offered. It consisted of roast turkey, roast pork, potatoes, beets, cole slaw, rice pudding, peach pie, pumpkin pie, and tarts. Potatoes, beets, cabbage, and pumpkin are mentioned as the vegetables.

Actually, many fruits and vegetables were not raised or eaten at all. The usual vegetables which served as staple items of diet with fish and meat were beans, turnips, carrots, and cabbage.

The food situation in Philadelphia and its environs was different from many colonial towns in that from the beginning Penn's city had excellent markets. There, one could find a huge supply of all kinds of provisions— vegetables, meats, poultry, fruits, and many foreign delicacies, available because of that town's active trade with all parts of the world.

For the most part, those vegetables which were prepared had herbs added for special seasoning, as will be noted in the recipes which follow.

BEANS. TO DRESS FRENCH BEANS: Trim some nice young French beans, and boil them in salt and water; drain them quite dry, and pour over them the following sauce:—Boil a little sauce tournée, and thicken it with the beaten yolks of two eggs and a little finely-chopped parsley, with a piece of fresh butter, a little pepper, salt, and the juice of a lemon added, and all stirred till hot. Or, put them into a stew-pan, and when quite hot, add a quarter of a pound of fresh butter, a little pepper, salt, and the juice of half a lemon; shake the stew-pan frequently, but do not use a spoon. If the butter does not mix well, add half a spoonful of sauce tournee.

The Practice of Cookery, 1830

CELERY, STEWED: Trim and cut to the same length a number of heads of celery; split them in two lengthwise; tie them in bundles with thread, and parboil them for ten minutes in salted water; drain them and arrange them in a saucepan over slices of bacon, with a bundle of sweet herbs, a couple of onions, pepper and salt to taste, and a blade of mace; add enough stock just to cover the contents, and set the saucepan to simmer gently till the celery is quite tender. Having removed the string, dispose the celery neatly on a dish; take some of the stock in which it has been stewed, remove all fat from it, add a small piece of fresh butter, pour it over the celery, and serve.

Mrs. Winslow's Domestic Receipt Book, 1878

CUCUMBERS (TO STEW): Pare the cucumbers, and let them lie in vinegar and water, with a little salt in it; drain them, and put them into a sauce-pan with a pint of gravy, a slice of lean ham, an onion stuck with one or two cloves, a bunch of parsley and thyme; let them stew, closely covered, till tender. Take out the cucumbers, strain and thicken the gravy with a piece of butter rolled in flour. Boil it up and pour it over the cucumbers.

The Practice of Cookery, 1830

Poppy

EGG PLANT, STEWED: The purple egg plants are better than the white ones. Put them whole into a pot with plenty of water, and simmer them till quite tender. Then take them out, drain them, and (having peeled off the skins) cut them up, and mash them smooth in a deep dish. Mix with them some grated bread, some powdered sweet marjoram, and a large piece of butter, adding a few pounded cloves. Grate a layer of bread over the top, and put the dish into the oven and brown it. You must send it to table in the same dish. Egg plant is sometimes eaten at dinner, but generally at breakfast.

Miss Leslie's Directions for Cookery, 1839

EGG PLANTS, STUFFED: Parboil them to take off their bitterness. Then slit each one down the side, and extract the seeds. Have ready a stuffing made of grated bread-crumbs, butter, minced sweet herbs, salt, pepper, nutmeg, and beaten yolk of egg. Fill with it the cavity from whence you took the seeds, and bake the egg plants in a Dutch oven. Serve them up with a made gravy poured into the dish.

Miss Leslie's Directions for Cookery, 1839

HERB PIE: Pick two handfuls of parsley from the stems, half the quantity of spinach, two lettuces, some mustard and cress, a few leaves of borage, and a little mint. Wash and boil them a little, then drain, press out the water and chop small; mix a batter of flour, two eggs well beaten, half a pint of milk and a pint of cream, and pour it upon the herbs. Cover in with a good crust, and bake. *Practical Housweeife,* 1860

MUSHROOMS, TO DRESS: Take very white button mushrooms, remove the stalks, wash well, put into a stewpan, with the juice of two lemons, a little white pepper, half a glass of white wine, a faggot of sweet herbs, and a table-spoonful of sweet oil. Put all over the fire, and after two boilings take it off, let it cool, and serve hot. *Practical Housewife,* 1860

POT-HERBS: (Mentioned by Theophrastus) Lettuce, onion, cabbage, radish, turnip, beet, cucumber, gourd (squash), leek, celery, garlic, cardoon, mushroom, horseradish, lentil, pea and shallot. (Also, asparagus is noted as growing wild).

Enquiry into Plants, 4th. Century B.C.

POT-HERBS: (Mentioned by Dioscorides) Bean,

lentil, turnip, cabbage, radish, beet, cucumber, garlic, onion, leek, carrot, lettuce, mustard. Also, rocket, plantain, lupin, flax, sow thistle, etc.

The Greek Herbal of Dioscorides, c. 512

POTATO CROQUETTES (PARSLEY): Season cold mashed potatoes with pepper, salt and nutmeg. Beat to a cream with a teaspoon of melted butter to every cupful of potato; bind with two or three well-beaten eggs, and add some minced parsley (if you like). Roll into oval balls, dip in beaten egg, then in bread crumbs, and fry in hot lard or drippings. Pile in a pyramid upon a flat dish, and serve.

Mrs. Winslow's Domestic Receipt Book, 1875

SWEET POTATOS, STEWED: Wash and wipe them, and if they be large, cut them in two lengths; put them at the bottom of a stew pan, lay over some slices of boiled ham; and on that, one or two chickens cut up with pepper, salt, and a bundle of herbs; pour in some water, and stew them till done, then take out the herbs, serve the stew in a deep dish—thicken the gravy, and pour over it.

Virginia Housewife, 1856

VINEGAR RECIPES

A loaf of bread, the walrus said,
    Is what we chiefly need:
Pepper and vinegar besides
Are very good indeed—
Now if you're ready, oysters, dear,
    We can begin to feed!
        LEWIS CARROLL,
        The Walrus and the Carpenter

INTERESTING VINEGARS can be concocted with the use of herbs. Mrs. Webster's *The Improved Housewife or Book of Receipts* (1858) contains a recipe for Celery Vinegar which can be adapted to many different herbs. It reads, "take two gills of celery seed; pound and put it in a bottle, and fill it

with sharp vinegar; shake it every day, for two weeks; then strain it, and keep it for use. It will impart an agreeable celery flavor to everything with which it is used. A delicious flavor of thyme may be obtained, if gathered when in full perfection. It should be picked from the stalks, a large handful of it put into a jar, and a quart of vinegar or brandy turned on it; cover it very close. Next day, take all the thyme out, and put in as much more. Do this a third time; then strain, bottle, and *seal* the cork. This is far preferable to dried thyme. Mint may be prepared in a similar manner. The flavor of both these kinds of herbs must be preserved by care in the preparation. If permitted to remain more than twenty hours in the liquid, they will impart an unsavory taste."

Possibly, these were American innovations in the realm of herb vinegars, for Dr. Salmon (1710) suggests few other than "Fennel or Dill to Pickle" (though he does

Prickly Ash

Red Raspberry

Rhubarb

include many remarks relative to the making of various kinds of non-herb vinegars). As has already been noted, Salmon's Dill or Fennel Vinegar is made by letting "your water boil, then having your Fennel tied up in Bunches, half a dozen walms will be enough; drain it, and let your pickle be Vinegar."

CELERY, THYME, OR MINT VINEGAR: Pound two gills of celery seed, put it into a bottle and fill it with strong vinegar; shake it every day for a fort-night, then strain it, and keep it for use. It will impart a pleasant flavour of celery to any thing with which it is used. A very delicious flavour of thyme may be obtained, by gathering it when in full perfection; it must be picked from the stalks, a large handful of it put into a jar, and a quart of vinegar or brandy poured on it; cover it very close—next day, take all the thyme out, put in as much more; do this a third time; then strain it, bottle and seal it securely. This is greatly preferable to the dried thyme commonly used, during the season when it cannot be obtained in a fresh state. Mint may be prepared in the same way. The flavour of both these herbs must be preserved by care in the preparation; if permitted to stand more than twenty hours in the liquor they are infused in, a coarse and bitter taste will be extracted, particularly from mint.
Virginia Housewife, 1856

PRIMROSE VINEGAR: To fifteen quarts of water put six pounds of brown sugar; let it boil ten minutes, and take off the scum: pour on it half a peck of primroses; before it is quite cold, put in a little fresh yeast, and let it work in a warm place all night; put it in a barrel in the kitchen, and when done working, close the barrel, still keeping it in a warm place.
Family Receipt Book, 1819

TARRAGON VINEGAR: Tarragon should be gathered on a dry day, just before the plant flowers. Pick the green leaves from the stalks, and dry them a little before the fire. Then put them into a wide-mouthed stone jar, and cover them with the best vinegar, filling up the jar. Let it steep fourteen days, and then strain it through a flannel bag. Pour it through a funnel into half-pint bottles, and cork them well.

Miss Leslie's Directions for Cookery, 1839

SALAD RECIPES

> *Oh, herbaceous treat!*
> *'Twould tempt the dying anchorite to eat;*
> *Back to the world he'd turn his fleeting soul,*
> *And plunge his fingers in the salad bowl;*
> *Serenely full the epicure would say,*
> *'Fate cannot harm me,—I have dined to-day.'*
> SYDNEY SMITH, *A Receipt for a Salad*

ALTHOUGH SALADS are referred to as early as 1710 in Dr. Salmon's *The Family Dictionary*, mention is made of only a few possible ingredients—such as, hard boiled eggs, oil, vinegar, mustard, anchovies, parsley, lobsters, cucumber, "hot pickles," beetroot, lettuce, cresses, sorrel, young onions, celery, cabbage, radishes "in spring," and sage. Not all of these items appeared in the same salad. But from the listing, one detects a number of modern salad items among the missing. Nowhere could the writer find a recipe which included fruit, for example. Tuna, frequently resorted to in modern recipes for salad, does not even appear in Dr. Salmon's *Dictionary*. The herb, nasturtium, shows up as a garnish for a salad and is spelled somewhat differently from today's equivalent.

Interesting directions are given for raising the "greens," for a salad, rather quickly. In these days before chemical fertilizers we find the use of "pigeon's dung" instead, com-

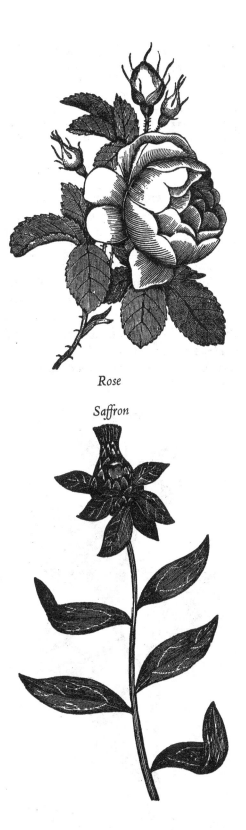

Rose

Saffron

bined with mould and powdered slacked lime. A typical "receipt" follows:

TO RAISE A SALAD QUICKLY: Steep lettuce-seed, mustard, cresses, & c. in aquavitae. Mix a little pigeon's dung with some mould, and powdered slacked lime. In forty-eight hours the salad will be produced.   *Family Receipt Book,* 1819

Again, as with the summer soup and winter vegetable one, there is the same distinction made between a Summer and a Winter Salad. The former includes lettuce, mustard, cresses, sorrel and young onions. The dish is "garnished with Nasturtiam flowers." For the Winter Salad, one relied on endive, celery, mustard and cresses, red cabbage, boiled beet-root, an onion, mixed together with salad sauce. It is pointed out that "In spring, add radishes, and also garnish the dish with them."

Sarsaparilla

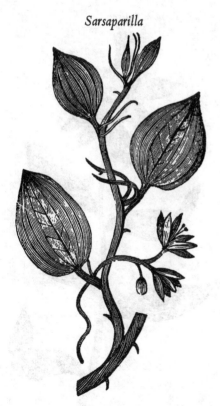

HINTS ABOUT SALADS: This is a point of proficiency which, with care, it is easy to attain. The main point is, to incorporate the several articles required for the sauce, and to serve up at table as fresh as possible. The herbs should be "morning gathered," and they will be much refreshed by lying an hour or two in spring water. Careful picking, and washing, and drying in a cloth, in the kitchen, are also very important, and the due proportion of each herb requires attention. The sauce may be thus prepared:— Boil two eggs for ten or twelve minutes, and then put them in cold water for a few minutes, so that the yolks may become cold and hard. Rub them through a coarse sieve with a wooden spoon, and mix them with a table-spoonful of water or cream, and then add two table-spoonfuls of fine flask oil, or melted butter; mix, and add by degrees, a tea-spoonful of salt, and the same quantity of mustard; mix till smooth, when incorporate with the other ingredients about three table-spoonfuls of vinegar; then pour this sauce down the side of the salad-bowl, but do not stir up the salad till wanted to be eaten. Garnish the top of the salad with the white of the eggs cut in slices; or these may be arranged in such manner as to be ornamental on the table. Some may fancy they are able to prepare a salad without previous instruction, but like everything else, a little knowledge in this case may not be thrown away.

          Practical Housewife, 1860

FRENCH SALLAD: Chop three anchovies, a shalot, and some parsley small; put them in a bowl with two tablespoonfuls of vinegar, one of oil, a little mustard, and salt. When well mixed, add by degrees some cold roast or boiled meat in the very thinnest slices; put in a few at a time, they being small, not exceeding two or three inches long; shake them in the seasoning, and then put more; cover the bowl close; and let the sallad be prepared three hours before it be eaten. Garnish with parsley, and a few slices of the fat.

     A New System of Domestic Cookery, 1807

LOBSTER SALAD: Take three yolks of hard eggs, two yolks of raw eggs, two tea-spoonfuls of mustard, a little salt and cayenne pepper, four table-spoonfuls of salad oil, one and a half table-spoonful of tarragon vinegar, and one of essence of anchovies; mix well, and add three table-spoonfuls of cream. Cut two large lobsters up small, and mix with finely-cut salad,

116

cucumber, hot pickles, and beet-root. Pour the mixture given above over the salad, put in a dish, not a bowl, and garnish with hard boiled eggs cut in thin slices. *Practical Housewife, 1860*

SALAD, ASPARAGUS: Asparagus should be sodden in flesh broth, and eaten, or boiled in fair water, then seasoned with oil, pepper and vinegar, being served up as a salad.
The Herball or Generall Histoire of Plantes, 1597

SALAD, BEET: The Roots of the Red Beet, pared into thin Slices and Circles, are by the French and Italians contriv'd into curious Figures to adorn their Sallets. *Acetaria, 1697*

SALAD, BROOM BUD: (Pickled broom buds are suggested for a) Sallet of great delight serving all the year which do helpe to stir up an appetite to meat. *Adam in Eden, 1657*

SALAD, MINT: Garden mints were universally used for sauces in Pliny's time; and much commended for their singular Vertues, especially the young red buds in the Spring with a due proportion of Vinegar and Sugar, refresh the Spirits and stirreth up the appetite, and is one of the best Sallads the Garden affords. There are divers sorts of Mint but the red Garden Mint is the best. *Systema Horticulturae, 1677*

SALAD, NASTURTIUM: Nasturtiums . . . are now become an acceptable Sallad as well the leaf as the blossom. *Art of Gardening, 1677*

SALAD, TURNIP AND CABBAGE: Some make a very acceptable boil'd Sallet of the young and tender stalks of both Turneps, and of Cabbages when they first run up in the Spring, they boil them and peel them and put Butter, Vinegar and Pepper to them. *English Gardner, 1670*

SALAD: (Sweet Chervil roots are) most excellent in a sallade, if they be boiled, and after dressed, as the cunning Cooke knoweth how better than myself; notwithstanding I do use to eate them with oile and vinegar, being first boiled, which is very good for old people that are dull and without courage, it rejoiceth

and comforteth the hart, and increaseth their lust and strength.
The Herball or Generall Histoire of Plantes, 1597

SALAD: The seedes (of Sweet Chervil) eaten as a sallade whilest they are yet greene, with oile, vinegar and pepper, exceede all other sallade by many degrees, both in pleasantnes of taste, sweetnesse of smell, and holsomnesse for the cold and feeble stomach. . . . The leaves are exceeding good, holsome, and pleasant among other sallade herbes giving the taste of Anise seede unto the rest.
The Herball or Generall Histoire of Plantes, 1597

SALAD: (Made from 'cooling and Succory-like Herbss)—purslane, sorrel, orach, beets, chickweed, borage, bugloss, endive, chicory, dandelion, lettuce. (The latter item was considered excellent as a salad material). *Theatrum Botanicum, 1640*

THE PERFECT SALAD:
1. Let your *Herby Ingredients* be exquisitely cull'd . . . discreetly sprinkl'd, than over-much sob'd with Spring-Water, especially Lettuce . . . let them remain awhile in the Cullender to drain the superuous

Sassafras

moisture: And lastly, swing them altogether gently in a clean course Napkin.

2. (The *Oyl* must be) very clean, not high-colour'd nor yellow: but with an Eye rather of a pallid olive green, without Smell, or the least touch of rancid, or indeed of any sensible taste or Scent at all. . . .

3. *Vinegar* and other liquid Acids, perfectly clear, neither sawre, Vapid or spent. . . .

4. (The *Salt* should be) detersive, penetrating, quickning (and of the) brightest Bay grey-Salt.

5. (*Mustard* should be) of the best Tewksberry; or else compos'd of the soundest and weightiest York-shire Seed.

6. (*Pepper* should) be not bruised to too small a dust.

7. *Yolks* of fresh and new-laid Eggs, boil'd moderately hard, to be mingl'd and mash'd with the Mustard, Oyl and Vinegar: and part to cut into quarters, and eat with the Herbs.

8. (The *Knife*) with which the Sallet Herbs are cut be of Silver and by no means of Steel, which all Acids are apt to corrode, and retain a Metalic relish of.

9. (The *Saladiere* ought to be) of Porcelane, or of the Holland-Delft Ware.

Acetaria, 1697

SUMMER SALAD: Buddus of Stanmache, Vyolette flourez, Percely, Redmynt, Syves (chives), Cresse of Boleyn, Purselan, Ramson, Calamynt, Prime Rose buddus, Dayses, Rapounses, Daundelion, Rokette, Red Nettle, Borage flourers, Croppes of Red Fennell, Selbestryn, Chykyn-wede.

Book of Culinary Recipes, c. 15th. C.

A SUMMER SALAD: Wash very clean one or two heads of fine lettuce, divide it, let it lie some time in cold water; drain and dry it in a napkin, and cut it small before serving. Mustard and cresses, sorrel and young onions, may be added, and the dish garnished with Nasturtiam flowers.

The Practice of Cookery, 1830

WINTER SALAD: alexanders, artichokes, blessed thistle, cucumbers, endive, mustard, musk-million, mints, purslane, radish, rampions, rocket, sage, sorrel, spinage, sea holly, asparagus, skirrets, chicory, tarragon, and violets of all colors.

Five Hundred Points of Good Husbandry, 1573

A WINTER SALAD: Wash very clean one or two heads of endive, some heads of celery, some mustard and cresses; cut them all small, add a little shredded red cabbage, some slices of boiled beet-root, an onion, if the flavour is not disliked; mix them together with salad sauce. In spring, add radishes, and also garnish the dish with them.

The Practice of Cookery, 1830

SALADS: We are by Sallets to understand a particular Composition of certain crude and fresh Herbs, such as usually are, or may safely be eaten with some Acetous Juice, Oyl, Salt etc. to give them a grateful Gust and Vehicle.   *Acetaria, 1697*

SALADS, COMPOUND: Your compound Sallets are, first the young Buds and Knots of all manner of wholesome Herbs at their first springing as red Sage, Mint, Lettice, Violets, Marigolds, Spinage, and many others mixed together, and then served up to the table with Vinegar, Sallet-Oyle and Suger.

English Housewife, 1615

SALADS, FLOWER: Chiefly of the Aromatick Esculents and Plants are preferable, as generally endow'd with the Vertues of their Simples, in a more intense degree; and may therefore be eaten alone in their proper Vehicles, or Composition with other Salleting sprinkled among them; But give a more palatable Relish, being Infused in Vinegar; Especially those of the Clove Gillyflower, Elder, Orange, Cowslip, Rosemary, Arch-Angel (dead nettle), Sage, Nasturtium Indicum, etc.

Acetaria, 1697

SALADS FOR WINTER: Put with white-wine Vinegar and Sugar for Winter sallets (such ingredients as clove gillyflowers, and flowers of cowslips, bugloss, borage and archangel).

The English Gardner, 1670

SALADS, HEALTHFUL: (Salads are) proper for all seasons, but particularly from the beginning of February to July, in which period they are in greatest perfection, and consequently act most effectually in cleansing and attenuating the blood. . . . So again from the middle of September to the end of January, fresh salading of every kind is grateful to the stomach, and will have the effect of removing obstructions, relieving shortness of breath and correcting the humours generated by gross food.

Domestic Oracle, 1826

SALADS, KINDS OF: Your preserved Sallats are of two kinds, either pickled, as are Cucumbers, Samphire, Purslan, Broom and such like; or preserved with Vinegar, as Violets, Primrose, Cowslip, Gilly flowers of all kinds; Broom-flowers, and for the most part any wholesome flower whatsoever. . . . For the pickling of Sallats, they are only boyled (drained, spread on a table, salted; after they have cooled, they are placed in an earthenware pot and covered by a solution made of water, salt, and vinegar. Then the jar is sealed. If one wished to preserve flowers, sugar and vinegar were used.) Now for Sallets for shew only, and the adorning and setting out of a table with number of dishes, they be those which are made of Carret roots . . . cut into many shapes and proportions, or some into Knots, some in the manner of Scutions and Armes, some like Birds, and some like Wild Beasts, according to the Art and cunning of the Workman; and these for the most part are seasoned with Vinegar, Oyl, and a little Pepper.

English Housewife, 1615

SALADS OF MARIGOLD ETC:: (Suggestion is made by Markham in the 17th. Century that marigold and violets be used as salad materials.)

English Housewife, 1615

SALAT: Take parsel, sawge, garlec, chibollas (young onions), onyons, leek, borage, myntes, porrectes (kind of leek), fenel, and ton tressis (cresses), rew, rosemarye, purslarye (purslane); lave, and waisshe hem clene; pike hem, pluk hem small with thyn (thine) honde, and myng (mix) hem wel with raw oile. Lay on vynegar and salt, and serve it forth.

The Forme of Cury, c. 1390

SALLET OF COLD CAPON ROSTED: It is a good Sallet, to slice a cold Capon thin; mingle with it some Sibbolds, Lettice, Rocket and Tarragon sliced small. Season all with Pepper, Salt, Vinegar and Oyl, and sliced limon. A little Origanum doth well in it.

Closet Opened, 1669

SALLETS: By this name we here mean cold Sallets made of raw Herbs: Some as the French make a Medly of all sorts of Herbs; but we in England use only some few choice ones, as Lettices, Cabbage-

Seneca Snake-root

Senna

119 ✦ CULINARY USES OF HERBS

Skullcap

green Coffin of the Flower, and with the Purslan stalks, make the stalk of the flower, and the divisions of the leaves and branches; then with the thinne slices of Cowcumbers, make their leaves in true proportions, jagged or otherwise: and thus you may set forth some full blown, some halfe blown, and some in the bud, which will be pretty and curious. And if you will set forth yellow flowers, take the pots of Primroses and Cowslips, if blew flowers, then the pots of Violets, or Buglosse flowers; and these Sallets are both for shew and use, for they are more excellent for taste, then for to look on.

The English Housewife, 1615

PICKLE RECIPES

I am a shell-fish just come from being saturated with the waters of the Lucrine lake, near Baiae; but now I luxuriously thirst for noble pickle.

MARTIAL, *Epigrams*

PERHAPS THE FACT that there were so many pickled foods is due to the housewife's ingenuity in devising a method of preserving, in these days before generally accepted refrigeration.

From the recipes which follow, one discovers that nasturtium seed, when pickled, is often preferred to capers. Several months must pass after processing them, however, before they are fit for consumption.

The liquor from pickled walnuts is recommended as a catsup for fish. The same is true of the vinegar from pickled butternuts.

Mrs. Cornelius in *The Young Housekeeper's Friend* (1846) suggests a recipe for pickling small musk-melons by making an incision in the side of the fruit and stuffing it with cloves, mustard-seed, pepper-corns, horseradish, and chopped onion, if desired. One proceeds

Lettices, Lambs-Lettice, Sage, Sorrel, Parsley, Cresses, Tarragon, the white part of young Onions, or Shalots; which are mix'd in such proportion as each one likes; and being pick'd, well wash'd and prepared, just before eating, they make a mixture of choice Oil 3 parts, Wine Vinegar 2 parts, Mustard one part, and a little Salt, well beaten together, which is either poured over the whole Sallet, or put in on one side of the Dish, in which every one may rowl their Sallet as they please. In Winter Time they make it of the whitest, tenderest, and sweetest Cabbage they can get; which being shaved very fine, and chopt small with some small Onions or Shalots, they pour over it the former mixture, and so eat it.

Dr. Salmon's Recipes, 1710

THE MAKING OF STRANGE SALLETS: Now for the compounding of Sallets, of these pickled and preserved things, though they may be served up simply of themselves, and are both good and dainty; yet for better curiosity, and the finer adorning of the Table, you shall thus use them. First, if you would set forth any Red flower, that you know or have seen, you shall take your pots of preserved Gilliflowers, and suting the colours answerable to the flower you shall proportion it forth, and lay the shape of the Flower in a Fruit dish; then with your Purslan leaves, make the by "sewing on the piece with a needle and coarse thread, or bind a strip of old cotton around each one and sew it on." After they are placed in a jar and covered with boiling vinegar, they are "covered close."

As for jar covers, mention is made of a bladder followed by a piece of leather.

From one recipe, one learns that pickled lemons are "quite equal to the West India lime."

Let us examine the following recipes to discover the great variety of pickles, including "pickled martinoes," whatever they may be.

DIRECTIONS FOR PICKLING:

Musk-melons should be picked for mangoes, when they are green and hard. They should be cut open after they have been in salt water ten days, the inside scraped out clean, and filled with mustard-seed, allspice, horseradish, small onions, & c., and sewed up again. Scalding vinegar poured upon them.

When *walnuts* are so ripe that a pin will go into them easily, they are ready for pickling. They should be soaked twelve days in very strong cold salt and water, which has been boiled and skimmed. A quantity of vinegar, enough to cover them well, should be boiled with whole pepper, mustardseed, small onions, or garlic, cloves, ginger, and horseradish; this should not be poured upon them till it is cold. They should be pickled a few months before they are eaten. To be kept close covered; for the air softens them. The liquor is an excellent catsup to be eaten on fish.

Put *peppers* into strong salt and water, until they become yellow; then turn them green by keeping them in warm salt and water, shifting them every two days. Then drain them, and pour scalding vinegar over them. A bag of mustard-seed is an improvement. If there is mother in vinegar, scald and strain it.

Cucumbers should be in weak brine three or four days after they are picked; then they should be put in a tin or wooden pail of clean water, and kept slightly warm in the kitchen corner for two or three days. Then take as much vinegar as you think your pickle jar will hold; scald it with pepper, allspice, mustard-

seed, flag-root, horseradish, & c., if you happen to have them; half of them will spice the pickles very well. Throw in a bit of alum as big as a walnut; this serves to make pickles hard. Skim the vinegar clean, and pour it scalding hot upon the cucumbers. Brass vessels are not healthy for preparing anything acid. *Red cabbages* need no other pickling than scalding, spiced vinegar poured upon them, and suffered to remain eight or ten days before you eat them. Some people think it improves them to keep them in salt and water twenty-four hours before they are pickled.

If you find your pickles soft and insipid, it is owing to the weakness of the vinegar. Throw away the vinegar, (or keep it to clean your brass kettles,) then cover your pickles with strong, scalding vinegar, into which a little allspice, ginger, horseradish and alum have been thrown. By no means omit a pretty large bit of alum. Pickles attended to in this way, will keep for years, and be better and better every year.

Some people prefer pickled *nasturtion-seed* to *capers*. They should be kept several days after they are gathered, and then covered with boiling vinegar, and bottled when cold. They are not fit to be eaten for some months.

Skunk Cabbage

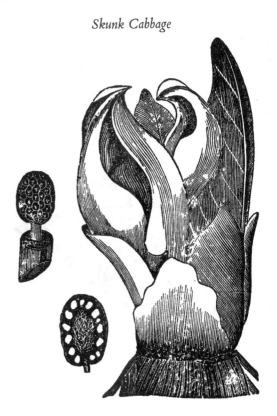

Martinoes are prepared in nearly the same way as other pickles. The salt and water in which they are put, two or three days previous to pickling, should be changed every day; because martinoes are very apt to become soft. No spice should be used but allspice, cloves, and cinnamon. The martinoes and the spice should be scalded *in* the vinegar, instead of pouring the vinegar *over* the martinoes.

American Frugal Housewife, 1833

ASSORTED PICKLES FOR WINTER USE: (Mention is made that the housewife pickled cucumbers, mangoes, codlins (green apples), kidney beans, samphire, walnuts, barberries, parsley, nasturtiums, radishes, elder shoots and buds, beets, cauliflower, red cabbage, grape, artichokes, mushrooms, and onions.)

The Experienced Housekeeper, 1782

BROOM BUDS, PICKLED: (A strong brine made of white wine vinegar and salt is poured over the buds which have been placed in a glass jar.) They should be frequently shaken till they sink under it and keep it (the jar) well stopt and covered.   *Acetaria,* 1699

BROOM BUDS, PICKLED: (Young buds of broom pickled are) to be eaten all the yeare after as a sallet of much delight, and are called Broome capers, which doe helpe to stirre up an appetite to meate, that is weak and dejected.

Theatrum Botanium, 1640

BUTTERNUTS: Gather them between the twenty-fifth and thirtieth of June. Make a brine of boiled salt and water, strong enough to bear up an egg after it is cold. Skim it while it boils. Pour it on the nuts, and let them lie in it twelve days. Then drain them; lay

Slippery Elm

them in a jar, and pour over them the best of vinegar, boiled with pepper-corns, cloves, allspice, mustard, ginger, mace and horseradish. This should be cooled before it is poured on. Cover close, and keep them a year before you use them. Walnuts are done in the same way. The vinegar becomes an excellent catsup, by many persons preferred to any other.

Young Housekeeper's Friend, 1846

CLOVE GILLIFLOWERS: (These) being pickled with Vinegar and Sugar, are a pleasant and dainty Sawce, stir up the Appetite and are also of a Cordiall faculty.   *Adam in Eden,* 1657

COLLYFLOWER (CAULIFLOWER) PICKLE: Boil them till they fall in Pieces: then with some of the stalk, and most of the flower, boil it in a part of the Liquor till pretty strong: then being taken off, strain it; and when settled, clear it from the Bottom. Then with Dill, Gross Pepper, a pretty Quantity of Salt, when cold, add as much Vinegar as will make it sharp, and pour all upon the Collyflower.

Acetaria, 1699

COWCUMBER PICKLE: It (dill) is put among pickled Cowcumbers, wherewith it doth very well agree, giving unto the cold fruit a pretty spicie taste or rellish.   *Seventeenth Century Recipe*

COWSLIP PICKLE: Pick very clean; to each Pound of Flowers allow one Pound of Loaf Sugar, and one Pint of White-Wine Vinegar, which boil to a Syrup and cover it scalding hot. Thus you may pickle Clove-gilly flowers, Elder, and other Flowers, which being eaten alone, make a very agreeable Salletine.

Acetaria, 1699

ELDER BUDS, PICKLED: (Buds are) gathered when the size of hop buds (aar) put in strong salt and water for nine days, stirring two or three times a day. Then put them in a pan, cover them with vine leaves and pour on them the water they came out of. Set them over a slow fire till they be quite green, make a pickle of allegar (vinegar made from ale), mace, shalots, and some ginger sliced. Boil them two or three minutes, and pour it upon your buds. Tie them down, and keep them in a dry place for use.

London Art of Cookery, 1801

A GOOD CHOW-CHOW: Boil in one quart of vinegar a quarter of a pound of mustard, mixed as for table use, two ounces of ginger, two ounces of white pepper, a very little mace, with a few cloves. Take one dozen large cucumbers, peeled and sliced, place in a sieve with a handful of salt, let them stand ten minutes, then put in jars. When the Vinegar is cold enough pour it over and tie down tight. It will be fit for use in one week, and will keep good a year.

Mrs. Winslow's Domestic Receipt Book, 1878

GREEN TOMATO PRESERVES: Eight pounds small, green tomatoes; pierce each one with a fork; seven pounds sugar, juice of four lemons, one ounce ginger and mace mixed, heat all together slowly, and boil till the fruit is clear. Then take out the fruit in a perforated skimmer; boil the syrup down thick. Put the fruit into jars and pour the hot syrup over it.

Mrs. Winslow's Domestic Receipt Book, 1875

HARDEN PICKLES AFTER THEY ARE TAKEN OUT OF THE BRINE: A lump of alum put in the vinegar, and horse-radish cut in strips, will make them crisp.

Mrs. Winslow's Domestic Receipt Book, 1878

MANGOES: Select small musk-melons, (the common kind are much better for this purpose than cantelopes); cut an oval piece out of one side. You must have a sharp knife, and be careful to make a smooth incision. Take out the seeds with a teaspoon. Fill the melons with a stuffing made of cloves, mustard-seed, pepper-corns, scrapings of horseradish, and chopped onion, if you like it. Sew on the piece with a needle and coarse thread, or bind a strip of old cotton around each one and sew it on. Lay them in a jar, and pour boiling vinegar on them with a little salt in it. Do it two or three times, then lay them in fresh vinegar and cover them close.

Young Housekeeper's Friend, 1846

NASTURTIUM BUDS, PICKLED: Gather the Buds before they are open to flower; lay them in the Shade three or four Hours, and putting them into an Earthen Glazed Vessel, pour good vinegar on them, and cover it with a Board. Thus letting it stand for eight or ten Days; then being taken out, and gently press'd, cast them into fresh Vinegar, and let them so remain as long as before. Repeat this a third time, and Barrel them up with Vinegar, and a little Salt.

Acetaria, 1699

PECCALILLI—INDIAN METHOD: This consists of all kinds of pickles mixed and put into one large jar—girkins, sliced cucumbers, button onions, cauliflowers, broken in pieces. Salt them, or put them in a large hair sieve in the sun to dry for three days, then scald them in vinegar a few minutes; when cold put them together. Cut a large white cabbage in quarters, with the outside leaves taken off and cut fine, salt it, and put it in the sun to dry for three or four days; then scald it in vinegar, the same as cauliflower, carrots, three parts, boiled in vinegar and a little bay salt. French beans, rack samphire, reddish pods, and nasturchions, all go through the same process as girkins, capsicums, & c. To one gallon of vinegar put four ounces of ginger bruised, two ounces of whole white pepper, two ounces of allspice, half an ounce of chillies bruised, four ounces of tumeric, one pound of the best mustard, half a pound of shallots, one ounce of garlic, and half a pound of bay salt. The vinegar, spice, and other ingredients, except the mustard, must boil half an hour; then strain it into a pan, put the mustard into a large basin, with a little vinegar; mix it quite fine and free from lumps, then add more; when well mixed put it to the vinegar just strained off, and when quite cold put the pickles into a large pan, and the liquor over them; stir them repeatedly, so as to mix them all; finally, put them into a jar, and tie them over first with a bladder, and afterwards with leather. The capsicums want no preparation.

Mackenzie's 5,000 Receipts, 1829

Solomon's Seal

PICCALILLI: To half a bushel of nicely chopped tomatoes, which must be squeezed dry, add two dozen onions chopped fine, one dozen green peppers chopped, one box of ground mustard, one large root of grated horse-radish, nearly a pint of salt, four tablespoonfuls ground cloves, four of allspice. Mix thoroughly in a stone jar and cover with vinegar, making a hole in the centre to let the vinegar to the bottom.

Mrs. Winslow's Domestic Receipt Book, 1878

PICKLED CAULIFLOWER: Cook the cauliflower till tender, then put it in jars and pour vinegar and ground mustard-seed, previously scalded together, over the cauliflower.

Mrs. Winslow's Domestic Receipt Book, 1875

PICKLED LEMONS: Cut the lemons in quarters—not entirely apart—and put a teaspoonful of salt in each one; put them where they will dry, either in the hot sun or by the stove; when they are dried so that they are black, and look good for nothing, prepare the

Spearmint

vinegar with cloves, cinnamon, nutmeg, ginger-root, onion, and a little mustard-seed, and pour it boiling hot over the lemons; keep a year before using. They are quite equal to the West India lime. They require more vinegar than other pickles as the lemons will swell to their natural size.

Mrs. Winslow's Domestic Receipt Book, 1878

PICKLED PEACHES: Take out of free-stone peaches the pits; fill with large and small mustard-seeds, mixed with some grated horse-radish; tie them up with a thread; pour over them a hot syrup, made of one pound of brown sugar to a quart of vinegar. The peaches must not be too hard to pickle in this way.

Mrs. Winslow's Domestic Receipt Book, 1878

TO PICKLE PEPPERS: Take green peppers, take the seeds out carefully, so as not to mangle them, soak them nine days in salt and water, changing it every day, and keep them in a warm place. Stuff them with chopped cabbage, seasoned with cloves, cinnamon, and mace; put them in cold spiced vinegar.

Beecher's Domestic Receipt Book, 1857

PICKLETTE: Four large, crisp cabbages chopped fine, one quart onions chopped fine, two quarts vinegar, or enough to cover the cabbage, two pounds brown sugar, two tablespoons ground mustard, two tablespoons black pepper, two tablespoons cinnamon, two tablespoons celery seed, one tablespoon allspice, one tablespoon mace, one tablespoon alum pulverized. Pack the cabbage and onions in alternate layers with a little salt between them; let them stand over night; then scald the vinegar, sugar and spiecs together, and pour over the cabbage and onions. Do this three mornings in succession; on the fourth, put all together over the fire and heat to a boil. Let them boil five minutes, when cold, pack in small jars. It is fit for use as soon as cool, but keeps well.

Mrs. Winslow's Domestic Receipt Book, 1875

PICKLED WALNUTS: Take a hundred nuts, an ounce of cloves, an ounce of allspice, an ounce of nutmeg, an ounce of whole pepper, an ounce of race ginger, an ounce of horseradish, half pint of mustard seed, tied in a bag, and four cloves of garlic.

Beecher's Domestic Receipt Book, 1857

SPICED CUCUMBER PICKLE—NICE: Two

dozen large cucumbers sliced and boiled in vinegar enough to cover them one hour; set them aside in hot vinegar. To each gallon of cold vinegar, allow one pound sugar, one tablespoon cinnamon, one tablespoon ginger, one tablespoon black pepper, one tablespoon celery seed, one teaspoon mace, one teaspoon allspice, one teaspoon cloves, one tablespoon scraped horse radish, one tablespoon sliced garlic, one-half teaspoon cayenne pepper. Put in the cucumbers, and stew two hours. The pickle is ready for use as soon as cold.

Mrs. Winslow's Domestic Receipt Book, 1875

TOMATO CHOW-CHOW: One-half bushel green tomatoes, one dozen onions, one dozen green peppers; chop all finely together, sprinkle over all one pint of salt, let it stand over night, then drain off the brine, cover with good vinegar and cook slowly for one hour, then drain and pack in a jar. Take two pounds brown sugar, two tablespoons cinnamon, one tablespoon allspice, one tablespoon cloves and one tablespoon pepper, all ground; one-half cup ground mustard, one pint grated horse radish, and vinegar enough to mix thin, when boiling hot, pour over the contents of jar and cover tight, and it is ready for use, and will keep for months.

Mrs. Winslow's Domestic Receipt Book, 1875

TOMATO KETCHUP: To one gallon tomatoes add four tablespoons salt, four tablespoons cloves, one tablespoon mace, one tablespoon cayenne, two tablespoons allspice, eight tablespoons white mustard-seeds, two whole peppers, one ounce of garlic, one pint good vinegar. Boil away nearly half. Strain and bottle. Cork tight.

Mrs. Winslow's Domestic Receipt Book, 1875

BEVERAGE RECIPES

COUNTLESS RECIPES for making various kinds of beverages are found among the writings of the early "receipt books." Many of these utilize herbs, as will be noted in the concoctions which follow.

Tea, coffee, and chocolate made from

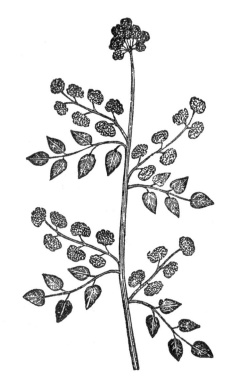

Spikenard

cocoa beans, called "cocoa nuts" in the colonial era, were the principal non-alcoholic or "sober liquors." It is likely that tea was probably drunk more generally in the towns and among the upper classes. Often, it was the poorer people who used native herbs as substitutes for the imported article. Sometimes, there were political reasons for making berry leaf teas. Anne Hollingsworth Wharton in her *Colonial Days and Dames* (1895) points out, "From that early and solitary Virginia witch, Grace Sherwood, who outwitted her persecutors by swimming when she was expected to sink, to the highborn and patriotic dames of North Carolina who banded themselves together to drink a decoction of raspberry leaves instead of tea until the odious tax should be taken off,

Colonial women faced perils and difficulties with unfailing heroism and patience."

After the Boston Tea Party of December 16, 1773, an association had been formed in the fall of the following year which had as its pledge the following statement: "We the Ladys of Edenton do hereby solemnly engage not to conform to that Pernicious Custom of Drinking Tea, or that we the aforesaid Ladys will not promote ye wear of any manufacture from England, untill such time that all Acts which tend to enslave our Native Country shall be repealed." Women who signed this agreement included Mrs. Penelope Barker, who presided over the association, Mrs. Elizabeth King, Mrs. Sarah Valentine, Miss Isabella Johnston, a sister of Governor Johnston of North Carolina, Mrs. Hoskins, and forty-six others.

Large amounts of "hard liquors" were available throughout the settlements. Drinking was engaged in at every drawing up of a contract, the signing of a deed, the selling of a farm, the purchase of goods, and the arbitration of a suit. Every transaction and every happening in the community in both public and private life were usually accompanied by the use of beverages. It has been reported that if either party backed out of a bargain before signing, he had to furnish half a barrel of beer or a gallon of rum to relieve the pangs of disappointment. Weddings, funerals, church openings, deacon ordainings, house raisings, births, "set suppers," patriotic celebrations, political rallies, and harvests all called for drinking and toasts.

Sydney George Fisher in *Men, Women and Manners in Colonial Times* (1898) writes that "John Adams, when he came to Philadelphia

to the Continental Congress in 1774, fresh from Boston, stood aghast at this life into which he was suddenly thrown, and thought it must be sin. But he rose to the occasion, and, after describing in his diary some of the 'mighty feasts' and 'sinful feasts' which he attended, says that he drank Madeira 'at a great rate' and found no 'inconvenience.'"

In writing of Chastellux who wrote so much concerning various aspects of colonial life, Fisher says, "The drinking habits were also trying to him. They had, he said, the barbarous British practice of drinking each others' healths at a dinner party, calling out names from one end of the table to the other, so that it was difficult to eat or converse while you had to inquire the names or catch the eyes of five and twenty or thirty persons, being incessantly called to on the right and left, or pulled by the sleeve by charitable neighbors, who were so kind as to acquaint you with the politeness you were receiving." Fisher adds, "Some would call out four or five names at once. 'The bottle is then passed to you, and you must look your enemy in the face, for I can give no other name to the man who exercises such an empire over my will: you wait till he likewise has poured out his wine and taken his glass; you then drink mournfully with him, as a recruit imitates the corporal in his exercise.'"

In some colonies it was customary to drink "egg nog" at Christmas. There is frequent reference in wills, inventories, and account books to decanters, wineglasses, punch bowls, and syllabub glasses. In reading original records of Ethan Allen's activities, for example, one often finds mention of his stopping by the punch bowl.

Stramonium

The European settlers of this country were not as accustomed as we to drinking water as a constant beverage. Some considered it very dangerous to experiment with drinking water. In many cases they were forced to do so; to their surprise they found it agreed with them very well.

Dwight, who traveled throughout New England and New York during the last decade of the eighteenth century and the first years of the next, wrote that here the principal drink is cider. "Wine, which is very cheap, is extensively used: so in the mild season is punch. Porter, also, is drunk by fashionable people; and in small quantities, ale."

Evelyn in his seventeenth century writings suggests the following beverage. "Small ale in which Elder flowers have been infused is esteemed by many so salubrious that this is to be had in most of the eating-houses about our town."

Parkinson in his *Paradisus,* (1629) describes

the many virtues of the calendula. "The herbe and flowers are of great use with us among other pot-herbs, and the flowers eyther green or dryed, are often used in possets, broths and drinkes as a comforter of the heart and spirits."

Dr. Andrew Borde in *Regyment of Helth,* (16th. century), defines the difference between "meade" and "metheglyn." "Meade is made of honny and water boyled both togyther; yf it be fyred and pure, it preserveth helth; but it is not good for them the which have the Ilyacke or the Colyche. . . . Metheglyn is made of honny and water and herbs, boyled and sodden togyther; yf it be fyred and stale, it is better in the regyment of helth than meade."

In the *English Housewife,* (1615), by Gervase Markham, directions are given for a spicy drink called Hippocras. "To make Ipocras, take a pottle of wine, two ounces of good cinamon, $\frac{1}{2}$ ounce of ginger, nine cloves and six peppercorns, and a nutmeg,

Striped Alder

and bruise them and put them into the wine with some Rosemary flowers, and so let them steep all night, and then put in Sugar, a pound at least, and when it is well settled, let it run through a wollen bag made for that purpose; thus if your wine be claret, the Ipocras will be red; if white, then of that colour also."

Charles A. Goodrich in *The Universal Traveller* (1847) indicates that "Cider, beer and porter, are in considerable use in the Southern and Western States. The rich at the South bestow much care and expense upon their wines, which are chiefly sherry and Madeira, except in Louisiana, where claret is more in use."

It should be remembered that the concoctions of so many beverages were not always intended for human consumption. There were innumerable uses to which they were put in the management of the household. For example, a pint of small beer added to black lead and a bit of soap was a mixture used to clean the back of the grate, the inner hearth, and the fronts. One boiled pipemakers' clay, water, a quart of small beer, and put in some blue stone to clean stone stairs and halls. Beer was even used to rid the house of insects by being left hanging in open bottles—the scent of which was sure to attract them.

Wine combined with saffron, yellow amber, gum-lac, and "forty grains of dragon's blood in tears" were ingredients from which brass or silver could be gilded. Isinglass dissolved in brandy and then strained made excellent glue. Isinglass dissolved in gin over a low heat made cement for wood or paper. For shoe blacking, "In three pints of small beer, put two ounces of ivory black,

and one penny worth of brown sugar. As soon as they boil, put a desert-spoonful of sweet oil, and then boil slowly till reduced to a quart. Stir it up with a stick every time it is used; and put it on the shoe with a brush when wanted."

There was even the ironic practice of pouring brandy into the boots or shoes, when the feet got wet, "with a view to prevent the effects of cold." Later, it was found that this practice, though very common, often proved fatal. It was finally suggested that "if such a remedy is to be at all employed it ought, undoubtedly, to be taken into the stomach."

CREAMS

ABSINTHE OR WORMWOOD CREAM: In seven pints of common brandy infuse, for two days, half a pound of the heads of wormwood and the zests of two lemons, or, which is better, two oranges thinly sliced; distil the liquor to half the quantity; dissolve six pounds of fine sugar in three pints of common water; let it cool, and mix it well with the brandy; strain it, and put in bottles tightly corked.

Wormwood, ½ lb.; oranges, 2; brandy, 7 pts.; sugar, 6 lbs.; water, 3 pts. Infuse two days.

The Art of Confectionery, 1866

MINT CREAM: Take one pound of freshly gathered mint, and the zests of five lemons; cut fine; macerate them for eight days in seven pints of brandy; distil to one-half, then add half a drachm of essence of peppermint. Dissolve four pounds of sugar in three pints of water, let it cool; mix it thoroughly with the distilled liquor, filter, and keep it in bottles in a cool and shady place.

Mint, 1 lb.; zests of lemons, 5; brandy, 7 pts.; essence peppermint, 2 drs.; sugar, 4 lbs.; water, 3 pts. Steep eight days.

The Art of Confectionery, 1866

LIQUEURS OR CORDIALS

ANISEED CORDIAL: Take of aniseed, bruised, 2 lbs.—proof spirit, 12½ gallons,—water, 1 gallon. Draw off 10 gallons with a moderate fire. This water should never be reduced below proof: because the large quantity of oil with which it is impregnated, will render the goods milky and foul, when brought down below proof. But if there is a necessity for doing this, their transparency may be restored by filtration. *Mackenzie's 5,000 Receipts,* 1829

ANISETTE: Oil of anise-seed, ten drops; alcohol, three pints; sugar, two pounds; pure water, one and a half pounds. Make the syrup with the sugar and water cold, and mix the liquors.

ANOTHER ANISETTE: Star anise-seed, eight ounces; bitter almonds pounded, and coriander, each, eight ounces; powdered Florence iris, four ounces; alcohol, five gallons. Macerate in the alcohol for five days; distil in the water-bath, and add twelve pounds of sugar dissolved in seven pints of distilled water. *The Art of Confectionery,* 1866

ANISETTE DE BOURDEAUX: Take of sugar, 9 oz.; oil of aniseed, 6 drops. Rub them together, and add by degrees, spirit of wine, 2 pints; water, 4 pints. Filter. *Mackenzie's 5,000 Receipts,* 1829

ANISETTE DE BOURDEAUX: Green anise-seed, ten ounces; hyson tea, two ounces; star anise-seed, four ounces; coriander, one ounce; fennel, one ounce. Macerate for fifteen days in three and a half gallons of alcohol; distil in the water-bath; then make a syrup with ten pounds of sugar and seven pints of water; mix well, and filter.

ANOTHER ANISETTE DE BOURDEAUX: Dill, one pound; green anise-seed, eight ounces; fennel, four ounces; coriander, four ounces; sassafras-wood cut fine, four ounces; pearl gunpowder tea, four ounces; musk-seed, one ounce. Macerate all these substances in three and a half gallons of alcohol for six days; then distil in the water-bath; add a syrup made with twenty-eight pounds of fine sugar, two and a half gallons of distilled water, one quart of double-distilled orange-flower water, and one quart of pure water. *The Art of Confectionery,* 1866

Sumac

Swamp Dogwood

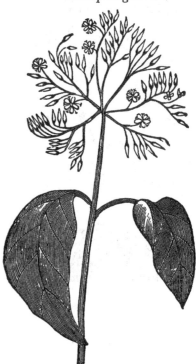

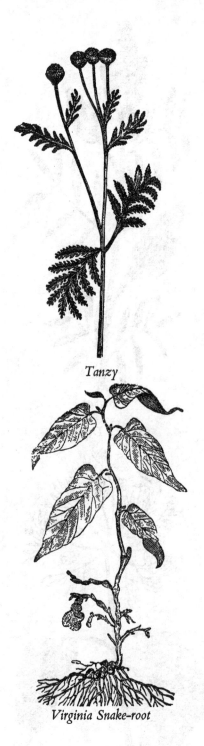

Tanzy

Virginia Snake-root

BALM, OR WITH SAGE: Balm, or lemon balm alone, or with sage, is much recommended, with a few flowers of lavender; it has a most delicious flavour and taste, but is most agreeable when green.

Family Receipt Book, 1819

BALM OF MANKIND: Peruvian balsam, one ounce; cashew-nuts, eight ounces; coriander, four drachms; dried heads of wormwood, one ounce; yellow rinds of six lemons. Macerate these in two gallons of alcohol for eight days; distil the liquor in the water-bath to nearly one-half; add a syrup made with five and a half pounds of sugar; filter, and color green. *The Art of Confectionery, 1866*

CARAWAY CORDIAL: For 20 gallons. Take 1½ ounces of oil of caraway, 20 drops of cassia-lignea oil, 5 drops of essence of orangepeel, 5 drops of the essence of lemon, 13 gallons of spirits, one in five, and 8 lbs. of loaf sugar. Make it up and fine it down.

Mackenzie's 5,000 Receipts, 1829

GODFREY'S CORDIAL: Dissolve 2½ drachms of sal tartar in 3¼ pints of water; to which add one pint of thick sugar house molasses, and afterwards 3 oz. laudanum. Dissolve ½ a drachm oil sassafras in 4 oz. alcohol, and add to the above; shake well, and it is ready for use. *Family Hand-Book, 1855*

GOLD CORDIAL: Take of the roots of angelica, sliced, 4 lbs. raisins, stoned, 2 lbs. coriander seeds, ½ lb. caraway seeds and cinnamon, each ½ lb. cloves, 2 oz. figs and liquorice root, sliced, each, 1 lb. proof spirit, 11 gallons, water 2 gallons. Digest two days; and draw off by a gentle heat, till the feints begin to rise; hanging in a piece of linen, fastened to the mouth of the worm, an ounce of English saffron. Then dissolve 8 lbs. of sugar in three quarts of rose-water, and add to it the distilled liquor.

The above cordial derives its name from a quantity of leaf gold being formerly added to it; but this is now generally disused.

Mackenzie's 5,000 Receipts, 1829

HUILE DE VENUS (a liqueur): Take of flowers of the wild carrot, picked, 6 oz.—spirit of wine, 10 pints. Distil in a bath heat. To the spirit add as much syrup of capillaire; it may be coloured with cochineal. *Mackenzie's 5,000 Receipts, 1829*

NECTAR: White honey, four ounces; coriander, two ounces; fresh zests of lemon, one ounce; storax calamite, benzoin, and cloves, each, one ounce; tincture of vanilla, half a drachm; tincture of orange-flower water, four ounces; highly rectified spirits, five quarts. Pulverize the substances which require it, and macerate them for fifteen days in the alcohol; then distil the liquor to four quarts in the water bath; add a syrup made with six pounds of fine sugar, with the tincture of vanilla. Color a deep red.
The Art of Confectionery, 1866

PERFECT LOVE, ANOTHER: Lemon zests, two pounds; cinnamon, half a pound; rosemary-leaves, quarter of a pound; orange-flowers, three-eighths of a pound; pinks, one ounce and a half; mace, one ounce; cardamom, one ounce. Macerate in thirty quarts of spirits and fifteen quarts of water; then distil the liquor to twenty-seven quarts; add a syrup made of thirty pounds of sugar in thirteen quarts of water, and color with cochineal.
The Art of Confectionery, 1866

TINCTURE JAPONICA: Take of the best English saffron, and dissolve one ounce; mace bruised, one ounce; infuse them into a pint of brandy till the whole tincture of the saffron is extracted, which will be in seven or eight days; then strain it through a linen cloth, and to the strained tincture add two ounces of tartar Japonica powdered fine; let it infuse till the tincture is wholly impregnated.
Mackenzie's 5,000 Receipts, 1829

RATAFIAS

ABSINTHE OR WORMWOOD RATAFIA: Steep four pounds of bruised wormwood leaves, eight ounces of juniper berries, and two ounces of ground cinnamon, in four drachms of angelica rum and seventeen pounds of brandy, for fifteen days; distil the mixture to twelve pounds of liquor, and redistil this upon the residuum to ten pounds; then add two and a half pounds of powdered sugar, two

pounds of pure water, and eight ounces of double-distilled orange-flower water.
Wormwood leaves, 4 lbs.; juniper berries, 8 oz.; cinnamon, 2 oz.; angelica rum, 4 drs.; brandy, 17 lbs.; sugar, 2½ lbs.; water, 2 lbs.; orange-flower water, 8 oz. Steep fifteen days.
The Art of Confectionery, 1866

ANGELICA RATAFIA: Take four ounces of fresh angelica stalks, one ounce of angelica seed, one drachm of nutmeg, half a drachm of Ceylon cinnamon, and one drachm of coriander; bruise the seeds in a mortar, and steep the whole for eight days in seven pints of alcohol; then pass it through a sieve; add a syrup made with four and a quarter pounds of sugar and two and a half pints of water, and filter.
Angelica stalks, 4 oz.; angelica seed, 1 oz.; nutmeg, 1 dr.; cinnamon, ½ dr.; coriander, 1 dr.; sugar, 4¼ lbs.; water, 2½ pts. Steep eight days.
The Art of Confectionery, 1866

ANISE-SEED RATAFIA: Take two ounces of green anise-seed and four ounces of star anise-seed; bruise the seeds, and steep them in seven quarts of alcohol for eight days; then pass it through a sieve; add a syrup made with six and a half pounds of sugar and two quarts of spring water, and filter.
Green anise-seed, 2 oz.; star anise-seed, 4 oz.; alcohol, 7 qts.; sugar, 6½ lbs.; water, 2 qts. Steep eight days. *The Art of Confectionery, 1866*

BLACK-CURRANT RATAFIA: Take six pounds of fully ripe black currants, four ounces of black-currant leaves, half a drachm of cloves, half a drachm of Ceylon cinnamon, and half a drachm of coriander; bruise the berries, and steep the whole for one month in ten quarts of brandy; then express the liquor; add a syrup made with seven pounds of sugar and three and a half pints of water, and filter.
Black currants, 6 lbs.; black-currant leaves, 4 oz.; cloves, ½ dr.; cinnamon, ½ dr.; coriander, ½ dr.; sugar, 7 lbs.; water, 3½ pts. Steep one month.
The Art of Confectionery, 1866

JUNIPER-BERRY RATAFIA: Take eight ounces of juniper berries, one drachm of cinnamon, two drachms of coriander, and half a drachm of mace; bruise the whole, and steep them for fifteen days in fourteen pints of brandy; squeeze through a cloth, and add a syrup made with seven pounds of sugar, and filter.

Juniper-berries, 8 oz.; cinnamon, 1 dr.; coriander, 2 drs.; mace, ½ dr.; brandy, 14 pts.; sugar, 7 lbs. Steep fifteen days.

The Art of Confectionery, 1866

RATAFIA D'ANGELIQUE: Take of angelica seeds, 1 drachm; stalks of angelica, bitter almonds, blanched, each 4 oz.; proof spirit, 12 pints; white sugar, 2 lbs. Digest, strain, and filter.

Mackenzie's 5,000 Receipts, 1829

SEED RATAFIA: Take one ounce each of dill, angelica, fennel, caraway, carrot, coriander, and green anise seed; pound them, and steep them for a month in six quarts of alcohol; strain, and add a syrup of eight pounds of sugar with one quart of water; then filter.

Dill, angelica, fennel,.caraway, carrot, coriander, and anise seeds, 1 oz. each; alcohol, 6 qts.; sugar, 8 lbs.; water, 1 qt. Steep one month.

The Art of Confectionery, 1866

USQUEBAUGH, ANOTHER: Saffron, one ounce; dates and nuts without stones and seeds, each, two ounces; juniper-berries, four drachms; pounded jujubes, four drachms; pounded cinnamon, two drachms; green anise, mace, coriander, and cloves, each, one ounce; alcohol, four quarts; syrup boiled to a bead, three quarts. Macerate fifteen days, then strain and add the syrup.

The Art of Confectionery, 1866

SPIRITUOUS WATERS

ANGELICA WATER AND COMPOUND SPIRIT: Take of the Roots of Angelica, of the leaves of Carduus Benedictus, each six ounces; Bawm and Sage, of each four ounces, of the Seeds of Angelica six ounces, of sweet Fennel seeds nine ounces, to the dried Herbs and Seeds grosly poudered; add of the Species called *Aromatick Rosat*, and sweet *Diamosch*, of each an ounce and an half; infuse them two days in sixteen quarts of *Spanish Wine*, and then distil them

with a gentle Fire; add to every pint two ounces of Sugar dissolved in Rose-water: The first three pints are called Spirits, the rest is the Compound Water.

The Family Dictionary, 1710

ANGELICA, WATER OF: Take strong Spirits ten Gallons, Water six Gallons, Aniseeds one pound, or two Drams of Oil of Aniseeds, *Spanish* Angelica-Roots bruised two pound, mix and distil them; draw ten Gallons of Water, and add to every Gallon a pound of D.L.S. (Double Refined Loaf-Sugar).

The Family Dictionary, 1710

ANISE-SEED WATER (COMPOUND): Rub four ounces each of green anise, angelica, and star anise seed, to a very fine powder in a mortar; macerate the whole in five pints of alcohol for five or six days; then distil in a water-bath.

Green anise, angelica, and star anise seed, each, 4 ozs.; alcohol, 5 pts. Macerate six days.

The Art of Confectionery, 1866

ANISEED WATER: Take ten Gallons of good low Wines, or proof Spirits, one pound of Aniseed, or more, as you will have it in strength; now, if your Spirits are high proof, you may add a little Water in the Distillation, and then draw off the same quantity you put on: This Rule serves well for Seeds, but only the quantity is diversified, according as they may be in strength; for of Cardamums you must put two pound to the like quantity of Spirits.

The Family Dictionary, 1710

BARLEY WATER (COMPOUND): Take two pints of simple barley water, a pint of hot water, two and a half ounces of sliced figs, half an ounce of liquorice root sliced and bruised, and two ounces and a half of raisins. Boil all down to two pints, and strain it. This is slightly aperient.

Domestic Receipt Book, 1857

BAWM WATER: Take of Spirits ten Gallons, Water five Gallons, Aniseeds one pound, Bawm-Leaves eight handfuls; mix and Distil them, draw nine Gallons of Water, and sweeten it with D.L.S. (Double Refined Loaf-Sugar).

The Family Dictionary, 1710

EAU DE BARBADES: Take of fresh orange peel, 1

oz.; fresh lemon-peel, 4 oz.; cloves, ½ drachm; coriander, 1 do.; proof spirit, 4 pints. Distil in a bath heat and add white sugar in powder.

Mackenzie's 5,000 Receipts, 1829

ROSEMARY WATER: Take strong Spirits ten Gallons, Water five Gallons, as many Rosemary-Leaves as may be had for Six-Pence, one pound of Aniseeds, or an ounce of the Oil of it, mix and distil them; draw ten Gallons and a half, and add to every Gallon a pound of D.L.S. (Double Refined Loaf-Sugar) in fine Pouder.

The Family Dictionary, 1710

WORMWOOD WATER: Take two Gallons of White Port, half a pound of Aniseeds, and a like quantity of Liquorice, bruise them together very fine, then take three handfuls of the tender Tops of Roman Wormwood, and put them with the other Ingredients into the Wine, let them infuse twelve Hours, and then distil them in an Alembick. The Water will be stronger, if instead of Wine you put Brandy, or Sugar Spirit.   *The Family Dictionary, 1710*

WORMWOOD, ANOTHER: Take four pound of Wormwood chop'd, one pound of Liquorice scraped, Two Pennyworth of Mace, one ounce of Nutmegs, cut them in pieces, bruise the Seeds and Liquorice, and infuse all 24 Hours in 4 Gallons of strong Ale, and Distil it in a Limbeck.

The Family Dictionary, 1710

WORMWOOD, ANOTHER: Take of Wormwood four pound, Aniseeds and Liquorice, of each one pound; Raisons of the Sun ston'd one pound; Figgs one pound cut in twain, infuse all in four Gallons of strong Ale and Beer, and Distil it.

The Family Dictionary, 1710

WINES

BALM WINE: Take 40 pounds of sugar and 9 gallons of water, boil it gently for 2 hours, skim it well, and put it into a tub to cool. Take 2 pounds and a half of the tops of balm, bruise them, and put them into a barrel, with a little new yeast; and when the liquor is cold, pour it on the balm. Stir it well together, and let it stand 24 hours, stirring it often. Then close it up, and let it stand 6 weeks. Then rack it off and put a lump of sugar into every bottle. Cork it well, and it will be better the second year than the first.

Mackenzie's 5,000 Receipts, 1829

CIDER WINE: Prof. Horsford, a celebrated chemist, communicated the following recipe to the Horticultural Society of Massachusetts, and recommends it for general trial:

"Let the new cider from sour apples, (ripe, sound fruit preferred,) ferment from 1 to 3 weeks, as the weather is warm or cool. When it has attained to a lively fermentation, add to each gallon, according to its acidity, from ½ a lb. to 2 lbs. of white crushed sugar, and let the whole ferment until it possesses precisely the taste which it is desired should be permanent. In this condition pour out a quart of the cider and add for each gallon ¼ oz. of *sulphite of lime*, not sulphate. Stir the powder and cider until intimately mixed, and return the emulsion to the fermenting liquid. Agitate briskly and thoroughly for a few

Water Horehound

moments, and then let the cider settle. Fermentation will cease at once. When after a few days, the cider has become clear, draw off carefully, to avoid the sediment, and bottle. If loosely corked which is better, it will become a sparkling cider wine, and may be kept indefinitely long.

This has been tried with varied success; those who do not think it too much to follow the directions, obtain a good article, but others, supposing it to do just as well without sugar, or drawing off, or bottling, have found but little satisfaction—they have no reason to expect any; and yet they might be well satisfied to obtain a good wine from the orchard, even with all the above requisitions.

Dr. Chase's Recipes, 1869

CIDER RED WINE: Take of cold soft water, 3 gallons, cider, 16 gallons, honey, 10 pounds. Ferment. Add raw sugar, 4 pounds, beet-root, sliced, 4 pounds, red tartar, in fine powder, 6 oz. Mix sweet marjoram and sweetbriar, 3 handsful, rum, 1 gallon. This will make 18 gallons.

Mackenzie's 5,000 Receipts, 1829

GRAPE WHITE WINE: Take of cold soft water, 13 gallons, white grapes, 50 pounds. Ferment. Mix refined sugar, 25 pounds, white tartar, in powder, 3 ounces. Add clary seed bruised, 3 ounces, or clary flowers, 6 handsful, rum, 1 gallon. This will make 18 gallons. *Mackenzie's 5,000 Receipts,* 1829

JUNIPER-BERRY WINE: Take of cold soft water, 18 gallons, Malaga or Smyrna raisins, 35 lbs. juniper berries, 9 quarts, red tartar, 4 ounces, wormwood and sweet marjoram, each 2 handsful, British spirit, two quarts or more. Ferment for ten or twelve days. This will make eighteen gallons.

Mackenzie's 5,000 Receipts, 1829

MIXED BERRIES FROM A SMALL GARDEN: Take of cold soft water, 11 gallons; fruit, 8 do. Ferment. Mix, treacle, 14 or 16 lbs.; tartar, in powder, 1 oz. Put in ginger, in powder, 4 oz.; sweet herbs, 2 handsful: then add spirits, 1 or 2 quarts. This will make 18 gallons. *Mackenzie's 5,000 Receipts,* 1829

RED AND WHITE CURRANT WINE: Take of cold soft water, 12 gallons; white currants, 4 do.; red currants, 3 do. Ferment. Mix, raw sugar, 25 lbs.; white tartar, in fine powder, 3 oz. Put in sweet-briar leaves, 1 handful; lavender leaves, 1 do.; then add spirits, 2 quarts or more. This will make 18 gallons.

Mackenzie's 5,000 Receipts, 1829

SAGE WINE: Boil 26 quarts of spring water a quarter of an hour, and when it is blood warm, put 25 pounds of Malaga raisins, picked, rubbed, and shred, into it, with almost half a bushel of red sage shred, and a porringer of ale yeast; stir all well together, and let it stand in a tub, covered warm, six or seven days, stirring it once a day; then strain it off, and put it in a runlet. Let it work three or four days, and then stop it up; when it has stood six or seven days, put in a quart or two of Malaga sack; and when it is fine bottle it.

Mackenzie's 5,000 Receipts, 1829

WHITE CURRANT WINE: Take of cold soft water, 9 gallons; white currants, 9 do.; white gooseberries, 1 do. Ferment. Mix, refined sugar, 25 lbs.; white tartar, in powder, 1 oz.; clary seed, bruised, 2 oz. or clary flowers, or sorrel flowers, 4 handsful: then add white brandy, 1 gallon. This will make 18 gallons.

Mackenzie's 5,000 Receipts, 1829

WHITE MEAD WINE: Take of cold soft water, seventeen gallons, white currants, six quarts. Ferment. Mix honey, 30 pounds, white tartar, in fine powder, 3 oz. Add balm and sweetbriar, each 2 handsful, white brandy, 1 gallon. This will make 18 gallons.

Mackenzie's 5,000 Receipts, 1829

WORTLEBERRY OR BILBERRY WINE: Take of cold soft water, 6 gallons; cider, 6 gallons; berries, 8 gallons. Ferment. Mix, raw sugar, 20 pounds; tartar, in fine powder, 4 ounces. Add ginger, in powder, 4 ounces; lavender and rosemary leaves, 2 handsful; rum or British spirits, 1 gallon. This will make 18 gallons.

Mackenzie's 5,000 Receipts, 1829

CHAPTER FIVE

Other
Household Uses of Herbs

FROM THE EARLIEST DAYS in America and in rural areas throughout the nineteenth century, spinning, weaving, and dyeing were important household enterprises. Textile-making at home had been stimulated by the non-importation regulations of the 1760's and the Revolution. It continued for many decades.

Home weaving of blankets in plaids, checks, and stripes dates back to the early 1700's. As late as 1851, the Reverend Horace Bushnell in a centennial address at Litchfield, Connecticut described the intervening one hundred years quite appropriately as the "age of homespun."

After the material was woven, it was first washed to remove the grease and then scraped to even the threads. Finally, the material was colored with dyes made from bark, berries, and the leaves and flowers of herbs.

Among the herb dyes were those concocted from balm blossoms steeped in water. The result is a "Pretty rose-color," according to the *American Frugal Housewife,* 1833. In

this book it is recommended for the linings of children's bonnets and for ribbons. To set the color to some degree, it is suggested that a small piece of alum might be added.

Saffron, steeped in earthenware and strained, produced a fine straw color. It was discovered, too, that "the dry outside skins of onions, steeped in scalding water and strained, color a yellow very much like 'bird of paradise' color."

In the 1860's, horseradish leaves were boiled in water for half an hour to create another yellow dye.

In a manuscript recipe book compiled by Charles P. Wheeler, Jr., dated 1831, there is recorded "No. 99—A Dye for the Hair." He writes, "M. Brandes has been analyzing a liquid sold at Berlin for dyeing the hair and finds it to be a spirituous infusion of the shell of green walnuts made aromatic by lavender water, and not in the least prejudicial to the health."

For a FURNITURE POLISH: According to the *Family Receipt Book,* 1819, one can concoct a mixture of "Three pennyworth of alkanet root, one pint of cold drawn linseed oil, two pennyworth of rose pink; put these into a pan, and let them stand all night: then take some of this mixture, rub it over the tables or chairs, and let it remain one hour; then take a linen cloth and rub it well off, and it will leave a beautiful gloss on the furniture." This was excellent for cleaning and polishing mahogany furniture.

GREASE REMOVAL: Another recipe included in Wheeler's manuscript is for oil soap which can be used in a variety of ways including grease or paint removal. "Take of white Soap cut fine 2 oz. alcohol, 1 pint oil of rosemary. . . . Mix and set the bottle in the sun until the soap is dissolved. Useful for removing grease, paint, etc. from cloth or silk, also in strains, swelling, rheumatism, etc."

MOTH PREVENTIVES AND SACHETS: Among other curious uses of herbs are included *penny-royal* for the expelling of insects; "The odour of it destroys some and drives away others. At seasons when fresh green bunches of penny-royal are not to be obtained, get oil of penny-royal, pour some into a saucer, and steep in it small bits of wadding or raw cotton; lay them about in corners, closet-shelves, bureau-drawers, boxes, and all places where you have seen cockroaches or ants, or wherever they are likely to be found." So recommended the *Practical Housewife,* 1860. Anything which in any way aided in expelling insects in those days before insecticides must have been most welcome!

Mackenzie points out in his *Five Thousand Receipts,* 1829, that one may "sprinkle bay leaves, or Worm-wood, or lavender, or walnut leaves, or rue, or black pepper in grains," to drive away caterpillars.

The May, 1864 issue of *Godey's Lady's Book* contains this recipe, "Cloves, in coarse powder, one ounce; cassia, one ounce; lavender flowers, one ounce; lemon peel, one ounce. Mix and put them into little bags, and place them where the clothes are kept, or wrap the clothes round them. They will keep off insects."

Perfumed woods were used by the ancient Greeks and Romans in the clothes chests where their robes were kept. Slices of pungent Florentine iris root were sewn directly into Elizabethan garments.

Early sources in this country recommend that crushed herbs and cloves may be used scattered for such a purpose, as can bags and pads filled with similar ingredients. It is also suggested that dried tops of such herbs as rosemary, southernwood, thyme, mint, wormwood, lavender, tansy, and the dried, sliced roots of sweet flag may diffuse a pleasant perfume and also serve as an insect repellent among clothing. About a pound of herbs mixed with a couple of tablespoonfuls of crushed spices is an effective combination.

Culpepper's particular favorite as a moth preventive is wormwood. "This herb, wormwood, being laid among cloaths will make a moth scorn to meddle with cloaths as much as a lion scorns to meddle with a mouse or an eagle with a fly."

A 1525 herbal by Banckes suggests that you "take the flowers of rosemary and put them in thy chest among thy clothes or

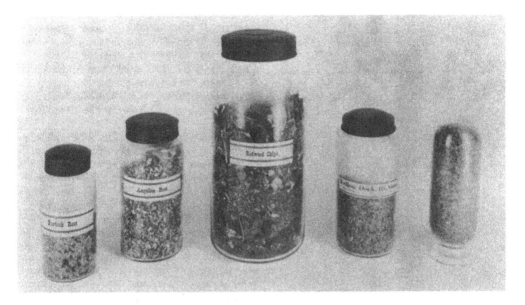

Plate 23. *Jars containing roots and chips used in dying. These include burdock root, angelica root, redwood chips, yellow dock, and saffron. (Courtesy Shelburne Museum, Inc.)*

among thy Bookes and Moths shall not destroy them."

In 1579, William Langham in his *Garden of Health* gave a method for perfuming clothes which would also act as an insect repellent. "Boyle it (lavender) in water and wett thy shirt in it and dry it again and weare it."

A curious use of garlic in preparing ivory leaves for miniature painters is mentioned in the *Family Receipt Book*, 1819. Apparently the juice of the garlic took off any greasiness which might prevent the "colours from taking on the ground."

Sage was used, when boiled in strong vinegar, to soften bones or ivory, according to the 1819 book mentioned above.

A strong tea made of fig leaves was used to sponge black worsted dresses. Also, Mrs. Winslow in her 1875 *Domestic Receipt Book*

notes that "this process restores crispness" to alpaca and bombazine.

The use of herbs in the making of confections, or conserves and preserves was quite usual in the sixteenth, seventeenth, and eighteenth centuries, as one can observe from the recipes that follow.

CONFECTIONS

CANDIED FLOWERS: (To preserve) Whole Roses, Gilliflowers, Marigolds, etc. .... Dip half open flowers in a boiling sugar syrup and open the leaves carefully with a smooth bodkin: lay the flowers on paper in the Sun or warm room or oven.
Delightes for Ladies, 1602

FLOWER SYRUP: Clip your Flowers, and take their Weight in Sugar, then take a high Gallypot, and put a row of Flowers, and a strewing of Sugar, till the Pot is full; then put in two or three spoonfuls of the

Wild Indigo

Wild Carrot

same (sugar) Syrup or still'd (distilled) water; tye a Cloth on the top of the Pot, and put a Tile on that, and set your Gallypot in a kettle of water over a gentle Fire, and let it infuse till the strength is out of the Flowers, which will be in four or five hours; then strain it thro a Flannel, and when 'tis cold, bottle it up.
Compleat Housewife, 1728

FLOWERS, CANDIED: (Put the flowers in boiling sugar syrup), take them out as quick as you can, with as little of the Syrup as may be, and lay them in a Dish over a gentle Fire, and with a Knife spread them, that the Syrup may run from them; then change them upon another warm Dish, and when they are dry from the Syrup, have ready some double-refin'd Sugar, beaten and sifted and strew some on your Flowers; then take the Flowers in your Hands, and rub them gently in the hollow of your Hand, and that will open the Leaves; a Stander-by strewing more Sugar into your Hand, as you see convenient; then pour your Flowers into a dry Sieve, and sift all the Sugar clean from them. They must be kept in a dry place. Rosemary Flowers must be put whole into your Syrup. *Compleat Housewife*, 1728

ROSE DROPS: The Roses and Sugar must be beat separately into a very fine powder and both sifted; to a pound of Sugar, an ounce of red Roses: They must be mixed together and then wet with as much Juice of Lemon, as will make into a stiff Paste. Set it on a slow Fire, in a Silver Porringer, and stir it well; and when 'tis scalding hot quite thro' take it off, and drop it on Paper. Set them near the Fire the next day: they'll come off. *Compleat Housewife*, 1728

SUGAR-PLATE: A Way to Make Sugar-plate both of colour and taste of any flower. Take violets, and beat them in a mortar with a little hard sugar; then put into it a sufficient quantitie of Rose-water; then lay your gum (gum arabic) to steep in the water, and so work it into paste; and so will your paste be both of the colour of the violet and of the smell of the violet. In like sort you may worke with Marigolds, Cowslips or any other flower.
Delightes for Ladies, 1602

SYRUP OF VIOLETS: First make of clarified sugar by boiling a simple sirupe, of a good consistence, or meane thickness, whereunto put the flowers cleane, piked from all manner of filth, as also the white endes nipped away, a quantitie, according to the quantitie of the sirupe, to your owne discretion. (Infuse 24 hours in a warm place, strain, add more violets, repeating three or four times.) Then set them upon a gentle fire to simper, but not to boil in any wise. . . . some do but a little guantitie of the juice of Limons in the boiling that doth greatly increase the beautie thereof, but nothing at all the vertue.

The Herball or Generall Histoire of Plantes, 1597

CONSERVES AND PRESERVES

BETONY CONSERVE: (Leaves and flowers in the conserve of betony) by their sweete and spicie Taste, are comfortable both in meate and medicine.

Theatrum Botanium, 17th C.

CALENDULA CONSERVE: The herbe and flowers (of calendula) are of great use with us among other pot-herbs, and the flowers eyther green or dryed, are often used in possets, broths and drinkes as a comforter of the heart and spirits, and to expel any malignant or pestilential quality gathered neere thereunto. The Syrups and Conserve made of the fresh flowers are used for the same purposes to good effect.

Paradisus, 1629

CONSERVES AND PRESERVES: I understand by this preserve, taken properly, the preserving of things whole and not stampt and beaten into one bodie (as in making conserves). (For keeping flowers by both ways): take the leaves or flowers of such herbs as you will preserve, make them very cleane, afterward, without anie manner of stamping them, put them whole into some vessell wherein you will keepe them, cast upon them a sufficient competence of fine Sugar made in pouder, and so set them to Sunning in the Vessell. Also in this sort boyle them at a small fire with Sugar so long as till the Sugar become as thicke as a Syrrup, and after put them in a vessell. *Countrie Farme, 1600*

ROSE HIPS CONSERVE: Gather Hips before they grow soft, cut off the Heads and Stalks, slit them in Halves, take out all Seeds and white that is in them very clean, then put them into an earthen Pan, and

Witch Hazel

White Wood

stir them every Day, or they will grow mouldy. Let them stand until they are soft enough to rub thro' a coarse Hair-sieve, as the Pulp comes take it off the Sieve: They are a dry Berry, and will require Paines to rub them thro'; then add its Weight in Sugar, mix them well together without boiling and keep it in deep Gallipots for Use. *Art of Cookery*, 1747

ROSE, RED CONSERVE:

They are mildly astringent. Their conserve is recommended in weakness of the stomach, coughs, phthisis, Haemorrhages, & c. The honey of roses used as a gargarison, helps inflammations and ulcers in the mouth and tonsils. Infusions, acidulated mildly with the vitriolic acid and sweetened with sugar, are called cooling and restringent, good to stop bleeding, and for hectical patients. Dose. Of the powder of the leaves one drachm. Of the conserve from one to two drachms. *The American Herbal*, 1801

PASTRIES, CAKES, AND PIES

APEES: A pound of flour, sifted. Half a pound of butter. Half a glass of wine, and a table-spoonful of rose-water, mixed. Half a pound of powdered white sugar. A nutmeg, grated. A tea-spoonful of beaten cinnamon and mace. Three table-spoonfuls of caraway seeds.

Sift the flour into a broad pan, and cut up the butter in it. Add the caraways, sugar, and spice, and pour in the liquor by degrees, mixing it well with a knife; add enough of cold water to make it a stiff dough. Spread some flour on your pasteboard, take out the dough, and knead it very well with your hands. Cut it into small pieces, and knead each separately, then put them all together, and knead the whole in one lump. Roll it out in a sheet about a quarter of an inch thick. Cut it out in round cakes, with the edge of a tumbler, or a tin of that size. Butter an iron pan, and lay the cakes in it, not too close together. Bake them a few minutes in a moderate oven, till they are very slightly coloured, but not brown. If too much baked, they will entirely lose their flavour. Do not roll them out too thin.

The top of the oven should be hotter than the bottom, or the cakes will lose their shape.

Seventy-five Receipts, 1838

CROSS BUNS: Put 2½ lbs. of fine flour into a wooden bowl, and set it before the fire to warm; then add ½ a lb. of sifted sugar, some coriander seed, cinnamon and mace powdered fine; melt ¼ lb. of butter in half a pint of milk; when it is as warm as it can bear the finger, mix with it three table-spoonsful of very thick yeast, and a little salt; put it to the flour, mix it to a paste, and make the buns as directed in the last receipt. Put a cross on the top, not very deep.

Mackenzie's 5,000 Receipts, 1829

GINGERBREAD: Mix six pounds of flour with two ounces of caraway seeds, two ounces of ground ginger, two ounces of candied orange peel, the same of candied lemon peel cut in pieces, a little salt, and six ounces of moist sugar; melt one pound of fresh butter in about half a pint of milk, pour it by degrees into four pounds of treacle, stir it well together, and add it, a little at a time, to the flour; mix it thoroughly; make it into a paste; roll it out rather thin, and cut into cakes with the top of a dredger or wine glass; put them on floured tins, and bake them in rather a brisk oven. *Mackenzie's 5,000 Receipts*, 1829

HONEY CAKE: Sift into a pan a pound of flour, and rub into it three-quarters of a pound of butter; and then mix in a large tea-cup full of brown sugar that has been crushed fine with a rolling-pin; and three table-spoonfuls of ginger. Also, if you choose, two table-spoonfuls of caraway seeds. Beat five eggs very light, and stir them into the mixture alternately with a pint of strained honey. Stir the whole very hard; putting in, at the last, a very small-teaspoonful of pearl-ash, melted in a little lukewarm water.

Put the mixture into a square pan, well buttered; set it in a moderate oven, and bake it at least an hour. If thick, it must remain longer in the oven.

Cut it into squares, when cool. It will keep a week, but is best fresh. *Seventy-five Receipts*, 1838

ICING FOR CAKE: Two pounds double refined sugar, one spoonful of fine starch, one pennyworth of gum arabic in powder, five eggs, one spoon rose-water, the juice of one lemon. Make the sugar fine, and sift it through a hair seive, rub the fine, sift, and the gum arabic sift also; beat or stir all well together. Take the whites of the eggs, whisk them well, put one spoonful of rose-water, one spoon of the juice of lemon, beat well together; then put to the sugar by degrees, till you wet it, then beat it until the cake is baked; lay it on with a knife, and the ornaments, if you have any; and if it does not harden sufficiently from the warmth of the cake, return it to the oven. Be careful not to discolor.

Family Hand-Book, 1855

MACAROONS: Half a pound of shelled sweet almonds. A quarter pound of shelled bitter almonds. The whites of three eggs. Twenty-four large tea-spoonfuls of powdered loaf-sugar. A wine-glass of rose-water. A large tea-spoonful of mixed spice, nutmeg, mace and cinnamon.

Blanch and pound your almonds, beat them very smooth, and mix the sweet and bitter together; do them, if you can, the day before you make the macaroons. Pound and sift your spice. Beat the whites of three eggs till they stand alone; add to them, very gradually, the powdered sugar, a spoonful at a time; beat it in very hard, and put in, by degrees, the rose-water and spice. Then stir in, gradually, the almonds. The mixture must be like a soft dough; if too thick, it will be heavy; if too thin, it will run out of shape. If you find your almonds not sufficient, prepare a few more, and stir them in. When it is all well mixed and stirred, put some flour into the palm of your hand, and taking up a lump of the mixture with a knife, roll it on your hand with the flour into a small round ball; have ready an iron or tin pan, buttered, and lay the macaroons in it, as you make them up. Place them about two inches apart, in case of their spreading. Bake them about eight or ten minutes in a moderate oven; they should be baked of a pale brown colour. If too much baked, they will lose their flavour; if too little, they will be heavy. Let the top of the oven be hotter than the bottom. They should rise high in the middle, and crack on the surface. You may, if you choose, put a larger proportion of spice.

Cocoa-nut cakes may be made in a similar manner, substituting for the pounded almonds half a pound of finely grated cocoa-nut. They must be made into small round balls with a little flour laid on the palm of the hand, and baked a few minutes. They are very fine. *Seventy-five Receipts, 1838*

NEW YEAR'S COOKIES: Weigh out a pound of sugar, three-quarters of a pound of butter—stir them to a cream, then add three beaten eggs, a grated nutmeg, two table-spoonsful of caraway seed, and a pint

Wormwood

Yellow Dock

of flour. Dissolve a tea-spoonful of saleratus in a tea-cup of milk, strain and mix it with half a tea-cup of cider, and stir it into the cookies—then add flour to make them sufficiently stiff to roll out. Bake them as soon as cut into cakes, in a quick oven, till a light brown.   *Kitchen Directory*, 1846

PLAIN CAKE: Take as much dough as will make a quartern loaf, (either made at home, or procured at the baker's) work into this a quarter of a pound of butter, a quarter of a pound of moist sugar, and a handful of caraway seeds. When well worked together, pull into pieces the size of a golden pippin, and work it together again. This must be done three times, or it will be in lumps, and heavy when baked.
       Mackenzie's 5,000 Receipts, 1829

RHUBARB FOOL: Scald a quart or more of rhubarb, nicely peeled, and cut into pieces an inch long, pulp through a sieve, sweeten, and let it stand to cool. Put a pint of cream, or new milk, into a stewpan with a stick of cinnamon, a small piece of lemon-peel, a few cloves, coriander seeds, and sugar to taste; boil ten minutes. Beat up the yolks of four eggs, and a little flour, stir into the cream, set over the fire till it boils, stirring all the time; remove, and let it stand till cold. Mix the fruit and cream together, and add a little grated nutmeg.   *Practical Housewife*, 1860

SAFFRON CAKES: Take a quartern of fine flour, 1½ lbs. of butter, 3 oz. of caraway seeds, 6 eggs, well beaten, ¼ of an oz. of well beaten cloves and mace, a little pounded cinnamon, 1 lb. of sugar, a little rose-water and saffron, a pint and a half of yeast, and a quart of milk. Mix them thus: first boil the milk and butter, then skim off the butter, and mix it with the flour and a little of the milk. Stir the yeast into the rest and strain it; mix it with the flour, put in the eggs and spice rose-water, tincture of saffron, sugar, and eggs. Beat it all well up, and bake it in a hoop or pan well buttered. Send it to a quick oven, and an hour and a half will do it.
       Mackenzie's 5,000 Receipts, 1829

SEED CAKES (CARAWAY): Eight cups flour, three cups sugar, one cup butter, one cup cream—or milk, if you cannot get cream—one teaspoonful saleratus, one egg, caraway seed to suit your taste.
       Mrs. Winslow's Receipt Book, 1875

SHREWSBURY CAKES: Mix half a pound of butter well beat like cream, and the same weight of flour, one egg, six ounces of beaten and sifted loaf sugar, and half an ounce of caraway seeds. Form these into a paste, roll them thin, and lay them in sheets of tin; then bake them in a slow oven.
       Mackenzie's 5,000 Receipts, 1829

SPICE CAKES: Melt a tea-cup of butter, mix it with a tea-cup of sugar and half a tea-cup of molasses. Stir in a tea-spoonful of cinnamon, the same quantity of ginger, a grated nutmeg and a tea-spoonful each of caraway and coriander seed—put in a tea-spoonful of saleratus, dissolved in half a tea-cup of water, stir in flour till stiff enough to roll out thin, cut it into cakes, and bake them in a slow oven.
       Kitchen Directory, 1846

WIGGS: Put half a pint of warm milk to three quarters of a pound of fine flour; mix in it two or three spoonsful of light yeast. Cover it up, and set it before the fire an hour, in order to make it rise. Work into it four ounces each of sugar and butter, make it into cakes, or wiggs, with as little flour as possible, and a few caraway seeds, and bake them quick.
       Mackenzie's 5,000 Receipts, 1829

PUDDING RECIPES

BATTER PUDDINGS WITHOUT EGGS: Take six spoonfuls of flour, a teaspoonful of salt, two of ginger and two of the tincture of saffron. Mix them with a little less than a quart of milk. Add fruit if you choose. Boil the pudding in a cloth an hour. Eat it with cold sauce.
       Young Housekeeper's Friend, 1846

BERRY PUDDING WITHOUT MILK OR EGGS: To a quart of washed whortleberries, put a pint of flour in which you have put a small teaspoonful of salt. Add a very little water. That which is upon the berries will be nearly enough. Boil it two hours in a cloth tied close, allowing no room to swell. It may be eaten with a sauce made without butter,—with a large teacup full of sugar, a teacup of water, and another of rose-water.
       Young Housekeeper's Friend, 1846

BLANCMANGE: Four calf's feet. A pint and a half of thick cream. Half a pound of loaf-sugar, broken up. A glass of wine. A glass of rose-water. A teaspoonful of mace, beaten and sifted. Ten drops of essence of bitter almonds.

Get four calf's-feet; if possible some that have been scalded, and not skinned. Scrape and clean them well, and boil them in three quarts of water till all the meat drops off the bone. Drain the liquid through a colander or sieve, and skim it well. Let it stand till next morning to congeal. Then clean it well from the sediment, and put it into a tin or bell-metal kettle. Stir into it, the cream, sugar, and mace. Boil it hard for five minutes, stirring it several times. Then strain it through a linen cloth or napkin into a large bowl, and add the wine and essence of rose-water, and bitter almonds.

Set it in a cool place for three or four hours, stirring it very frequently with a spoon, to prevent the cream from separating from the jelly. The more it is stirred the better. Stir it till it is cool.

Wash your moulds, wipe them dry, and then wet them with cold water. When the blancmange becomes very thick, (that is, in three or four hours, if the weather is not too damp) put it into your moulds.

When it has set in them till it is quite firm, loosen it carefully all round with a knife, and turn it out on glass or china plates.

. *Seventy-five Receipts,* 1838

PUMPKIN PUDDING: Half a pound of stewed pumpkin. Three eggs. Quarter of a pound of fresh butter, or a pint of cream. Quarter of a pound of powdered white sugar. Half a glass of wine and brandy mixed. Half a glass of rose-water. One teaspoonful of mixed spice, nutmeg, mace and cinnamon.

Stew some pumpkin with as little water as possible. Drain it in a colander, and press it till dry. When cold, weigh half a pound, and pass it through a sieve. Prepare the spice. Stir together the sugar, and butter, or cream, till they are perfectly light. Add to them, gradually, the spice and liquor.

Beat three eggs very light, and stir them into the butter and sugar alternately with the pumpkin.

Cover a soup-plate with puff paste, and put in the mixture. Bake it in a moderate oven about half an hour.

Grate sugar over it when cool.

Instead of the butter, you may boil a pint of milk or cream, and when cold, stir into it, in turn, the sugar, eggs, and pumpkin.

Seventy-five Receipts, 1838

TANSY PUDDING: Blanch and pound a quarter of a pound of Jordan almonds; put them into a stewpan, add a gill of the syrup of roses, the crumb of a French roll, some grated nutmeg, half a glass of brandy, two table-spoonsful of tansy juice, 3 oz. of fresh butter, and some slices of citron. Pour over it a pint and a half of boiling cream or milk, sweeten, and when cold, mix it; add the juice of a lemon, and 8 eggs beaten. It may be either boiled or baked.

Mackenzie's 5,000 Receipts, 1829

Bibliography

ADAIR, J. M. (M. D.), *An Essay on Diet and Regimen.* London: 1804

Ancient English Cookery Recipes, compiled by master cooks for Richard II. c. 1390

ANDREWS, EDWARD D., *MS., No. 23, 1834–1848, Ledger, 1844–1848.* Herb Department, New Lebanon Church family

———, *MS., No. 25, 1846–1873, Ledger, 1846–1873.* Herb Department, New Lebanon Church family

———, *MS., No. 68; Elisha Myrick's Diary* kept for the Use and Convenience of the Herb Department. Harvard Church, Massachusetts; January 1, 1853

———, *MS., No. 17, Seeds Raised at the Shaker Gardens, 1795–1884*

The Art of Confectionery. (Collected from the best New York, Philadelphia, and Boston Confectioners, and include a large number from the French and other foreign nations). Boston: J. E. Tilton & Co., 1866

ASKHAM, ANTHONY, *A Lytel Herball.* London: 1550

AUSTIN, RALPH, *Treatise of Fruit Trees.* 1653

AVERY, SUSANNA, *Plain Plantain.* MS. 1688

BAGLEY, GEORGE K. (Dr.), *The Family Instructor, or Guide to Health.* Montpelier, Vermont: E. P. Walton and Sons, Printers, 1848

BAKER, GEORGE, *Jewell of Health.* London: 1599

BART, JOHN SINCLAIR (Sir), *The Code of Agriculture:* including observations on gardens, orchards, woods, and plantations. Hartford: Hudson and Company and Cooke & Hale, 1818

BEACH, W., (M. D.), *The American Practice Abridged, or the Family Physician:* Being the Scientific System of Medicine; on Vegetable Principles, Designed for Classes. N. Y.: Messrs. Andrews and Company, 1846

BEECHER, (Miss), *Domestic Receipt-Book:* Designed as a Supplement to Her Treatise on Domestic Economy. (Third Edition). New York: Harper and Bros., Publishers, 1857

BLAKE, STEPHEN, *The Compleat Gardener's Practice.* 1664

BORDE, ANDREW (Dr.), *Regyment of Helth.* (sixteenth century)

CHASE, A. W., *Dr. Chase's Recipes,* or, Information for Everybody: An Invaluable Collection of About Eight Hundred Practical Recipes, . . . Ann Arbor, Michigan: Published by the Author, 1869

CHILD, (Mrs.), *The American Frugal Housewife,* Dedicated to Those Who Are Not Ashamed of Economy. (Thirteenth Edition). Boston: Carter, Hendee, and Company, 1833

CHRISTISON, ROBERT, *A Dispensatory,* or Commentary on the Pharmacopoeias of Great Britain (and the United States). Philadelphia: Lea and Blanchard, 1848

COLES, WILLIAM, *The Art of Simpling.* London: 1656

———, *Adam in Eden.* London: 1657

CORNELIUS, (Mrs.), *The Young Housekeeper's Friend;* or, A Guide to Domestic Economy and Comfort. Boston: Charles Tappan and New York: Saxton and Huntington, 1846

CULPEPPER, NICHOLAS, *Complete Herbal.* 1652

DALGAIRNS, (Mrs.), *The Practice of Cookery,* Adapted to The Business of Every Day Life. Boston: Munroe and Francis, 128 Washington Street and New York: Charles S. Francis, 1830

DARLINGTON, WILLIAM, *American Weeds and Useful Plants*. New York: 1859

DARWIN, ERASMUS, *The Botanic Garden*. New York: T. and J. Swords, 1798

DIGBY, *The Closet of Sir Kenelm Digby (Knight) Opened*. (c. 1650)

DIOSCORIDES, *De Medica Materia*. Venice: 1558

———, *The Greek Herbal of* (c. 512), Englished by John Goodyer (1652–5)

DUNGLISON, ROBLEY, *New Remedies: the Method of Preparing and Administering Them; Their Effects on the Healthy and Diseased Economy*. Philadelphia: Lea and Blanchard, 1841

DWIGHT, TIMOTHY, *Travels in New England and New York*. New Haven: S. Converse, Printer, 1822

EARLE, ALICE M., *Old Time Gardens*. New York: 1901

Enquire Within Upon Everything. London: Houlston and Sons, 1875

EVELYN, JOHN, *Kalendarium Hortense*. London: 1706

———, *Acetaria*. (1697)

———, *The French Gardiner*. London: 1675

———, *Directions for the Gardiner at Says Court*, (MS. c. 1687)

———, *Fumifugium*. 1661

FAIRFAX FAMILY, Still-room book, (17th. Century)

Family Hand-Book, containing Many Valuable Recipes for Cooking, Dyeing, Making Perfumery, etc. c. 1855

The Family Receipt Book, Containing Eight Hundred Valuable Receipts in Various Branches of Domestic Economy; Selected from the Works of the Most Approved Writers, Ancient and Modern; and from the Attested Communications of Scientific Friends. (Second American Edition). Pittsburgh: published by Randolph Barnes, Third Street, 1819

FARLEY, JOHN, *London Art of Cookery*. 1801

FAVRETTI, RUDY J., *Early New England Gardens: 1620–1840*. Old Sturbridge Booklet Series, 1962

FERNIE, W. T., *Herbal Simples*. Philadelphia: 1897

FERRARIUS, *De Florum Cultura*. Rome: 1633

FESSENDEN, THOMAS G., *The Husbandman and House-wife*. Bellows Falls: Bill Blake and Company, 1820

FISHER, SYDNEY GEORGE, *Men, Women and Manners in Colonial Times*. Philadelphia: and London: J. B. Lippincott Co., 1898

FRANCATELLI, CHARLES ELME, *The Modern Cook*. London: 1845

GARDENER, JON, *Feate of Gardening*. 1440

GENTIL, *Le Jardinier Solitaire*. Paris: 1705

GERARDE, JOHN, *The Herball or Generall Histoire of Plantse*. London: 1597

———, *The Herball or Generall Histoire of Plantes*. Very Much Enlarged and Amended by Thomas Johnson. London: 1636

GLASSE, HANNAH, *The Art of Cookery*. London: 1747 and 1751

GOODRICH, CHARLES A., *Universal Traveler:* ... Hartford: Gurdon Robins, 1847

GOOD SAMARITAN, *The American Family Keepsake*. Boston: 66 Cornhill, 1849

GREEN, HORACE, (M. D.), *Selections from Favorite Prescriptions* of Living American Practitioners. New York: J. Wiley, 1860

GRIFFITH, R. EGLESFELD, *Medical Botany:* or Descriptions of the More Important Plants used in Medicine, with their History, Properties, and Mode of Administration. Philadelphia: Lea and Blanchard, 1847

HALE, SARAH J. (Mrs.), *The Way to Live Well, and To Be Well While We Live*. Hartford: Case, Tiffany and Company, 1849

HAWES, STEPHEN, *Pastime of Pleasure*. c. 1523

HENRY, SAMUEL, (Botanist), *A New and Complete American Medical Family Herbal*, wherein is displayed the True Properties and Medical Virtues of the Plants, Indigenous to the United States of America: Together with Lewis' Secret Remedy, Newly Discovered, which has been Found Infallible in the Cure of the Dreadful Disease Hydrophobia. ... New York: published by the Author, No. 6 Peck-Slip, 1814

HILL, GEORGIANA, *The Cook's Own Book*. London: 1860

HILL, Sir JOHN, *The Family Herball*. London: 1812

The Housekeeper's Receipt Book. London: 1813

HOWLAND, Mrs. E. A. (Esther Allen), *The American Economical Housekeeper and Family Receipt Book*. Worcester: 1850

HYLL, THOMAS, *Briefe and Pleasant Treatise*. 1563

———, *The Gardeners Labyrinth*. 1577

The Kitchen Directory, and American Housewife: Containing the most Valuable and Original Receipts, in All the Various Branches of Cookery; Together with a Collection of Miscellaneous Receipts, and Directions Relative to Housewifery. Also the Whole Art of Carving, Illustrated by Sixteen

Engravings. New York: Mark H. Newman and Company, 1844 and 1846

KNIGHT, Madame, *The Private Journal* Kept by Madam Knight, on a Journey from Boston to New York, in the Year 1704

LAMB, PATRICK, *Royal-Cookery*. London: 1716

LANGLEY, BATTY, *New Principles of Gardening*. 1728

LAWRENCE, JOHN, *The Clergyman's Recreation*. 1726

LAWSON, WILLIAM, *Country House-wifes Garden*. 1617

———, *A New Orchard and New Garden*. London: 1618 and 1638

LESLIE, (Miss), *Seventy-Five Receipts* for Pastry, Cakes, and Sweetmeats. (Tenth edition). Boston: Munroe and Francis, and Joseph H. Francis. New York: Charles S. Francis, 1838

———, *Directions for Cookery, In Its Various Branches*. (Sixth Edition). Philadelphia: E. L. Carey and A. Hart, Chestnut Street, 1839

LIGER, L., *Le Jardinier Fleuriste*. Paris: 1763

LINCOLN, WALD. *Bibliography of American Cookery Books*. 1742–1860. Worcester: American Antiquarian Society, 1929

LINOCIER, *Histoire de Plantes*. Paris: 1584

The London Complete Art of Cookery. London: Minerva Press, 1797

The London Distiller. London: 1652

LYTE, HENRY, *A New Herbal*. London: 1619

MACKENZIE, *Five Thousand Receipts in All the Useful and Domestic Arts*: constituting A Complete Practical Library. Philadelphia: James Kay, Jun. and Brother, 1829

MARKHAM, GERVASE, *English Husbandman*. 1613

———, *English Housewife*, 1615

———, *A Way to Get Wealth*. London: 1660

———, *Countrie Farme*. 1600

MEAGHER, LEONARD, *The English Gardner*. 1670

MURRAY, ALEXANDER, *The Domestic Oracle*. London: 1826

A New Family Encyclopedia, or Compendium of Universal Knowledge. Philadelphia: 1833

New System of Domestic Cookery, Formed upon Principles of Economy, and Adapted to the Use of Private Families. (Second Edition). Boston: Published by Andrews and Cummings, and L. Blake, 1807

PARKINSON, JOHN, *Theatrum Botanium*, 1640

———, *Paradisi in Sole*, 1629

PIERCE, R. V., *The People's Common Sense Medical Adviser*. (46th. Edition). Buffalo: World's Dispensary Medical Association, 1895

PLAT, Sir HUGH, *Jewell House of Art and Nature*. (Both parts). London: 1594

———, *Delights for Ladies*. 1602

The Practical Housewife: A Complete Encyclopaedia of Domestic Economy and Family Medical Guide. Philadelphia: J. B. Lippincott and Company, c. 1860

A Primer for Herb Growing. Boston, Mass.: Herb Society of America, 1958

RAFFALD, ELIZABETH, *The Experienced English Housekeeper*. London: 1782

RANDOLPH, MARY (Mrs.), *The Virginia Housewife*: or, Methodical Cook. Philadelphia: E. H. Butler and Company, 1856

REECE, RICHARD, (M. D.), *The Medical Guide*, for the Use of Families and Young Practitioners in Medicine and Surgery. Being a Complete System of Modern Domestic Medicine; Exhibiting a Comprehensive View of the Latest and Most Important Discoveries in Medicine, Pharmacy, etc. (First American, from the Fourth London Edition, Considerably Enlarged and Improved.) Philadelphia: B. B. Hopkins, and Company, No. 170 Market-Street, Fry and Kammerer, Printers, 1808

Report of the Commissioner of Agriculture for the Year 1862. Washington: Government Printing Office, 1863

ROBERTSON, F. K. and WILCOX, SILAS, *The Book of Health*, or Thomsonian Theory and Practice of Medicine . . . and Materia Medica. Bennington: J. I. C. and A. S. C. Cook, 1843

SALMON, WILLIAM, (M. D.), *The Family Dictionary: Or, Household Companion*. (The Fourth Edition with above Eleven Hundred Additions, intersperst through the Whole Work). London: Printed for D. Rhodes, at the Star, the Corner of Bride-Lane, in Fleet Street, 1710

———, *Botanologia, the English Herbal*. 1710

SMITH, E., *The Compleat Housewife or, Accomplished Gentlewomen's Companion*. 1728

STEARNS, SAMUEL, *The American Herbal, or Materia Medica*. Walpole: David Carlisle, 1801

SURFLET, RICHARD, *Maison Rustique*. London: 1616

TAYLOR, JOSEPH, *Nature of the best Physician; or, a Complete Domestic Herbal: Being a Brief, but Valuable Description of the Physical Properties of the*

Most Generally Known Herbs and Plants. . . .
London: printed for Dean and Murray, 1818

THACHER, JAMES, (M. D.), *The American New Dispensatory*. (Second Edition). Boston: Thomas B. Wait and Company, 1813

THEOPHRASTUS, *Enquiry into Plants*. (2 vols.) 300 B.C. (Trans., 1916)

THOMSON, ANTHONY TODD, (M. D. and F. L. S.), *A Conspectus of the Pharmacopoeias of the London, Edinburgh, and Dublin Colleges of Physicians, and of the U.S. Pharmacopoeia; Being a Practical Compendium of Materia Medica and Pharmacy.* (Third American Edition). New York: Henry G. Langley, 8 Astor House, 1845

THOMSON, SAMUEL, *The Thomsonian Materia Medica, or Botanic Family Physician: Comprising a Philosophical Theory, the Natural Organization and Assumed Principles of Animal and Vegetable Life: To Which are Added the Description of Plants and Their Various Compounds: Together with Practical Illustrations. . . .* (Thirteenth Edition). Albany: Printed by J. Munsell, State Street, 1841

Toilet of Flora. London: 1779

TURNER, WILLIAM, *The Names of Herbes A. D. 1548.* London: 1881

TUSSER, THOMAS, *Five Hundred Points of Good Husbandry.* 1573

WAINWRIGHT, ELIZABETH, *The Receipt Book of a Lady of the Reign of Queen Anne.* 1711

WALLIS, GEORGE (M. D. & S. M. S.), *Art of Preventing Diseases, and Restoring Health, and Founded on Rational Principles, and Adapted to Persons of Every Capacity.* 1794

WARNER, RICHARD, *Antiquitates Culinarie.* 1791

Ways of Living on Small Means. Boston: Light and Stearns, 1837

WEBSTER, A. L. (Mrs.), *The Improved Housewife or Book of Receipts.* Boston: Phillips, Sampson and Company, 1858

WHARTON, ANNE HOLLINGSWORTH, *Colonial Days and Dames.* Philadelphia: J. B. Lippincott, 1895

WHEELER, CHARLES P., Jr., *Recipes.* MS., 1831

WINSLOW, (Mrs.), *Domestic Receipt Book,* for 1873: 1874: 1875: and 1878. Jeremiah Curtis and Sons and John I. Brown and Sons, 1872–1877

WINTHROP, JOHN, *The History of New England* from 1630 to 1649. Boston: T. B. Wait and Son, 1826

WORLIDGE, JOHN, *Systema Horticulturae.* 1677

———, *Art of Gardening.* 1677

WRIGHT, RICHARDSON, *Hawkers and Walkers in Early America.* Philadelphia: J. B. Lippincott Co., 1927

Index

BEVERAGES

Ale
Elder Flowers, 127

Creams
Absinthe or Wormwood, 128
Mint, 128

Liquers or Cordials
Aniseed, 129
Anisette, 129
Anisette de Bourdeaux, 129
Balm, or with Sage, 130
Balm of Mankind, 130
Caraway, 130
Godfrey's, 130
Gold, 130
Huile de Venus, 130
Nectar, 131
Perfect Love, 131
Tincture Japonica, 131

Ratafias
Absinthe or Wormwood, 131
Angelica, 131
Anise-Seed, 131
Black-Currant, 131
Juniper-Berry, 131
Ratafia d'Angelique, 132
Seed Ratafia, 132
Usquebaugh, 132

Spirituous Waters
Angelica and Compound Spirit, 132
Angelica, Water of, 132
Anise-Seed (Compound), 132
Barley (Compound), 132
Bawm, 132
Eau de Barbades, 132
Rosemary, 133
Wormwood, 133

Wines
Balm, 133
Cider, 133
Cider Red, 134
Grape, White, 134
Hippocras, 127
Juniper-Berry, 134
Mixed Berries, 134
Red and White Currant, 134
Sage, 134
Syllabub, 69
White Currant, 134
White Mead, 134
Wortleberry or Bilberry, 134

CONFECTIONS
Candied Flowers, 137, 138
Flower Syrup, 137
Rose Drops, 138
Sugar-Plate, 138
Syrup of Violets, 138

CONSERVES
Betony, 139
Calendula, 139
Conserves and Preserves, 139
Lavender, 38
Marigold, 36
Marjoram, 36
Pennyroyal, 38
Rose Hips, 139
Rose, Red, 140
Sage Flowers, 57

DYES
Balm Blossoms, 135
Horseradish Leaves, 135
Lavender Water, 135
Onion Skins, 135
Saffron, 135

FISH
Black Fish, Stewed, 105
Carp, Stewed, 105
Crabs, Dressed, 105
Eel Pie, 106
Matelote of Firm Fish, 106
Oysters, Pickled, 106
Pike to Stew, 106
Salted Fish, 107
Shad, Baked, 107

FOWL
Birds, to Stew, 107

FOWL (continued)
Boudin a la Richlieu, 108
Chicken-au-Soliel, 108
Chicken Croquets & Rissoles, 108
Chicken, Fricassee, 108
Chicken Pie, 108
Chicken Pudding, 109
Ducks, Nottingham Fashion, 109
Duck, to Stew, 109
Fowl a la Conde, 110
Goose, to Roast, 110
Pheasant, Larded and Roasted, 110
Turkey, Boned, 110
Turkey, Roast, 111

FURNITURE POLISH
Cleaner and Polish, 135

GRAVIES AND SAUCES

Gravies
Clear, 92
Gravy, 92
Gravy Cakes, 92
Gravy, Rich, 92
Gravy, Veal, 92

Sauces
Aspic, 91
Cullis, or Brown, 93
Fennel, 91
Fish-a-la-Craster, 93
For Boiled Rabbits, 93
For Fowls, 90
For a Goose or Duck, 90
For a Pig, 90
For Turtle, of Calf's Head, 94
General's, 91, 93
Gooseberry Sauce, 91
Ham Cullis, 91
Italienne, 93
Piquante, 94
Poor Man's, 91
Roast Lamb, 93
Soy Sauce, 94
White Sauce for Fowls, 94
To Melt Butter, 94

INSECTICIDES
Bay Leaves, 136
Lavender, 136, 137
Mint, 136
Pennyroyal, 136
Rosemary, 136
Rue, 136
Southernwood, 136
Thyme, 136
Wormwood, 136

MEAT
Beef a la Mode, 80
Beef a-la-Daube, 81
Beef Bouilli, 81
Beef Collared, 81
Beef Steak, Stuffed, 82
Beef Stew, 82
Black Puddings, 82
Bologna Sausages, 82
Calf's Feet, to Fry, 82
Calf's Head, Hashed, 82
Calf's Head, to Roast, 83
Calf's Liver, Roasted, 83
Ducks (Wild), to Stew, 83
First-Watch Stew, 79, 83
Hams, Tongues, Glazing for, 83
Ham Dumplings, 84
Head Cheese, 79, 84
Lamb, Shoulder of, Grilled, 84
Lamb, Stuffed, 84
Mutton Cutlets a-la-Maintenon, 84
Mutton Harico, 85
Mutton and Lamb, Roast, 85
Mutton, Shoulder of, 85
Mutton Chops, Stewed, 86
Oxford Sausages, 86
Pigs, Baked or Roasted, 86
Pork Collared, 86
Pork, Portuguese, Loin, 86
Pork Steaks, 86
Rabbit, Fricassee of, 87
Rabbits, Roast, 87
Sausages, Fine, 87
Sausages, to Make, 87
Tripe, Pepper Pot, 88
Veal a la Maintenon, 88

Veal, Breast of, 88
Veal or Mutton, to Boil a Leg, 88
Veal, Savory Dish of, 88
Veal, Shoulder on Galantine, 88
Veal, Stewed Breast of ,89
Veal, to Stuff a Shoulder, 89

MEDICINAL REMEDIES
Ague, 43
Apoplexy, 38, 47, 62
Arthritis, 41
Asthma, 30, 37, 38, 43, 62
    Elixir Asthmatic, 47
    Essence of Peppermint, 48
Biliousness, 42, 62
Bitters for Stomach, 48
Bladder Ailments, 36
Bleeding, 48, 63
Blood Builder, 37
Blood Purifier, 40, 48, 49, 62
Boils, 62
Brain, 37, 39, 62
Bruises, 62
Burns, 49
Cancers, 49, 62
Cankers, 49
Catarrh, 35, 38, 62
Cauterization, 43
Colic, 43, 55, 62
Colds, 40, 43, 63
Consumption, 38, 40, 49, 50, 62
Convulsions, 62
Corns, 50, 63
Coughs, 35, 38, 39, 42, 43, 62
Cough Syrup, 51
Cure-All, 51
Cuts, 42, 51
Dentifrice, 51
Diarrhea, 51, 63
Digestion, 37, 38, 39, 63
Diuretic, 38, 63
Dog Bite, 36, 37
Dropsy, 37, 40, 43, 52, 63
Dysentery, 52, 63
Dyspepsia, 41, 43, 44
Earache, 36, 37, 41
Eclectic Emetic, 52
Emollient, 38

Empyema, 52
Epilepsy, 38, 40, 63
Eyes, 52, 63
Eye Inflammation, 36
Eyesight, 37, 38
Fainting, 38
Felons, 52
Fever, 30, 34, 35, 38, 39, 43, 44, 52, 53, 58, 63
Footbaths, 38, 43, 63
Gargle, 53
Germicide, 53
Giddiness, 39
Gout, 37, 38, 54, 63
Gravel, 38, 63
Gunshot Wounds, 54
Head, 37
Headache, 36, 37, 38, 39, 43, 54, 63
Heart, 36, 38, 54
Herpes, 40
Hiccough, 37, 55
Hoarseness, 43, 63
Hot Drops, 55
Humors, 63
Hysterics, 30, 43, 55, 63
Indigestion, 44, 55, 63
Inflammation, 42, 43, 44
Influenza, 43
Insomnia, 55
Intestinal Distress, 55, 63
Irritating Plaster, 56
Jaundice, 37, 38, 39, 56, 63
Lethargy, 37, 38, 63
Loss of appetite, 62
Lungs, 38, 42, 43, 63
Memory, 37, 64
Menses, 64
Miscarriage, 37
Muscle Ache, 56
Nausea, 56
Nerve Tonic, 57
Nervous Irritability, 64
Nightmare, 38, 39, 64
Nosebleed, 37, 57
Oils of Flowers, 57
Pain, 39
Palsy, 38, 57, 58, 64
Paralysis, 37, 64

Physic, 43, 58
Piles, 58, 64
Plague, 36, 58
Pleuresy, 35, 64
Poison, Insect, 58
Pox, French, 37
Purge, 64
Quinsies, 31, 35
Refrigerant, 42
Rheumatism, 30, 40, 58, 64
Ringworm, 58, 64
Salt Rheum, 40
Scalds, 64
Sciatica, 30, 36, 64
Scurvy, 39, 64
Shortness of Breath, 39, 62
Skin Diseases, 40
Snuff, 37
Sore Throat, 31, 39, 42, 59, 64
Spasms, 38, 64
Spirit, Cheerful, 38, 64
Spirits, Medicinal, 60
Splinters, 60
Steam Baths, 60
Stimulant Aperient Pills, 60
Stomach, Weak, 36, 38, 42, 43
Stomach Complaints, 41
Sunburn, 30, 57, 60, 64
Swellings, 64
Thirst Quencher, 39, 40, 42, 43
Tinctures, 60
Tonics, 58, 61
Toothache, 31, 36, 50, 64
Tranquilizer, 43
Trembling, 38, 64
Ulcers, 30, 40, 49, 64
Veins, Weak, 43
Venereal Disease, 61
Vertigo, 38, 64
Warts, 50, 61, 65
Weakness, 43
Wounds, 36, 43, 61, 64, 65
Wrinkles, 57

PASTRIES, CAKES, PIES
Apees, 140
Cross Buns, 140
Gingerbread, 140
Honey Cakes, 140

Icing for Cake, 140
Macaroons, 141
New Year's Cookies, 141
Plain Cake, 142
Rhubarb Fool, 142
Saffron Cakes, 142
Seed Cakes (Caraway), 142
Shrewsbury Cakes, 142
Spice Cakes, 142
Wiggs, 142

PICKLES
Assorted Pickles for Winter, 122
Broom Buds, Pickled, 122
Butternuts, 120, 122
Chow-Chow, Good, 123
Clove Gilliflowers, 122
Collyflower, 122
Cowcumber, 122
Cowslip, 122
Cucumbers, 121
Green Tomato Preserves, 123
Mangoes, 123
Martinoes, 121, 122
Muskmelons, 120, 121
Nasturtium Buds, 123
Nasturtium Seed, 120, 121
Peccalilli, Indian Method, 123
Peppers, 121, 124
Piccalilli, 124
Pickled Cauliflower, 124
Pickled Lemons, 121, 124
Pickled Peaches, 124
Picklette, 124
Pickled Walnuts, 120, 121
Red Cabbage, 121
Spiced Cucumber Pickle, 124
To Harden Pickles, 123
Tomato Chow-Chow, 125
Tomato Ketchup, 125

PUDDINGS
Batter Puddings, 142
Berry Pudding, 142
Blanc Mange, 143
Pumpkin Pudding, 143
Tansy Pudding, 143

SALADS
Asparagus, 117
Beet, 117
Broom Bud, 117
Compound, 118
Flower, 118
French, 116
Healthful, 118
Hints, 118
Ingredients, 116
Kinds, 119
Lobster, 116
Marigold, 119
Mint, 117
Nasturtium, 117
Perfect, 117
Salat, 119
Sallet of Cold Capon Roasted, 119
Sallets, 119
Strange Sallets, 120
To Raise a Salad Quickly, 116

SHAVING MATERIAL, 73

SOAPS
Jamaica Vegetable, 74
Substitutes, 74
Windsor and Castile, 75

SOUPS
Asparagus, 96, 97
Beef Gravy, 97
Beef or Black, 97
Bouillabaisse, 95
Brown, 97
Broth, 97
Broth of Beef, Mutton, and Veal, 97
Cheap Soup for the Poor, 97
Chicken or Turkey, 97
Common, 97
Fasting-Day, 98
Flemish, 98
General Remarks, 96
Giblet, 98, 99
Gravy, 99
Green Pea, 99

Hare or Rabbit, 99
Herb, 99
Hessian, 96, 100
Hodge-Podge, 99, 100
Macaroni, 100
Meg Merrilies, 100
Mock Turtle, or Calf's Head, 96, 100
Oyster, 101
Pease-Porridge, or Soop, 94
Pigeon, 95, 101
Pottage, 101
Roast Beef Bone, 101
Soup for the Poor, 102
Soup Cressy, 102
Soup Herb Spirit, 102
Soup Maigre, 102
Soup Powder, 95, 102
Southern Gumbo, 103
Spring, 96, 103
Veal, 103
Vermicelli, 103
White, 95, 104
Winter Vegetable, 96, 104

SPOT REMOVER, 136

TOILET WATERS, 75

TOILETRIES, PERFUMES, POMATUM

Colognes
Cologne Water, 70
Eau de Cologne, 70
Eau de Melisse de Carmes, 70

Deoderizers
Incense Perfume, 70
Sweet Jars, 70
Vinegar of the Four Thieves, 70

Hair Invigorators
Erasmus Wilson's Lotion to Promote Growth of Hair, 93
Macassar Oil to make hair Grow and Curl, 71
To Promote Growth of Hair, 71

Perfumes
Orris, 71
Perfume Bags for Drawers, 71
Perfume, 71, 72
Perfumed Washing Waters, 72
Perfumed Scent, 72
Pleasant Perfume, and Moth Preventive, 71
To Perfume Linen, 71
To Perfume Hair Powder, 71
Pot Pourri, 72

Pomades
Pomade Divine, 72
Pomatum, Dutch, 67
Pomatum, Rare, 72
Rosewater, 68
Rosemary Pomatum, 72
Soft Pomatum, 72

TOOTH BRUSHES 75

TOOTH POWDERS
Tooth Powder, 76
Turkish Rouge, 76

VEGETABLES
Beans, To Dress French, 111
Celery, Stewed, 112
Cucumbers, To Stew, 112
Egg Plant, Stewed, 112
Egg Plants, Stuffed, 112
Herb Pie, 112
Mushrooms, To Dress, 112
Pot Herbs, 112
Potato Croquettes, 113
Sweet Potatos, Stewed, 113

VINEGARS, 114

A CATALOG OF SELECTED DOVER
BOOKS IN ALL FIELDS OF INTEREST

100 BEST-LOVED POEMS, Edited by Philip Smith. "The Passionate Shepherd to His Love," "Shall I compare thee to a summer's day?" "Death, be not proud," "The Raven," "The Road Not Taken," plus works by Blake, Wordsworth, Byron, Shelley, Keats, many others. 96pp. 5³⁄₁₆ x 8¼. 0-486-28553-7

100 SMALL HOUSES OF THE THIRTIES, Brown-Blodgett Company. Exterior photographs and floor plans for 100 charming structures. Illustrations of models accompanied by descriptions of interiors, color schemes, closet space, and other amenities. 200 illustrations. 112pp. 8⅜ x 11. 0-486-44131-8

1000 TURN-OF-THE-CENTURY HOUSES: With Illustrations and Floor Plans, Herbert C. Chivers. Reproduced from a rare edition, this showcase of homes ranges from cottages and bungalows to sprawling mansions. Each house is meticulously illustrated and accompanied by complete floor plans. 256pp. 9⅜ x 12¼. 0-486-45596-3

101 GREAT AMERICAN POEMS, Edited by The American Poetry & Literacy Project. Rich treasury of verse from the 19th and 20th centuries includes works by Edgar Allan Poe, Robert Frost, Walt Whitman, Langston Hughes, Emily Dickinson, T. S. Eliot, other notables. 96pp. 5³⁄₁₆ x 8¼. 0-486-40158-8

101 GREAT SAMURAI PRINTS, Utagawa Kuniyoshi. Kuniyoshi was a master of the warrior woodblock print — and these 18th-century illustrations represent the pinnacle of his craft. Full-color portraits of renowned Japanese samurais pulse with movement, passion, and remarkably fine detail. 112pp. 8⅜ x 11. 0-486-46523-3

ABC OF BALLET, Janet Grosser. Clearly worded, abundantly illustrated little guide defines basic ballet-related terms: arabesque, battement, pas de chat, relevé, sissonne, many others. Pronunciation guide included. Excellent primer. 48pp. 4³⁄₁₆ x 5¾. 0-486-40871-X

ACCESSORIES OF DRESS: An Illustrated Encyclopedia, Katherine Lester and Bess Viola Oerke. Illustrations of hats, veils, wigs, cravats, shawls, shoes, gloves, and other accessories enhance an engaging commentary that reveals the humor and charm of the many-sided story of accessorized apparel. 644 figures and 59 plates. 608pp. 6⅛ x 9¼. 0-486-43378-1

ADVENTURES OF HUCKLEBERRY FINN, Mark Twain. Join Huck and Jim as their boyhood adventures along the Mississippi River lead them into a world of excitement, danger, and self-discovery. Humorous narrative, lyrical descriptions of the Mississippi valley, and memorable characters. 224pp. 5³⁄₁₆ x 8¼. 0-486-28061-6

ALICE STARMORE'S BOOK OF FAIR ISLE KNITTING, Alice Starmore. A noted designer from the region of Scotland's Fair Isle explores the history and techniques of this distinctive, stranded-color knitting style and provides copious illustrated instructions for 14 original knitwear designs. 208pp. 8⅜ x 10⅞. 0-486-47218-3

Browse over 9,000 books at www.doverpublications.com

ALICE'S ADVENTURES IN WONDERLAND, Lewis Carroll. Beloved classic about a little girl lost in a topsy-turvy land and her encounters with the White Rabbit, March Hare, Mad Hatter, Cheshire Cat, and other delightfully improbable characters. 42 illustrations by Sir John Tenniel. 96pp. 5³⁄₁₆ x 8¼. 0-486-27543-4

AMERICA'S LIGHTHOUSES: An Illustrated History, Francis Ross Holland. Profusely illustrated fact-filled survey of American lighthouses since 1716. Over 200 stations — East, Gulf, and West coasts, Great Lakes, Hawaii, Alaska, Puerto Rico, the Virgin Islands, and the Mississippi and St. Lawrence Rivers. 240pp. 8 x 10¾. 0-486-25576-X

AN ENCYCLOPEDIA OF THE VIOLIN, Alberto Bachmann. Translated by Frederick H. Martens. Introduction by Eugene Ysaye. First published in 1925, this renowned reference remains unsurpassed as a source of essential information, from construction and evolution to repertoire and technique. Includes a glossary and 73 illustrations. 496pp. 6⅛ x 9¼. 0-486-46618-3

ANIMALS: 1,419 Copyright-Free Illustrations of Mammals, Birds, Fish, Insects, etc., Selected by Jim Harter. Selected for its visual impact and ease of use, this outstanding collection of wood engravings presents over 1,000 species of animals in extremely lifelike poses. Includes mammals, birds, reptiles, amphibians, fish, insects, and other invertebrates. 284pp. 9 x 12. 0-486-23766-4

THE ANNALS, Tacitus. Translated by Alfred John Church and William Jackson Brodribb. This vital chronicle of Imperial Rome, written by the era's great historian, spans A.D. 14-68 and paints incisive psychological portraits of major figures, from Tiberius to Nero. 416pp. 5³⁄₁₆ x 8¼. 0-486-45236-0

ANTIGONE, Sophocles. Filled with passionate speeches and sensitive probing of moral and philosophical issues, this powerful and often-performed Greek drama reveals the grim fate that befalls the children of Oedipus. Footnotes. 64pp. 5³⁄₁₆ x 8 ¼. 0-486-27804-2

ART DECO DECORATIVE PATTERNS IN FULL COLOR, Christian Stoll. Reprinted from a rare 1910 portfolio, 160 sensuous and exotic images depict a breathtaking array of florals, geometrics, and abstracts — all elegant in their stark simplicity. 64pp. 8⅜ x 11. 0-486-44862-2

THE ARTHUR RACKHAM TREASURY: 86 Full-Color Illustrations, Arthur Rackham. Selected and Edited by Jeff A. Menges. A stunning treasury of 86 full-page plates span the famed English artist's career, from *Rip Van Winkle* (1905) to masterworks such as *Undine, A Midsummer Night's Dream,* and *Wind in the Willows* (1939). 96pp. 8⅜ x 11. 0-486-44685-9

THE AUTHENTIC GILBERT & SULLIVAN SONGBOOK, W. S. Gilbert and A. S. Sullivan. The most comprehensive collection available, this songbook includes selections from every one of Gilbert and Sullivan's light operas. Ninety-two numbers are presented uncut and unedited, and in their original keys. 410pp. 9 x 12. 0-486-23482-7

THE AWAKENING, Kate Chopin. First published in 1899, this controversial novel of a New Orleans wife's search for love outside a stifling marriage shocked readers. Today, it remains a first-rate narrative with superb characterization. New introductory Note. 128pp. 5³⁄₁₆ x 8¼. 0-486-27786-0

BASIC DRAWING, Louis Priscilla. Beginning with perspective, this commonsense manual progresses to the figure in movement, light and shade, anatomy, drapery, composition, trees and landscape, and outdoor sketching. Black-and-white illustrations throughout. 128pp. 8⅜ x 11. 0-486-45815-6

Browse over 9,000 books at www.doverpublications.com

THE BATTLES THAT CHANGED HISTORY, Fletcher Pratt. Historian profiles 16 crucial conflicts, ancient to modern, that changed the course of Western civilization. Gripping accounts of battles led by Alexander the Great, Joan of Arc, Ulysses S. Grant, other commanders. 27 maps. 352pp. 5⅜ x 8½. 0-486-41129-X

BEETHOVEN'S LETTERS, Ludwig van Beethoven. Edited by Dr. A. C. Kalischer. Features 457 letters to fellow musicians, friends, greats, patrons, and literary men. Reveals musical thoughts, quirks of personality, insights, and daily events. Includes 15 plates. 410pp. 5⅜ x 8½. 0-486-22769-3

BERNICE BOBS HER HAIR AND OTHER STORIES, F. Scott Fitzgerald. This brilliant anthology includes 6 of Fitzgerald's most popular stories: "The Diamond as Big as the Ritz," the title tale, "The Offshore Pirate," "The Ice Palace," "The Jelly Bean," and "May Day." 176pp. 5⅜ x 8½. 0-486-47049-0

BESLER'S BOOK OF FLOWERS AND PLANTS: 73 Full-Color Plates from Hortus Eystettensis, 1613, Basilius Besler. Here is a selection of magnificent plates from the *Hortus Eystettensis,* which vividly illustrated and identified the plants, flowers, and trees that thrived in the legendary German garden at Eichstätt. 80pp. 8⅜ x 11.
0-486-46005-3

THE BOOK OF KELLS, Edited by Blanche Cirker. Painstakingly reproduced from a rare facsimile edition, this volume contains full-page decorations, portraits, illustrations, plus a sampling of textual leaves with exquisite calligraphy and ornamentation. 32 full-color illustrations. 32pp. 9⅜ x 12¼. 0-486-24345-1

THE BOOK OF THE CROSSBOW: With an Additional Section on Catapults and Other Siege Engines, Ralph Payne-Gallwey. Fascinating study traces history and use of crossbow as military and sporting weapon, from Middle Ages to modern times. Also covers related weapons: balistas, catapults, Turkish bows, more. Over 240 illustrations. 400pp. 7¼ x 10⅛. 0-486-28720-3

THE BUNGALOW BOOK: Floor Plans and Photos of 112 Houses, 1910, Henry L. Wilson. Here are 112 of the most popular and economic blueprints of the early 20th century — plus an illustration or photograph of each completed house. A wonderful time capsule that still offers a wealth of valuable insights. 160pp. 8⅜ x 11.
0-486-45104-6

THE CALL OF THE WILD, Jack London. A classic novel of adventure, drawn from London's own experiences as a Klondike adventurer, relating the story of a heroic dog caught in the brutal life of the Alaska Gold Rush. Note. 64pp. 5³⁄₁₆ x 8¼.
0-486-26472-6

CANDIDE, Voltaire. Edited by Francois-Marie Arouet. One of the world's great satires since its first publication in 1759. Witty, caustic skewering of romance, science, philosophy, religion, government — nearly all human ideals and institutions. 112pp. 5³⁄₁₆ x 8¼. 0-486-26689-3

CELEBRATED IN THEIR TIME: Photographic Portraits from the George Grantham Bain Collection, Edited by Amy Pastan. With an Introduction by Michael Carlebach. Remarkable portrait gallery features 112 rare images of Albert Einstein, Charlie Chaplin, the Wright Brothers, Henry Ford, and other luminaries from the worlds of politics, art, entertainment, and industry. 128pp. 8⅜ x 11. 0-486-46754-6

CHARIOTS FOR APOLLO: The NASA History of Manned Lunar Spacecraft to 1969, Courtney G. Brooks, James M. Grimwood, and Loyd S. Swenson, Jr. This illustrated history by a trio of experts is the definitive reference on the Apollo spacecraft and lunar modules. It traces the vehicles' design, development, and operation in space. More than 100 photographs and illustrations. 576pp. 6¾ x 9¼. 0-486-46756-2

A CHRISTMAS CAROL, Charles Dickens. This engrossing tale relates Ebenezer Scrooge's ghostly journeys through Christmases past, present, and future and his ultimate transformation from a harsh and grasping old miser to a charitable and compassionate human being. 80pp. 5‰6 x 8¼. 0-486-26865-9

COMMON SENSE, Thomas Paine. First published in January of 1776, this highly influential landmark document clearly and persuasively argued for American separation from Great Britain and paved the way for the Declaration of Independence. 64pp. 5‰6 x 8¼. 0-486-29602-4

THE COMPLETE SHORT STORIES OF OSCAR WILDE, Oscar Wilde. Complete texts of "The Happy Prince and Other Tales," "A House of Pomegranates," "Lord Arthur Savile's Crime and Other Stories," "Poems in Prose," and "The Portrait of Mr. W. H." 208pp. 5‰6 x 8¼. 0-486-45216-6

COMPLETE SONNETS, William Shakespeare. Over 150 exquisite poems deal with love, friendship, the tyranny of time, beauty's evanescence, death, and other themes in language of remarkable power, precision, and beauty. Glossary of archaic terms. 80pp. 5‰6 x 8¼. 0-486-26686-9

THE COUNT OF MONTE CRISTO: Abridged Edition, Alexandre Dumas. Falsely accused of treason, Edmond Dantès is imprisoned in the bleak Chateau d'If. After a hair-raising escape, he launches an elaborate plot to extract a bitter revenge against those who betrayed him. 448pp. 5‰6 x 8¼. 0-486-45643-9

CRAFTSMAN BUNGALOWS: Designs from the Pacific Northwest, Yoho & Merritt. This reprint of a rare catalog, showcasing the charming simplicity and cozy style of Craftsman bungalows, is filled with photos of completed homes, plus floor plans and estimated costs. An indispensable resource for architects, historians, and illustrators. 112pp. 10 x 7. 0-486-46875-5

CRAFTSMAN BUNGALOWS: 59 Homes from "The Craftsman," Edited by Gustav Stickley. Best and most attractive designs from Arts and Crafts Movement publication — 1903–1916 — includes sketches, photographs of homes, floor plans, descriptive text. 128pp. 8¼ x 11. 0-486-25829-7

CRIME AND PUNISHMENT, Fyodor Dostoyevsky. Translated by Constance Garnett. Supreme masterpiece tells the story of Raskolnikov, a student tormented by his own thoughts after he murders an old woman. Overwhelmed by guilt and terror, he confesses and goes to prison. 480pp. 5‰6 x 8¼. 0-486-41587-2

THE DECLARATION OF INDEPENDENCE AND OTHER GREAT DOCUMENTS OF AMERICAN HISTORY: 1775-1865, Edited by John Grafton. Thirteen compelling and influential documents: Henry's "Give Me Liberty or Give Me Death," Declaration of Independence, The Constitution, Washington's First Inaugural Address, The Monroe Doctrine, The Emancipation Proclamation, Gettysburg Address, more. 64pp. 5‰6 x 8¼. 0-486-41124-9

THE DESERT AND THE SOWN: Travels in Palestine and Syria, Gertrude Bell. "The female Lawrence of Arabia," Gertrude Bell wrote captivating, perceptive accounts of her travels in the Middle East. This intriguing narrative, accompanied by 160 photos, traces her 1905 sojourn in Lebanon, Syria, and Palestine. 368pp. 5⅜ x 8½. 0-486-46876-3

A DOLL'S HOUSE, Henrik Ibsen. Ibsen's best-known play displays his genius for realistic prose drama. An expression of women's rights, the play climaxes when the central character, Nora, rejects a smothering marriage and life in "a doll's house." 80pp. 5‰6 x 8¼. 0-486-27062-9

Browse over 9,000 books at www.doverpublications.com